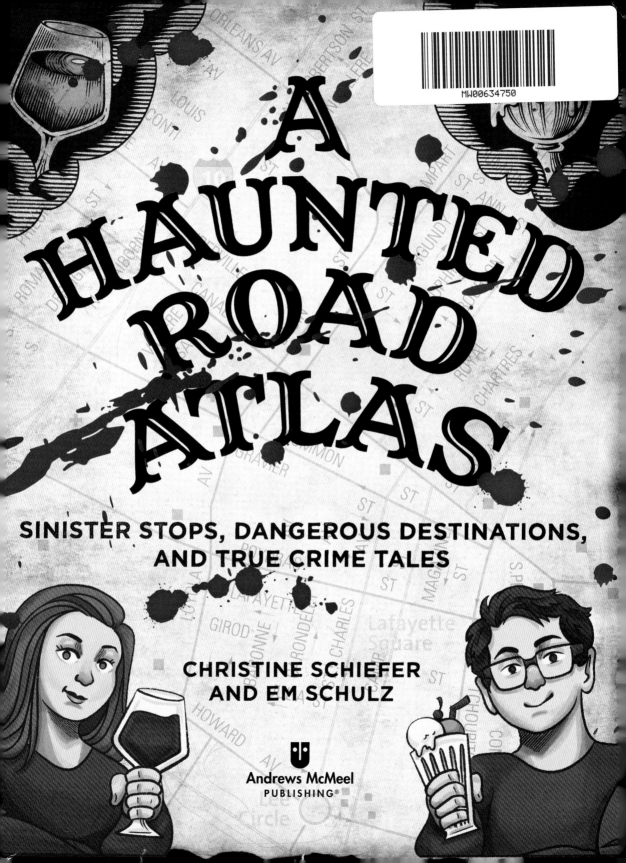

A HAUNTED ROAD ATLAS

SINISTER STOPS, DANGEROUS DESTINATIONS, AND TRUE CRIME TALES

CHRISTINE SCHIEFER
AND EM SCHULZ

Andrews McMeel
PUBLISHING®

A HAUNTED ROAD ATLAS

Andrews McMeel Publishing
a division of Andrews McMeel Universal
1130 Walnut Street, Kansas City, Missouri 64106

www.andrewsmcmeel.com

22 23 24 25 26 SHO 10 9 8 7 6 5 4 3 2 1

ISBN: 978-1-5248-7210-6

Library of Congress Control Number: 2021948611

Illustrations by James Mied

Editor: Charlie Upchurch
Art Director/Designer: Holly Swayne
Production Editor: Jasmine Lim
Production Manager: Tamara Haus

ATTENTION: SCHOOLS AND BUSINESSES
Andrews McMeel books are available at quantity discounts with bulk purchase for educational, business, or sales promotional use. For information, please e-mail the Andrews McMeel Publishing Special Sales Department: specialsales@amuniversal.com.

CONTENTS

INTRODUCTION

Em and Christine wrote a book?!

Trust us, we're just as surprised as you are. When we met way back in 2014, we had no clue we'd one day be best friends, let alone author a book together. But when we realized there was no haunted road trip guide on the market, we knew we could be the ones to fill that gap. And thus, *A Haunted Road Atlas* was born!

Compiling this book was a great way to reminisce on our past travels and get excited about future tours. Whether you pick up this book for your next road trip or simply for your coffee table, we hope it will inspire some incredibly boozy, haunted adventures. (Please tag us in your pictures!)

We'd also like to apologize to any cities we didn't feature in this edition. Our original list of cities was absurdly long, but it quickly became apparent that an encyclopedia-sized travel guide wasn't the most convenient of travel companions.

If you're a listener of *And That's Why We Drink*, thank you for your endless support. We wouldn't have gotten here without you. And if you're new here, well . . . we're sorry. And we hope you like lemons.

Love,
Em and Christine

S. DUPRE ST
S. WHITE ST
S. BROAD AV
CLEVELAND ST
PALMYRA
BANKS
TULANE AV
S. DORGENOIS
S. ROCHEBLAVE
ST
ST
ST
ST
ST
N. MIRO ST
N. GALVEZ ST
JOHNSON
PRIEUR
BIENVILLE AV
LOUIS
CONTI
ST
ST
ST
90
PERDIDO
POYDRAS
S. TONTI
S. MIRO
S. GALVEZ
ST
S.
ST
ST
ST
ST
S. ROMAN
DERBIGNY
N. CLAIBORNE AV
BOLIVAR
S.
S.
IBER
CANA
VILLIERE
LA SALLE
Med. Ctr. of La.-
Univ. Campus
LAFAYETTE
ST
V.A.
Med. Ctr.
Public
Library
EARHART
ST
City Hall
GALVEZ ST
S. ROMAN
BL
CLIO
ERATO
Louisiana
Superdome
New Orleans
Arena
LOYOLA
AV
P.O. &
Fed. Bldg.
MARTIN
LUTHER
KING
MAGNOLIA ST
ST
FRERET ST
BUS
90
Union
Passenger
Terminal
JACKSON
IGNY
90

ROAD TRIP GAME

I SPY: *ATWWD* EDITION

- [ ] A LEMON
- [ ] THE NAME "GIO"
  "Giovani" counts too!
- [ ] "TM"
- [ ] A TYPO SO YOU CAN YELL, "ENGLISH ISN'T MY FIRST LANGUAGE!"
- [ ] SOMEONE'S PRONOUNS
- [ ] A PILLAR
- [ ] A CLOWN THAT WOULD MAKE SASSY PROUD
- [ ] A BUTT CURTAIN
- [ ] CRIME SCENE TAPE
- [ ] BUFFALO PLAID
- [ ] A CREEPY OLD HOUSE THAT'S DEFINITELY HAUNTED
- [ ] A CEMETERY
- [ ] A CANADIAN FLAG
- [ ] THE NAME "MEGAN"
  The more unnecessary vowels, the better
- [ ] A DISCARDED SHOE
  May or may not contain a disembodied foot
- [ ] A CREEPY VAN
- [ ] BONUS POINTS: A GHOST, A CRYPTID, OR A UFO

NORTHEAST

BOSTON, MA

Boston is where Christine and I met! It took a few years for us to get our friendship cooking, but I wouldn't have it any other way. On tour, we were in town for two days, and I luckily got to see some friends and family, but I loved reminiscing with Christine about how different our lives were the last time we were both there before we really knew each other. My favorite part of the *And That's Why We Drink Does Boston* experience was seeing our faces on the marquee of the Wilbur Theatre, our "hometown" theater (which we sold out!). It was such a surreal feeling looking up and seeing ourselves on the sign of a theater I used to go to when I lived in the city. After our show, I stood outside FaceTiming my friends to show them the marquee so we could all scream about it together, and I'll never forget that feeling. While I was there, I also made about three stops to Toscanini's, my favorite ice cream place in the world. If you want to try my order, I always get a scoop of Earl Grey and a scoop of B3!

Em and I lived across the street from each other on Bay State Road and had no idea we'd one day be best friends! One time I hosted a Super Bowl party at my apartment, and within minutes of Em's arrival, all the chicken wings had mysteriously vanished . . . Now that I know Em better, I can't believe I was ever surprised.

PARANORMAL

THE WITCH OF LIME STREET, AKA MINA "MARGERY" CRANDON

10 LIME ST · BOSTON, MA

Of the incredible feats Harry Houdini is known for, too few of us know about his *passion project,* debunking fraudulent mediums. Among his psychic rivals, without question, Houdini's archnemesis was Mina Crandon.

In 1918, Mina married Dr. Leroi Crandon and moved to 10 Lime Street in Boston. Five years later, her husband got into the spiritualism movement and had friends over for a séance. When Mina wasn't taking it seriously, she was scolded by the group, and soon she was "overcome" by a spirit that made her "move" the table. Her husband was amazed (and an idiot) and soon had her regularly working on growing her powers. Soon enough, she was making tables levitate and making objects and spirits materialize in front of his eyes. Mina (going now by Margery) became a massive success, and one of her biggest fans was devout believer in the afterlife, Sir Arthur Conan Doyle.

With this rebirth of spiritualism, *Scientific American* launched an investigation and was offering $2,500 for a true physical or photographed phenomenon under test conditions. When Margery came to show her talents, one of the people reviewing her was Harry Houdini: (1) a staunch skeptic who, as an illusionist, believed that anything "unbelievable" is just an act and (2) someone who was out for justice after losing his mother and being taken advantage of by several mediums. As expected, Houdini caught Margery in several tricks during the séance but decided he would not expose her until he had more evidence.

Unfortunately, in his desperation to make her out as a fraud, he was caught contaminating the panel's tests to "catch her" in more damning ways, which then made him and *Scientific American* look bad. So Margery was still being written up as a legitimate medium, and Houdini felt even more threatened as both an illusion artist and someone openly against spiritualists. Since the

Scientific American committee wasn't ready to side with him or call Margery a fraud, Houdini took matters into his own hands.

He published a pamphlet that explained exactly how "mediums" were performing their tricks (with pictures!) and even began performing the same stunts at his own magic shows. Houdini publicly challenged all mediums: if they wanted him to stop, he would pay them up to $10,000 (or $150,000 today) to perform an act he couldn't replicate. Margery's "abilities" suddenly got more powerful, and before you knew it, she was materializing ectoplasm at almost every one of her séances.

I'm sorry, but mediums and magicians going after each other at the combined height of spiritualism and Houdini's stardom? This would have been TMZ headlining news, and I would have eaten it up.

Many skeptics on Houdini's side started reporting that Margery's "ectoplasm" looked a lot like animal entrails that were stuffed up and coming out of . . . her orifices. (And now the gossip is X-rated? I could not be more invested in this.)

Some of these skeptics in defense of Houdini were Eric Dingwall and "Father of Parapsychology," J.B. Rhine. This led Sir Arthur Conan Doyle to defend Margery by taking out spots in local papers that said, "J.B. Rhine is an ass." Although hysterical, this was also the first big rift that divided spiritualists from parapsychologists. Scientific and psychical committees began taking sides and breaking off to form new research organizations that still exist today. In 1928, Mina was officially proven guilty of fraud when a "spirit's" fingerprint perfectly matched Margery's.

She is known as the twentieth century's most controversial medium, and although a fraud, she did once predict during a séance that "Houdini will be gone by November." On October 31, a fan went backstage to Houdini's show, punched him in the stomach, and Houdini died of a ruptured appendix. To this day, some believe it was a planned murder by a spiritualist in defense of Margery's mediumship. Today you can still see Margery's home, 10 Lime Street . . . from afar! It is a private property but also right in Boston proper, where you can enjoy several other spooky locations and tourist experiences.

For a crash course in the coolest battle ever, Harry Houdini vs. Psychics, go listen to And That's Why We Drink *Episode* 155.

    For the much longer spiel on Houdini vs. Margery Crandon, listen to And That's Why We Drink *Episode* 156: "The Chairman of the Haunted House Committee and Too Many Walters."

TRUE CRIME

BOSTON STRANGLER

Sometimes referred to by the more glamorous name of the "Silk Stocking Murders," the Boston Strangler's murders of thirteen women in the early 1960s shook the Boston area. Though some believed the killings to be the work of multiple perpetrators, there were some eerie similarities between the victims. Despite their ages ranging from nineteen to eighty-five, the women all lived alone, and there appeared to have been no forced entry. What's more, the killer's MO included sexually assaulting his victims before strangling them with a stocking, pillowcase, or other object, which he would leave around the victim's neck, tied in what authorities called an "ornamental bow."

The killer was dubbed the "Mad Strangler of Boston," and it was believed he had gained entry to his victims' homes by posing as a maintenance man, delivery man, or other service industry worker as a means to disarm his victims. Despite the media hype surrounding this high-profile killer, the attacks persisted. Struck with fear, residents of Boston began purchasing tear gas and dead bolts. Some even went as far as to move out of the city altogether.

An unexpected connection to an existing crime spree helped break the case. Albert DeSalvo, age 28, had been arrested in 1960 for a series of sex offenses in the Cambridge, Massachusetts, area. He had been visiting homes door-to-door and introducing himself to young women as a talent scout for a modeling agency. He would grope the women as he took their "measurements," leading to yet another moniker, the "Measuring Man."

After DeSalvo was arrested for the crimes, he was released after only eleven months for good behavior.

I think we all know where this is going . . . His good behavior persisted and he never attacked again! NOT.

DeSalvo immediately began another crime spree, breaking into over 400 homes and sexually assaulting over 300 women. Yes, you read that right—300. For god-knows-what reason, DeSalvo wore green during every attack, earning him yet another moniker, though perhaps not the most creative: the "Green Man."

The Boston Strangler attacks were taking place simultaneously, and they weren't connected to the attacks of the Green Man until a woman came forward with a description of her attacker. From her detailed description (my guess is, "He wore all green"), it was quickly determined that the man police were looking for was their "well-behaved" pal Albert DeSalvo.

After his arrest, DeSalvo confessed to his attorney that he was indeed the Boston Strangler. But here's the catch—turns out DeSalvo had a budding bromance with convicted murderer George Nassar, and the two had allegedly worked out a deal to split the reward money if one of them confessed to being the Boston Strangler. That being said, DeSalvo was able to describe the crimes in eerie detail, leading authorities to believe they had the right man. In fact, he even nailed some details that his own victims had misremembered. For example, he had described a blue chair in a woman's living room, though she had insisted it was brown. Photographic evidence proved DeSalvo was indeed correct.

Although he was never tried for the Boston Strangler murders, DeSalvo was thankfully put away for life for the Green Man attacks. In February of 1967, DeSalvo escaped with two fellow inmates, triggering a full-scale manhunt. He disguised himself as a US Navy petty officer but quickly turned himself in because he was tired of running.

Sounds like a very Em-and-Christine move, if you ask me.

As a result of his stunt, DeSalvo was transferred to the maximum security Walpole State Prison, where he was stabbed and killed in his cell six years later.

But that's not all! Fast-forward to July 2013—a savvy surveillance expert had snatched a discarded water bottle left at a worksite by none other than DeSalvo's nephew, Tim DeSalvo. The DNA on the bottle was a "near certain match" to the samples collected from the scene of the Strangler's final murder—that of 19-year-old Mary Sullivan of Beacon Hill. DeSalvo's body was exhumed and DNA was extracted from his femur and teeth. It was determined that DeSalvo was indeed the man who killed Mary Sullivan!

Although Sullivan's family has gained some closure from this discovery, there remains some doubt as to whether DeSalvo committed all of the Boston Strangler's homicides. Some are still convinced that the murders were committed by multiple perpetrators, and still others are sure that DeSalvo's confession was simply the result of his desperate desire for fame and notoriety.

To this day, no one has ever been charged as the Boston Strangler.

FUN FACTS

The Strangler was given a number of monikers throughout his career. Some fans of alliteration insisted on calling him the "Phantom Fiend."

Visit Cambridge for your very own "I went to Harvard" shirt.

TEAM WINE HAUNTS

WARREN TAVERN GHOST
Haunted

UNION OYSTER HOUSE
Haunted. As both captain of Team Wine and Team Seafood, Christine may be spotted here enjoying a Sam Adams (or three) with a dozen oysters.

DRINK

DARRYL'S CORNER BAR & KITCHEN
Black-owned

PUBLICK HOUSE
Christine recommends the moules-frites with a pint of Allagash White.

TEAM MILKSHAKE HAUNTS

TOSCANINI'S
"The World's Best Ice Cream" by the *New York Times* (and Em Schulz)

LIZZY'S
Woman-owned

CHRISTINA'S

HAUNTED HOTELS

CHARLESGATE HOTEL

LIBERTY HOTEL

THE WAYSIDE INN

OMNI PARKER HOUSE HOTEL

SPOOKY TOURS

BOSTON GHOST TOURS BY GHOSTS
AND GRAVESTONES

DEATH AND DYING GHOST TOUR

HAUNTED BOSTON GHOST AND PUB
WALKING TOUR

SPELLBOUND MUSEUM, VAMPIRE,
AND GHOST HUNT TOUR

GHOSTS OF BOSTON TOUR

BOSTON CRIME TOUR

BOSTON BY FOOT TOUR: THE DARK
SIDE OF BOSTON

MOBSTERS AND LOBSTERS TOUR

OTHER WEIRD (WTF) PLACES TO CHECK OUT

LIZZIE BORDEN'S HOUSE

WORLD'S LARGEST CANDLE STORE

THE ORIGINAL DUNKIN' DONUTS

GLOW-IN-THE-DARK SWINGS

OLDEST WOODEN JAIL IN THE
COUNTRY

SALEM WITCHES' HANGING SITE

WITCHES' DUNGEON MUSEUM

CURSED GRAVESTONE

MUSEUM OF BAD ART

GRAVE OF THE BOSTON STRANGLER

WORLD'S SMALLEST MUSEUM

DR. SUESS'S AMAZING WORLD

FUN FACTS

Boston is the home of America's first public park, first public beach,
first subway system, and, most importantly, first chocolate factory!

The Boston Red Sox have a patent on their Green Monster's coloring;
the shade is called Fenway Green.

NEW YORK, NY

According to the people who were there, New York City was one of the creepier shows we've done. We were at the Gramercy in 2018, and Christine and I both picked great cases. Christine covered NXIVM, one of my favorite stories to date that she's discussed, and I covered Dear David, the documentation gone viral of a guy keeping tabs on the creepy experiences in his home. What freaked people out in particular was that at one of the scarier parts of my story, one of the stage lights' bulbs exploded and went out in a crackling hiss. The audience freaked out, and we later heard from the tech people that those were brand-new bulbs and they wouldn't have done that by themselves. Personally, my favorite parts of the night were when Lisa Lampanelli came to support us and when my girlfriend sent us "good luck" cookies. When I'm not on tour, I love the Jekyll and Hyde Club and all of their wild museums!

I will never forget our time in New York! Our show at the Gramercy was one for the books, but we also had an incredible time accepting our Webby there in 2019. As Em so rudely forgot to mention, New York is also the home of Em's and my love child, whose name is definitely spelled "Chremit," not "Chremmett."

PARANORMAL

GHOSTS OF BROADWAY

Apparitions in the wings? Actors hearing voices behind them mid-production? Instruments tuning themselves? That's show biz, baby! New York City is the home of Broadway, and with historic venues all over town, you can be certain that the living aren't the only ones enjoying the theater. Cast members see doppelgängers in the wings. Ghosts have woken up actors from naps just before showtime. Props will go missing and are sometimes seen *defying gravity.*

At the Palace Theatre, people have had encounters with the spirits of a man who roams the offices, a girl in the balcony, a boy in the mezzanine, a woman in the orchestra pit, and the spirit of Judy Garland.

Imagine working here and getting to be regularly haunted by Judy fucking Garland—are you kidding me?

This theater also has the spirit of Louie Borsalino, who fell to his death from the rafters mid-performance and is sometimes seen reenacting his death. Staff also report doors slamming by themselves, lights flickering, cold spots in rooms, and *all that jazz.*

The Belasco Theatre is haunted by its original owner, David Belasco. Witnesses claim he looks very real and is frequently seen in the halls, stairways, and the balcony, where he used to sit for shows. Some claim he has even walked right up to actors, shaken their hand, and complimented their performance. (A boss taking time to validate their staff? Dead or alive, it's a rarity, and we love to see it!) Curtains fly open, cigar smoke fills the air, and women feel their butts getting squeezed. (Ughhhh, you had to make it weird, David.)

People have spotted him in mirrors, gotten locked out of rooms, and heard David's sealed-off private elevator still running. They also hear footsteps and David yelling, and it's been said that *the "halls" are alive with the sound of music.* (After twenty years, my separate interests in musicals and ghosts have finally come together for these puns—please just let me have this.) When one usher bid David goodnight, all of the lobby doors swung open at once, one woman watched lights turn on and doors close for her on their own when grabbing her coat, and if a show has a bad night, the dressing rooms' furniture and decor will be thrown around by unknown forces. (. . . Okay, David, relax.)

The most active ghost in all of Broadway can be found at the New Amsterdam Theatre. Chorus girl Olive Thomas was cast in *Ziegfeld Follies*, a magazine cover girl, and a silent film actress. She is said to have died from swallowing a bottle of mercury bichloride pills (which eerily enough were shaped like coffins). Wearing a green dress, beaded headpiece, and holding a blue pill bottle, her apparition is seen all over the theater: hanging out backstage, walking through walls, walking across the empty stage, and appearing in the elevators. A *dead girl walking,* Olive is most active whenever the building is being renovated or when *Follies* plays here. Her customer service skills are also top-notch, as guests have reported being helped by her in a pinch.

In one instance, a woman requested a booster seat for her child, and by the time employees came back with one, Olive had already carried a seat over to the family. People have heard old music playing and tap dancing in empty rooms, and the stage will shake and light bulbs will burn out. She's also known to be flirty around men, so much so that security started hiring female guards at night, knowing that if fewer male guards were there, less paranormal activity would occur. (Not trying to shame you, girl, and I know it's been 100 years, but keep it together, Olive!!! Security had to change their entire protocol because of you.) Like Angelica Schuyler, she *will never be satisfied.* For even more of Broadway's ghosts, make sure to check out *Playbill*'s website, which happens to track spooky activity in each venue.

TRUE CRIME

MICHAEL MALLOY:
THE MAN WHO WOULDN'T DIE

This just sounds like one giant frat house initiation.

The story of "Iron Mike" has gone down in *ATWWD* history as one of our most memorable episodes. A down-on-his-luck Irishman living in New York during the Great Depression, Michael Malloy lived a somewhat unremarkable life, but in death became, as Gen Z might say, "iconic."

It all began on a summer evening in 1932, when 27-year-old bar owner Tony Marino was fed up with his struggling business. Sitting with friends Francis Pasqua and Daniel Kriesberg, Marino watched as patrons drank whiskey on credit with no intention of paying the bill.

Marino needed cash, and he needed it fast. Like many a desperate man before him, he decided to break the law to get it. It wouldn't take long for Marino to home in on loyal customer Michael Malloy as the perfect victim. The man, known as a local drunk, came into the bar every morning like clockwork and had no friends or family to speak of.

Marino and his friends hatched a plan. They would kill Malloy and collect the $3,500 in life insurance money, which equates to about $70,000 in today's currency. In January of 1933, the plan began in earnest. In what appeared to be a gesture of kindness, Marino offered Malloy unlimited credit at his bar, hoping the man would drink himself to death. Although Malloy drank on and on, and Marino's arm ached from pouring so many shots, it quickly became clear that Malloy wouldn't be dying of drink any-time soon. In fact, after three days of taking full advantage of his unlimited credit at Marino's bar, Malloy entered the speakeasy and shouted, "Boy, ain't I got a thirst?"

Marino was not amused. He and his friends, whom the press would later dub the "Murder Trust," decided to take their plan to the next level. They exchanged Malloy's whiskey for wood alcohol, but rather than succumb to the poisonous effects of this early version of antifreeze, Malloy simply asked for more.

When turpentine and horse liniment didn't do the trick either, they resorted to straight-up rat poison. When Malloy finally crumpled to the floor, the Murder Trust rejoiced. They'd done it! Or so they thought. After a few jagged breaths, Malloy emitted what they thought to be a death rattle. But, to their dismay, moments later he began snoring.

A "Drunk Superman," as Em called him in Episode 9, Malloy woke up from his slumber only to shout, "Gimme some of the old regular, m'lad!" Knowing Malloy loved seafood, they next resorted to feeding him oysters soaked in denatured alcohol. Malloy ate each and every oyster, downing his meal with a nice cold chaser of antifreeze.

Surprise, surprise: he survived.

At a certain point, the Murder Trust had grown to so many members that the $3,500 they stood to gain from Malloy's death wouldn't even be worth it. But rather than take these many, massive hints from the universe that *maybe you should stop trying to murder this man*, the gang only grew more determined to kill Malloy, just to prove to themselves that they could.

A man named Murphy was next to try his hand at murder. He let a tin of sardines rot for several days before mixing it with shrapnel, slathering the concoction between pieces of bread, and serving Malloy a "sandwich" that the group hoped would tear through his organs and kill him. Instead, he asked for seconds.

Next, the gang attempted to use nature to their advantage. They doused an intoxicated Malloy in ice water before leaving him on a park bench in the -14 degree Fahrenheit weather. When Marino opened his bar up the next morning, he found Malloy in the basement, half frozen. Turns out, he had trekked the half mile back to the bar, complaining of a "wee chill."

It had now been two months of these attempts, with no success. In February, another insurance payment was due—the group was not about to make the payment, so out of desperation they decided to drive over him with a car. The group lugged a drunk Malloy to a nearby road, hitting him head-on at fifty miles per hour before backing over him for good measure. The men fled the scene, but in order to collect their insurance payment, they had to find the body. They called every morgue in town, but Malloy was nowhere to be found.

A few days later, Michael Malloy limped into the bar and proclaimed, "I sure am dying for a drink."

Seven months after the Murder Trust had hatched their plan, Michael Malloy, "the man who wouldn't die," finally passed away. The group had grown so desperate that they threw caution to the wind and ran a rubber tube from a gas lamp fixture to Malloy's mouth. Within the hour, he was dead.

When the Trust attempted to cash in the policy with a phony death certificate in hand, the skeptical insurance company contacted the police. After exhuming the body, police arrested the men responsible. Marino, Pasqua, and Kriesberg were all convicted and sentenced to death. When it came to the men's own demise, I believe *Smithsonian* magazine said it best: "The charter members of the Murder Trust were sent to the electric chair at Sing Sing, which killed them all on the very first try."

For the full story of Malloy's heroics, check out Episode 9: "The Wandering Cowboy and the Pregnancy Pact, but for Boys."

TEAM WINE HAUNTS

EAR INN
Haunted

WHITE HORSE TAVERN
Haunted. Second-oldest continuously run tavern in New York City

ONE IF BY LAND, TWO IF BY SEA
Haunted. Romantic and full of ghosts—what more could you ask for on date night?

67 ORANGE STREET
Black-owned

NOWADAYS

THE DEAD RABBIT

JOYFACE EAST VILLAGE

TEAM MILKSHAKE HAUNTS

MORGENSTERN'S FINEST ICE CREAM

BIG GAY ICE CREAM

ODDFELLOW'S ICE CREAM CO.

HAUNTED HOTELS

HOTEL CHELSEA

THE ALGONQUIN HOTEL

WOLCOTT HOTEL

BOWERY HOTEL

SPOOKY TOURS

NYC GANGSTERS AND GHOSTS TOUR

NYC PHANTOM PUB CRAWL

TALES FROM THE GRAVE: GREENWICH VILLAGE

GHOST TOURS OF MANHATTAN

EAST VILLAGE GHOST TOUR

GHOSTS, MURDERS, AND MAYHEM: HELL'S KITCHEN

GANGS OF NEW YORK TOUR

THE ULTIMATE GREENWICH VILLAGE GHOST TOUR

OTHER WEIRD (WTF) PLACES TO CHECK OUT

MORBID ANATOMY MUSEUM

THE WORLD'S LARGEST KALEIDOSCOPE

HARRY HOUDINI MUSEUM

COUNTRY'S OLDEST MINI-GOLF

CAMP HERO
Alleged site of the Montauk Project and inspiration for *Stranger Things*

FILMING LOCATION FOR THE *GHOSTBUSTERS* HEADQUARTERS

JEKYLL AND HYDE CLUB
Em's favorite bar in NYC!

THE METRONOME CLOCK
"The World's Most Confusing Clock"

MUSEUM OF SEX
"If you aren't weirdly close with your mother, don't come here with her to bond like I did." —Em

SPYSCAPE: THE HOME OF SECRETS

HARRY HOUDINI'S GRAVE

SITE OF TESLA'S LAB

FUN FACTS

Einstein's eyeballs are kept in New York City in a safety-deposit box.

November 28, 2012, was the first documented day with not one violent crime reported in New York City.

WASHINGTON, DC

DC was the closest show to my hometown in Virginia. I was excited to visit home, but I knew by the end of the trip I would have to perform in front of tens of people I went to high school and college with, and I hadn't yet tackled my stage fright anxieties. Before the show, it took everything I had to keep my mother from buying out every ticket, so that actual listeners could be at the show. But Linda still found a way to show up in style. Christine and I drove to our own show in the back of my childhood best friend's car (shout-out to Deirdre), while my mom and her friends came to the venue in a fucking limousine. Back then we didn't have a lot of security at our shows, but luckily for us Deirdre wasn't just our driver that night. She volunteered to guard our greenroom door and came to the show dressed in a hot pink, full-body Juicy velour jumpsuit. Since this show, I've wanted all of our security to wear the same uniform, but so far nobody else seems on board with it.

Em definitely has a more storied past with DC, but not many people know I lived there for several years too! And Em is lucky I did, or else I'd never have met my wonderful roommate Allison, who later became Em's girlfriend . . . You're welcome, both of you.

PARANORMAL

THE WHITE HOUSE

1600 PENNSYLVANIA AVE NW • WASHINGTON, DC

The President's Palace, the Executive Mansion, or, as officially named in 1901, the "White House" really needs no introduction. Every president since John Adams has lived here, although George Washington chose the site for construction.

FUN FACT

A man named David Burnes already lived on this property and was ultimately pushed to sell it. (Nothing more American than taking somebody else's land to build the White House!)

Today the White House has ten recorded deaths, half of which were presidents and First Ladies, and the place is jam-packed with ghosts. In the attic, people hear two voices: President Harrison's and another saying, "I'm David Burnes." (Couldn't get rid of him that easily, Washington.) In the basement there is a ghost cat that is said to be an omen for looming national disasters. People have seen the ghosts of Grant, McKinley, several First Ladies, and others wandering the halls. In the Rose Garden, people see Dolley Madison, who leaves the scent of roses and scares those who attempt to dig up her roses.

In Jackson's old bedroom, the Rose Room, he is heard either laughing non-stop or swearing violently (#vibes). Lyndon B. Johnson's aide would even hear him in his room cussing up a storm. There is also the spirit of an unknown teenager called the "Thing" (wow, he's already dead; kick him while he's down) that scared Taft so much he threatened to fire his staff if they ever mentioned it. On the second floor where the first family sleeps, there are knocks, footsteps, and apparitions in bedrooms and the Yellow Oval Room. There is also the spirit of a British soldier who once set the White House on fire, sometimes still seen with a torch and lighting beds on fire while you sleep in them.

People have seen Lincoln's son Willie and heard Cleveland's wife giving birth. (Imagine your ghost having to relive childbirth for eternity.) In the East Room, Abigail Adams still hangs her laundry, and there's phantom banging on the front door from Anna Surratt, who once did so to beg for her mother to be spared after conspiring in Lincoln's assassination. The most common ghost seen in the White House is Abraham Lincoln, while his wife, interestingly, was the most active in the White House with spiritualism and even hosted séances there after losing their son. Just to name a few, Honest Abe (aka Attention-Seeking Abe) haunted the Hoovers, Kennedys, and Fords. The first person to see him was Calvin Coolidge's wife, Grace, who saw him looking out of the Oval Office window. People have seen him sleeping in bed, tying his shoes, standing at the window or next to the fireplace, sitting in a chair near the stairs, and vanishing before your eyes. Lincoln's spirit is most active during stressful points in the White House (soooo always?). Even eerier, Lincoln allegedly confided in his bodyguard that he knew he was going to die the night of his assassination. Lincoln's ghost is also known to pull pranks on people staying in his room, including George Bush's daughter, who woke up to loud music coming out of the fireplace. The staff told her later that Lincoln did that to prank kids.

Another time, Winston Churchill got out of the bathtub to get a cigar, and while walking through the room naked, he ran into Lincoln at the fireplace. (If that happened to me . . . for the rest of my life, every time I felt good about myself, my brain would remind me of this moment and humble me all over again.) Churchill grabbed his cigar and said, "Good evening, Mr. President. You seem to have me at a disadvantage." (He puts the "chill" in "Churchill," am I right?) Lincoln's ghost HEARD him, laughed, and faded away (oh my god). Among the presidents who have witnessed spirits here, Harry S. Truman seemed to have the most fun with it. He often wrote about his experiences here and even dressed up as a ghost and hid in his daughter's room to scare her. As Truman once wrote, "Damned place is haunted, sure as shooting."

Learn more about the White House in Episode 25: "Ghostly Frenemies and Alcala-ism."

TRUE CRIME

THE MURDER OF VIOLA DRATH

Ask a DC native about the Georgetown neighborhood, and you'll likely get a variety of answers. Some might describe the area as charming and trendy, while others might use more vivid adjectives like *uppity* or *pretentious*. However you feel about Georgetown, it can't be denied that the neighborhood is beautiful and filled with history. Its cobblestone streets, upscale boutiques, and waterfront dining make it one of the area's top spots for tourists and locals alike.

But this book is about the dark side of vacation destinations, and I intend to deliver. Enter: socialite Viola Herms Drath. Described by the *New York Times* as "the worst marriage in Georgetown," Viola's relationship with social climber Albrecht Muth is, as they say, one for the books.

Viola was raised in Germany but had lived in DC since 1968. She and her husband, Lieutenant Colonel Francis S. Drath, known more succinctly as the "Colonel," flourished in the capital. They were the ultimate power couple: the Colonel worked for the government and took care of their daughters, while Viola jetsetted to New York and Germany to cover fashion shows and build up her social circle, befriending Norman Mailer, Henry Kissinger, and other fancy folks. Viola was described as a notable figure in German-American relations, and in addition to German-American politics, she regularly wrote about culture, fine art, and political gossip.

In other words, she was a badass.

At a conference in the early 1980s, Viola met a young teenage intern from Germany. His name was Albrecht Muth, and he claimed to have been a big fan of her work "since his youth." He'd only recently moved to DC to study at American University,* but the two bonded over schnitzel, and Viola was impressed by his wit and ambition. The two struck up a sort of mentorship relationship, and Albrecht began visiting the Draths' Georgetown home regularly. Although he didn't seem threatening, there was no denying he was an odd duck. For example, he once showed up at the Drath residence wearing an eye patch, explaining that he had gotten in the way of an assassination attempt in Paraguay.

Meanwhile, the Colonel's health had been deteriorating, and on January 11, 1986, he lost his battle with cancer. After a happy and peaceful forty-year

---

*American University is known for notable alumni such as Judge Judy, Giuliana Rancic, and Christine Schiefer.

marriage, Viola was now left with an over-whelming amount of tasks that had previously been assigned to Francis. Gentleman that he was, the young Albrecht began stepping up to the various tasks that had once belonged to Francis. His visits to the home became more frequent, and he provided Viola with company and affection when she needed it most.

One day, Albrecht showed up unannounced wearing a tux and holding a bottle of French champagne. He proposed marriage, and Viola accepted. To give you some insight into their dynamic, Viola was seventy years old, and Albrecht was twenty-six. I'm not great at math, but my trusty calculator tells me that's a whopping forty-four-year difference. While I'm also the first to agree that "age is but a number," I think my insight into the story's ending gives me a right to raise at least one eyebrow.

During their marriage, Albrecht's "eccentricity" skyrocketed. He fabricated a story that an elderly German count had fallen from an elephant in India and needed to appoint a successor before dying—from that point forward, Albrecht insisted on being called either Count Albrecht or Count Albi.

Following the end of the Iraq War in 2003, Albrecht suddenly adopted the rank and wore the uniform of a brigadier general in the Iraqi army, going so far as to organize diplomatic events in DC that he claimed were for the new Iraqi regime. He even managed to arrange a ceremony at Arlington National Cemetery to honor fallen American soldiers on behalf of the Iraqi regime. Keep in mind, all of this is bullshit! To this day, there is no evidence whatsoever that Albrecht ever stepped foot in Iraq, though he was known to parade around the streets of Georgetown in an olive uniform and red beret. He even made up his own family crest.

If this story had stopped at eccentricities, it probably wouldn't be featured in this book. Unfortunately, however, it turns out there was an even darker side to Albrecht and Viola's relationship. In 1992, Albrecht was convicted of beating Viola, the beginning of a rap sheet that would chronicle numerous cases of domestic abuse, including punching her in the face for interrupting a phone call. During another instance, the two were staying at the Plaza Hotel when Albrecht threw Viola's clothes into the hall and locked her out of the room for the night.

Meanwhile, Albrecht was also actively having affairs with men. At one point, he even moved in with a boyfriend, whom he also abused before he was kicked out. Albrecht once insulted Viola's daughter, and Viola defended her, so Albrecht swung a chair at her and then repeatedly pounded her head against the floor. After she called 911 and had him arrested, Albrecht left for a while, claiming to be in Iraq working side by side with big-wig officials to end the war. Meanwhile, when he called Viola, his area code showed up as Miami, Florida. But despite all this, Albrecht was able to woo Viola back, as we see abusers do time and time again.

As expected, every time he wormed his way back into Viola's life, Albrecht's abusive behavior would escalate. By the time Viola was ninety, Albrecht was monitoring her emails and isolating her from friends and acquaintances. Unsurprisingly, Albrecht was not well-liked in the community. Enough people had called him on his bullshit at this point that he began spending most of his time at home, drinking and sending Viola abusive rants via email while she sat in the other room.

One afternoon in 2011, Albrecht met up with a friend he had found on potentially the one place you *shouldn't* find friends: Craigslist. During this meeting, Albrecht got belligerently drunk and ended up staggering home around 10 p.m.

Side note: Albrecht called Viola's home "The Albrechtory."

The following morning, August 12, 2011, police received a call from Albrecht, saying he had returned from his morning walk to find his wife, Viola, dead on the bathroom floor. Now ninety-one years old, Viola was presumed to have taken a fall due to her age. But the medical examiner quickly realized that Viola's scalp was bruised, her thumbnail torn, and the cartilage in her neck fractured. She had been strangled and bludgeoned to death.

As soon as Viola's death was ruled a homicide, Albrecht, as he was wont to do, fabricated a preposterous tale. He explained that Viola had been killed as a result of a failed Iranian assassination attempt on him.

It took police only four days to collect enough evidence to arrest Albrecht. During that period, they forbade him from entering his home, so instead, he slept in a Georgetown park wearing a perfectly tailored houndstooth blazer.

Albrecht's behavior during his trial was absolutely balloonatoons. Not only did he show up in his orange prison jumpsuit with a popped collar, but he also announced that he would serve as his own attorney and that he would begin "an unlimited fast." When doctors pleaded with him to eat, he told them that he was following orders from the Archangel Gabriel. They needn't worry about his ability to survive, because he was comparable to a camel, and also Jesus.

On January 16, 2014, a jury deliberated only three hours before declaring Albrecht Muth, 49, guilty of beating and strangling socialite and journalist Viola Herms Drath to death. He was sentenced to fifty years in prison, where he remains to this day. I can only assume his "unlimited fast" has ended by now, but jury's out on the whole camel-Jesus thing.

For more on Count Albi's crimes (and the introduction of Lemon!), listen to Episode 108: "The Kings of Banter and a Mummified Lemon."

TEAM WINE HAUNTS

GADSBY'S TAVERN
Haunted

BEN'S NEXT DOOR
Black-owned. Christine recommends the Froze-Aye!

OLD EBBITT GRILL
Haunted

OCCIDENTAL GRILL
Haunted

RHODES TAVERN
Haunted

TEAM MILKSHAKE HAUNTS

PITANGO GELATO

NICECREAM

SOUTHWEST SODA POP SHOP
Black-owned

HAUNTED HOTELS

OMNI SHOREHAM HOTEL

HAY-ADAMS HOTEL

SPOOKY TOURS

DC HAUNTED PUB CRAWL

DC HAUNTED BAR TOUR

DC GHOST TOURS & HAUNTED TOURS
Nightly spirits

WHITE HOUSE PUB TOUR
Nightly spirits

GHOSTS OF GEORGETOWN AND WHITE HOUSE GHOSTS

TRUE CRIMES OF WICKED GEORGETOWN

ALEXANDRIA'S ORIGINAL GHOST AND GRAVEYARD TOUR

CAPITOL HILL HAUNTS

OTHER WEIRD (WTF) PLACES TO CHECK OUT

INTERNATIONAL SPY MUSEUM

JFK'S PROPOSAL BOOTH

THE TECHNICOLOR CHURCH

ABE LINCOLN'S HITCHING POST

THE MANSION ON O&O ST. MUSEUM
One of Em's favorite museums!

THE EXORCIST STAIRS

TAXIDERMIED MARTHA, THE LAST PASSENGER PIGEON

FUN FACTS

Washington and DC were originally two different cities.

People who live in DC drink more wine (per capita) than any other people in the US.

This could be because Allison and I lived there together . . .

PITTSBURGH, PA

While on our tour's leg to Pittsburgh, Christine's mom made bread and gave some to Christine to bring with her on her trip. While Christine was out with Blaise for dinner, she left me with her hotel key (stupid), and I decided I wanted to eat the bread in their room. So with the (forced) help of Eva, I stole the bread, left hints all over Christine's room for her to find, and "decorated" her mirrors with hair conditioner. I planned on bringing them back (most) of the bread the next morning, but we left in a rush and I forgot the bread in the hotel when we drove off. In my defense, Christine never paid the ransom note that she found behind her toilet. Also, let's call it karma for the night before, when Christine did that whole Steelers/Bengals jersey switcheroo in front of the audience.

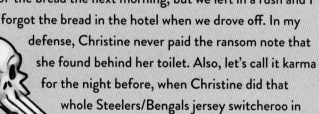

Yeah, I'm not sure Pittsburgh ever really forgave me for that stunt I pulled on stage. Incidentally, I've also never forgiven Em for the bread incident. Anyone who's tried it knows my mom's bread is a precious commodity. Unfortunately, I can't hold a grudge to save my life, but Renate sure can. Em, I advise you to stay far away if you know what's good for you.

PARANORMAL

HILL VIEW MANOR

2801 HILL VIEW MANOR DR · NEW CASTLE, PA

In 1926, the Lawrence County Poor Farm was built to house and employ the elderly, mentally ill, and destitute. By the 1970s it was renovated into a nursing home, which was originally going to be called the Lawrence County Home for the Aged. But at the last minute, the town held a contest that let the winner select the building's name, which is how we got the Hill View Manor. Unfortunately, it closed by 2004 and was auctioned off a year later.

It's said that while in operation, up to 10,000 deaths occurred on the property. Some of the causes of death were as common as suicides; others were as rare as a someone in a wheelchair rolling backward down the stairs. The most famous death was a resident here named Eli, who passed out in the boiler room after a night of drinking.

Not only were there several deaths in the past, but there are several ghosts today. There is the spirit of a boy named Jeffery, who may or may not be a literal demon disguising himself as a child. Throughout the building people hear whistling, laughter, singing, door slams, heavy thuds, dragging, footsteps, gurneys rolling, and the organ in hallway playing. Equipment malfunctions and gets thrown around, sometimes at people. People report getting grabbed and having their butt pinched all of the time.

Shadow figures are seen everywhere: in reflections, running down hallways, hiding in corners of the room, sitting in rocking chairs, and peering out of doorways. A lot of people have also said they feel like they're being choked in spaces where people have died, and one investigative team was able to debunk the story that someone jumped out of a window (they found out that the victim was actually pushed). There are spirits who don't like men, who scream at you to get out, and my personal favorite ghost in all of Pennsylvania, who will leave you alone if you shout, "Go, Steelers!"

Remember that time we performed in Pittsburgh and while on stage Christine wore a Steelers jersey, ripped it off, and showed the crowd her Bengals jersey that she was wearing underneath all along? Yeah, this ghost would HATE her.

Some of the spirits are said to answer questions through knocks, and there's one entity that is a solid black mass in the basement who will grow so large you can't see down the hallway. According to former employees, one time all of the lights went out at once, doors flew open, and animals didn't go down into certain parts of the building.

Eli, the man who died in the boiler room, seems to be very active. He screams a lot at people to leave and has been caught on audio saying, "I like to fuck with people." When Mr. Zak Bagans of the famed *Ghost Adventures* and his crew investigated Hill View Manor, they got a voice saying "Saari," which ended up being Eli's last name. While there, Zak also experienced shadow figures running by and someone rubbing his back. His team also caught some great EVPs (electronic voice phenomena) including "Hi, Zak," "Run," and in the geriatric wing, "Don't hurt your back."

There have been other teams who caught similarly great EVPs. When one team captured an EVP saying, "Please help," the team asked what kind of help. They then got an intelligent response back with a second EVP saying, "Doctor." Another time investigators asked, "Is anyone here?" to which they got back the perfectly creepy (but perfectly vague) response, "Me." Next time you're in the Pittsburgh area and looking for a way to scare yourself, check out the Hill View Manor. If you go and feel anything lurking nearby, just remember: Go, Steelers!

TRUE CRIME

THE BIDDLE BROTHERS

You know that quaint and evocative saying, "You can't make this shit up"? Well, I think this story deserves ample use of that phrase. The Biddle brothers have gone down in Pennsylvania history as one of the state's greatest scandals, and for good reason.

Brothers Jack and Ed Biddle were born in 1872 and 1876, respectively, and began a life of crime at a young age. As teenagers, they formed a gang known for knocking out their victims with chloroform- or ether-soaked rags before robbing them. This group of rapscallions, not-so-creatively nicknamed the "Chloroform Gang," committed twenty-seven burglaries throughout Pittsburgh before things escalated; while attempting to burglarize a grocery store in Mt. Washington in 1901, guns were drawn, and the store owner was killed.

When police entered the Biddle residence, things only got worse. An officer was shot, and the Biddle brothers were immediately arrested. They were convicted on all counts and were sentenced to hang on December 12, 1901.

While awaiting their execution in Allegheny County Jail, the brothers were visited by a woman named Kate Soffel, who was known for delivering Bibles and fruit to the prisoners in an attempt to convert them to Christianity and set them on the right path.

Am I the only one who questions her success rate?

Instead of bringing the brothers to Jesus, though, she fell in love with Ed Biddle. Oh, I should probably also mention that she just so happened to be the wife of the prison warden. Ruh-roh!

Deciding she could not allow the two brothers to die, *especially* her new crush, Ed, Kate instead hatched a plan to help them escape. She did so by smuggling in two revolvers and some saw blades, which she hid in the pages of her Bibles. At night, the Biddle brothers sawed away, and during the day they covered up their work by keeping the bars in place with chewing gum. The group even developed a coded language in which Kate would point at certain body parts to indicate which letter she was trying to communicate.

At 4 a.m. on January 30, 1902, Kate borrowed a tip from the Chloroform Gang and chloroformed her husband, the warden, knocking him out. While Kate was busy incapacitating her husband, Ed Biddle called out from his cell to one of the guards, James McGeary, announcing that his brother had suddenly fallen ill and needed immediate assistance. The unsuspecting guard rushed over with medication, not realizing that the brothers had already sawed through their prison bars and were simply luring him over as part of their plan. As the guard approached, Jack lunged through the opening in the bars, seized the guard by the waist, and threw him over a railing to the stone floor sixteen feet below. Meanwhile, Ed pulled out the revolver that Kate had smuggled in and shot a second guard. Amazingly, although both guards were severely wounded, both survived.

Jack and Ed stole the prison keys, locked the guards in the prison dungeon, and changed into the guards' clothes before walking out of jail. Kate Soffel had been waiting for them in the jail library, and the brothers swung by to pick her up. The three of them fled through downtown Pittsburgh and took a trolley to Perrysville. There, they bought some ham sandwiches and stole a sleigh. What did I say? *You can't make this shit up!*

Apparently, the sleigh they had stolen wasn't the classic toboggan-type we all recognize but was instead attached to a horse that would pull them to their next destination. It's been theorized that the group's goal was to escape into Canada, but because of the brutal winter cold they were forced to stop in Butler, Pennsylvania, for four hours. Apparently during this time, Ed and Kate decided to consummate their new relationship.

Aww?

After four hours of fun for everyone but brother Jack, I guess, it was time for them to hit the road again. But by this point, pursuing officers had caught up with them. The officers demanded they stop and put their hands up. In a panic, Ed turned his gun on himself. This prompted officers to shoot, but not before Ed had shot himself.

Jack was also riddled with bullets. Kate Soffel, thinking her lover had died, begged her own husband, the prison warden, to kill her too. Having just woken up from a chloroform nap to this sheer and utter chaos, the warden was probably very, very confused. When he refused to shoot his wife (duh), she responded by shooting herself in the chest. Amazingly, none of the three died that day, although neither brother ultimately survived their wounds.

Kate Soffel miraculously survived this whole ordeal. She ended up back in Pittsburgh and was put on trial for aiding in the Biddle brothers' escape. It didn't help that during the shoot-out, a letter from Ed Biddle fell from her pocket detailing his devotion to her and their plans to break out of jail. Kate was convicted of both aiding in the escape as well as adultery. She served a prison sentence of two years at the Western Penitentiary. Better than Allegheny County Jail, I guess? Because Kate wasn't one to keep things boring, she briefly attempted to make it in showbiz. She first worked as part of a traveling Vaudeville show called *The Biddle Boys*, before starring as herself in her own play called *A Desperate Chance*. The play was shut down by the Fayette County court in Pennsylvania due to claims that it was "illegal," whatever that means.

Her short-lived acting career over, Kate moved on to dressmaking, opening up a successful seamstress shop in the North Shore neighborhood of Pittsburgh. She also returned to her maiden name, Katherine Dietrich, in an attempt to distance herself from her notoriety.

Mrs. Soffel's ghost is said to haunt her old bedroom in the Allegheny County Jail. According to Haunted Pittsburgh Tours, the deputy warden experienced pictures moving on their own, sounds in the walls, and the cold touch of someone he believes to be Mrs. Soffel herself. An article published in 1907 even stated that prisoners complained about seeing the ghosts of the Biddle brothers roaming the halls.

Learn more about the hauntings at the old jail on the Haunted Pittsburgh Walking Tour, which runs from spring to early November each year.

FUN FACT

According to the president and CEO of Pittsburgh's Heinz History Center, "Ed Biddle was shot seventeen times, which coincidentally for you crime and violence buffs [by which I think he means us], is exactly the number of times that Clyde Barrow [of Bonnie and Clyde] was shot when he was killed."

The story was made into a 1984 film called *Mrs. Soffel*, starring Diane Keaton and Mel Gibson. During filming, MGM erected a headstone at the brothers' previously unmarked gravesite, which featured a poem found in Ed Biddle's pocket at his death.

The Biddle brothers' sleigh can be found at the Heinz History Center, still riddled with bullet holes.

To hear this story told live in Pittsburgh, listen to Episode 136: "A French Toast Ghost and the Pepper Spray Squad."

TEAM WINE HAUNTS

ST. CLAIR SOCIAL
Women-owned, Black-owned

ACACIA

BAR BOTANICO
Offers "Choose your own adventure" drinks!

HARMONY INN
Haunted

JEAN BONNET TAVERN
Haunted. This 1760s tavern is in Bedford, not Pittsburgh, but if you find yourself in the area, it's well worth grabbing a drink at this extremely haunted inn!

TEAM MILKSHAKE HAUNTS

KLAVON'S

THE MILKSHAKE FACTORY

MILLIE'S ICE CREAM

HAPPY DAY DESSERT FACTORY
Black-owned

HAUNTED HOTELS

RENAISSANCE HOTEL

OMNI WILLIAM PENN HOTEL

CENTURY INN

SPOOKY TOURS

HAUNTED PITTSBURGH GHOST TOUR

HAUNTED PITTSBURGH CRUISE

NOTORIOUS PITTSBURGH
WALKING TOUR

BLACK AND GHOST TOUR

OTHER WEIRD (WTF) PLACES TO CHECK OUT

MATTRESS FACTORY ART FACTORY

THE LAST WOODEN STREET IN
PENNSYLVANIA

ROBOWORLD

THE ORIGINAL BUBBLE MACHINE

FREDOSAURUS REX
Aka a dinosaur dressed like Mr. Rogers

RANDYLAND
One of Em's favorites!

WORLD'S OLDEST ROLLERCOASTER,
LEAP-THE-DIPS, AT LAKETON PARK
IN ALTOONA

THE CRAYOLA FACTORY

POTATO CHIP TOUR

CASTLE HALLOWEEN MUSEUM

THE FIFTIES PLACE MINI MUSEUM

FUN FACTS

From 1891 to 1911, Pittsburgh was officially spelled without its "h."

Pittsburgh has the steepest street in the United States:
Canton Avenue, at 37 degrees.

PHILADELPHIA, PA

Philly was one of the cities we traveled to during our small "practice" tour in 2018. We had two shows here, and luckily that meant we had some time to explore. Before one of our shows, we all got together and had Philly cheesesteaks on principle, and I checked out the Museum of Pizza Culture and the Mütter Museum, which was perfectly fun and perfectly weird. I personally liked the "Soap Woman" on display the most (a yellow fever victim whose body literally turned into soap due to how she was buried). I've also been to the World's Largest General Store in Leighton, and it was exactly what I was hoping for. I remember during our shows, *The Office* was playing in the greenroom the whole time, my sorority sister won one of the *And That's Why We Draw* prompts, and Christine appreciated the face masks one of our listeners gave her after the show.

Philly was a blast! I pretended to be a "runner" on that trip and attempted to jog around as a way to see the city. It was a great way to explore different neighborhoods, but let's just say the vegetarian Philly cheesesteak I had afterward was a much more physically enjoyable experience.

PARANORMAL

BALEROY MANSION

111 W MERMAID LN • PHILADELPHIA, PA

Built in 1911, the Baleroy Mansion is a thirty-two-room mansion documented as one of the most haunted places in the country. The original owner was a carpenter who allegedly killed his wife in the house, and in 1926 the Easby family moved in. George Meade Easby, great-grandson to General George Meade, who defeated Robert E. Lee at the Battle of Gettysburg, lived here most of his life. He says that stored in the mansion are thousands of historical items from world leaders, including the cannonball that killed his great-grandfather in battle.

Perhaps all of these significant items left behind residual energy in the home, which could explain many of the paranormal instances. George says he's had several experiences in the mansion, such as seeing apparitions floating around, rooms untidying themselves after being cleaned, getting grabbed at night, heavy footsteps running in the halls, and phantom cars coming up the driveway. He also claimed there were appearances from his late brother Steven. Before Steven died, George and his brother were out by the fountain looking at the water. George says that, at one point, his reflection did not change but Steven's morphed into a skeleton . . . excuse me?

Soon after, Steven was dead. George alleged Steven's spirit is still around and shows himself as a little boy looking out the window toward the yard. Staff also say they've seen a little kid looking out the window. Steven's portrait has also been lifted off of hooks and flown off of walls. His apparition has also been seen wandering the house and showing up in reflections. (I feel like when it's your brother, you're allowed to yell at him for creepy shit like this.) The mansion also has seen the apparition of Thomas Jefferson in the dining room, and during one dinner party a pot came out of nowhere and hit a guest in the head. During renovations, electricity will glitch, and construction workers have lost their breath or heard their names being called.

Some of George's most positive experiences, though, were whenever his late mother would visit and guide him toward answers or important heirlooms. One time, she led George to a secret drawer, in which he found a flag his great-grandfather had saved from the war. She also communicated with George through a medium named Judith. Judith heard a voice saying the name "Longfellow" and the phrase "Children's Hour," which George confirmed was "The Children's Hour" by Henry Wadsworth Longfellow, his mother's favorite poem. When he checked the bookshelf later, that book had her will and a note to him stuffed in the pages. One part of the will hinted that he was the rightful heir to the state of Florida.

Mom? When you come haunt me in the future, I would like to find out I'm the heir to Marvel Studios.

He also found a note from his skeptical father, admitting to having witnessed spirits, probably in the Baleroy Mansion. Although most of the spirits so far have seemed either nice or related to George, there is one more sinister ghost named Amanda. Amanda is attached to a 200-year-old chair in the drawing room. This chair is also known as the "Chair of Death" and was allegedly owned by Napoleon Bonaparte and made by a warlock (all of this sounds like it's so crazy it must be true, or it's just not true). According to the legend, Amanda tries to lure people over to the cursed chair so that they will die. Weirdly, many people have said they felt almost hypnotized to go sit in it, and at least three people have been documented sitting in the chair and dying a few weeks later, including George's innkeeper. Amanda is said to be very powerful and has thrown doors open and items across the room. She also manifests as a blue ectoplasm, sometimes even following people home after they've left the mansion. One person claimed to see Amanda after sitting in the Chair of Death—on the streets, in his car, at home, everywhere.

George's friend Robert later inherited the house and sold it in 2012. Honestly, though, imagine inheriting a demon, a chair that's trying to kill you, a mansion full of priceless historical items, and sometimes Thomas Jefferson's ghost? That's a lot of pressure—I get it, Rob. The Baleroy Mansion is now a private home, and for all of you wondering, the house has been blessed. Thanks, priests!

TRUE CRIME

ARSENIC INCORPORATED— THE STORY OF THE SOUTH PHILLY POISON RING

A tailor, a witch doctor, and a spaghetti salesman walk into a bar … and instead of a punch line, you're gonna hear the story of Philly's infamous Poison Ring.

Meet the Petrillo cousins: Paul was a reputable tailor who had emigrated from Naples in 1910, followed shortly thereafter by his cousin Herman, a spaghetti salesman. (Yes, I'm serious.) Like many faced with financial ruin due to the Great Depression, the men desperately sought a new way to make a living in 1930s Philadelphia.

They turned, naturally, to crime. Herman and Paul recruited a friend, Russian immigrant Morris Bolber, to join their new "business venture." Bolber himself had an interesting past. After graduating from university at age twelve, he had become obsessed with mysticism, studying under a sorceress for five years and learning to make potions and poison. He had recently emigrated to Philly and set up shop as a "faith healer," not-so-discreetly painting the letters "Dr." on his storefront.

This is like that time Em got ordained online and began calling themselves Reverend Schulz.

In 1932, one of Morris's patients complained of her husband's infidelity. A light bulb went off; Morris and the Petrillo cousins hatched a plan. Paul's role would be to seduce women unhappy in their marriage who might be interested in reaping the benefits of their husbands' deaths. Meanwhile, Herman would play the part of the husband and purchase life insurance. The group would then kill the *real* husband, an act they whimsically called "sending him to California."

Rather than enjoying a restful beach vacation, the group's victims were instead drowned, bludgeoned, or run over with a car. Meanwhile, the Depression worsened, and the group's crimes escalated. After about a dozen murders, the Petrillos had found themselves the leaders of an informal gang called Arsenic Incorporated (not to be confused with a band you might find on the back of a 2007 Warped Tour T-shirt).

Arsenic Inc., which later became the Philly Poison Ring, soon adopted a new member named Maria Carina Favato, another "faith healer" who also considered herself a matchmaker. She utilized curses and potions to help women move on from unhappy relationships, and amazingly, the potions actually worked. Not because they were magic, but because they were arsenic.

You see, the women's husbands would die from said "potion," leaving the women free to remarry and providing the gang a hearty life insurance payout. Like any successful business operation, Arsenic Inc. saw great growth, expanding to twenty-four members by 1938. With such rapid expansion, though, the operation became unwieldy, and the scam began to unravel.

Police had grown suspicious at the number of Italian men dying in the area, and it wasn't long before they caught a break in the case. You see, Arsenic Inc. had tried repeatedly and unsuccessfully to poison a man named Ferdinand Alfonsi. When an upholstery cleaner named George Myers approached Herman Petrillo to ask for a loan to save his business, Herman saw this as the perfect opportunity—he offered George Myers $500 in cash to kill Alfonsi. Myers was instructed to hit Alfonsi with a lead pipe, then throw him down the stairs to make it look like an accident.

Instead of bashing a stranger in the head with a pipe, Myers went straight to the police, who were already eyeing Herman for counterfeiting. To catch him once and for all, an undercover agent posed as a hitman and offered to kill Alfonsi for the same $500 offered to Myers. Before the deal could go through, though, Alfonsi ended up at Philadelphia's National Stomach Hospital with severe stomach pains. Upon his death, high levels of arsenic were found in his urine.

Herman Petrillo was arrested for homicide, but police worried they didn't have enough to hold him. That worry was short-lived, though, because to everyone's amazement, Herman wouldn't shut the hell up. He provided a mind-boggling list of victims and conspirators, describing Paul and Morris Bolber as the masterminds behind the whole operation.

On the stand, Morris confessed to fraud, explaining he regularly charged clients to rid their homes of so-called evil spirits. He had once put a frog in someone's basement, leading them to believe a devil lived there. He then charged them $75 and removed the frog. He once convinced a fellow Arsenic Inc. member named Salvatore Sortino to carry an egg under his armpit for nine days and nine nights, after which the special egg would hatch a devil. On the last day, Salvatore was to walk around a graveyard with outstretched arms before sitting in his basement to wait for the devil. Oh, to be a juror in this courtroom...

On February 2, 1939, the jury deliberated for only seven and a half minutes before convicting Herman Petrillo, Paul Petrillo, Stella Alfonsi, and Maria Favato of murder. The Petrillo cousins were sentenced to death by electric chair, and fifteen others, including many of the "poison widows," as they were called, were given life sentences.

It is interesting to note that many written accounts describe the Petrillos and Morris Bolber as witch doctors, but these allegations are probably nothing more than sensational journalism. The sole purpose of the Poison Ring was always money, obtained by murder and insurance fraud. It was later estimated that the group netted at least $100,000 ($1.7 million in today's currency), having killed anywhere from 50 to 100 people.

To hear this story told live in Philly, check out Episode 101*:* "A Ghost in the Nude and a Pasta Peddler."

TEAM WINE HAUNTS

TATTOOED MOM

MCGILLIN'S OLDE ALE HOUSE
Haunted

MONK'S CAFE

BOOKER'S RESTAURANT AND BAR
Black-owned

TEAM MILKSHAKE HAUNTS

THE FRANKLIN FOUNTAIN

VANNAH BANANA
Black-owned, vegan

WECKERLY'S

HAUNTED HOTELS

CORNERSTONE BED & BREAKFAST

WEDGWOOD INN

THE BLACK BASS HOTEL

SPOOKY TOURS

EASTERN STATE PENITENTIARY TOUR

GHOST TOURS OF PHILADELPHIA

GRIM PHILLY HISTORY AND GHOST TOURS

SPIRITS OF '76 GHOST TOURS

GHOST TOUR OF HAUNTED HISTORIC PHILADELPHIA

OTHER WEIRD (WTF) PLACES TO CHECK OUT

CHAINSAW SCULPTURE PARK

TOY ROBOT MUSEUM

LITTLE DEVIL'S CURIOSITIES SHOP

WORLD'S LARGEST OUIJA BOARD

WORLD'S LARGEST GENERAL STORE

MÜTTER MUSEUM OF MEDICAL HISTORY

HOUDINI MUSEUM

FIREWORKS MUSEUM

WALK-THROUGH HEART STATUE AT THE FRANKLIN INSTITUTE

POOR RICHARD'S FROM *THE OFFICE*

OLDEST BREWERY IN THE COUNTRY

MINE HORROR RIDE

THE CREEPER GALLERY SHOP

FUN FACTS

One out of every six doctors in the US is trained in Philly.

Philly is the mural capital of the US.

From 1943 to 1949, the Phillies were called the Blue Jays.

SOUTHEAST

NEW ORLEANS, LA

New Orleans was one of the best times I had on tour! I had about 1,000 beignets, stumbled upon the Zack and Addie House (Episode 35), and admired from afar (but actively avoided approaching) the Madame LaLaurie house. With only 24 hours before our show to do everything on my bucket list, I got up at 6 a.m. and started my day with a swamp tour. Even that early in the morning, the temperature was 103 degrees with 100 percent humidity. That day, I learned alligators like marshmallows and also that I hate holding them! I ate at Willie Mae's, Creole Creamery, and Hansen's Sno-Bliz, and before starting my second ghost tour of the trip, we all met a puppy named Waffle Fries. I spent the night in Christine's bed because the spirit of a little boy named Michael kept interacting with us in our hotel room, and I was too scared to be alone. At 4 a.m., neither of us could sleep, so I made Christine come with me to get yet another beignet.

As the hosts of a paranormal and true crime show, we consider New Orleans a home-away-from-home. In fact, Eva and I created our own aesthetic while visiting called *funeral chic.* While Em stood in a swamp holding alligators, Eva and I ate amazing seafood, drank hurricanes, and even got tattoos (shout-out to Electric Ladyland Tattoo!). At night, Em and I befriended a ghost boy named Michael, who knocked on my door repeatedly, turned my iPad on full blast when I was across the room, and loved when we played the Flintstones for him! Apparently, one visit to the Big Easy wasn't enough for me because Blaise and I went back only a few weeks later. I was off the clock this time, so I got to do the full drunken Bourbon Street experience, wandering the streets with a deliciously lime-green hand grenade cocktail.

PARANORMAL

THE LALAURIE MANSION

1140 ROYAL ST · NEW ORLEANS, LA

> I think this is probably the first time in podcast history that your story was more fucked up than mine, Em.

Hey there! Do you want to check out a place with a gut-churning and outrageously fucked-up past? Well, look no further! The LaLaurie Mansion is so chilling that even in a city bursting with spiritual energy, New Orleans locals have nicknamed this place the "Haunted House."

Marie Delphine was a prominent woman in the area, was widowed twice, and had five children: a son, Jean Pierre, and four daughters all named Marie (the first red flag of many). Marie #3 had back issues, which brought Madame Delphine to her third husband, Dr. LaLaurie. They bought this mansion in 1831 but a year later were separated, leaving Madame LaLaurie alone with her many enslaved people.

On April 10, 1834 (aka the most gruesome day I have ever reported on), a fire broke out at the LaLaurie Mansion. The fire was intentionally set by the cook, who was trying to "save" the enslaved people by putting them out of their misery . . . Get ready for the worst thing you've ever read. Once the fire was out, the house was checked, and several enslaved people were found upstairs in room where they were chained to the walls, locked in cages, and strapped to "makeshift operating tables."

These people were clearly being used for extreme and graphic experimental torture, including: gouged-out eyes, stomachs sliced open, intestines removed, mutilated sex change operations, and their own hands sewn to their sides. One person whose arms and legs were hacked off also had segments of her body carved off so she resembled a caterpillar. Another's limbs had been

broken and reset so she looked like a crab. One woman's mouth was stuffed with feces and then her lips were sewn shut. Arguably the worst torture of them all was the "brain stirring," which involved a hole being drilled into their skulls big enough that a stick could fit into their heads.

> Now would be a good/horrible time to remind you that most of these people were found still alive.

Note: Our only saving grace is that most of this information originally came from a tabloid magazine by someone who hated Madame LaLaurie, so fingers crossed this was just insanely fucked-up gossip and never happened. When the townspeople found out what Madame LaLaurie was doing, thousands of them destroyed her home, and she fled to France, where it's said she died in the 1840s.

The mansion then became an all-girls school, a music conservatory, a bar, a furniture store, and luxury apartments, all which had bad luck staying open. It is common lore in New Orleans that anyone who lives there—or even walks under its structure—will suffer bad luck either in wealth or in health. This includes the LaLaurie Mansion's most famous tenant, actor Nicolas Cage, who soon after purchasing the building went bankrupt. Before you rush over to this building, you have been warned!

People have claimed to have nosebleeds, migraines, and seizures after approaching the building, while others hear screaming, smell burning flesh, and see apparitions chasing them. One shadow figure, presumably Madame LaLaurie, allegedly tries to whip people, choke them in their sleep, and tug on their hair, clothes, and bags. People have seen the windows and front door open and close on their own, and some have snapped pictures of Madame LaLaurie herself walking down the street. Today, Madame LaLaurie is supposedly buried less than a mile away at the St. Louis Cemetery No. 1, another spooky destination that's worth the visit.

The LaLaurie Mansion was the inspiration for *American Horror Story: Coven*. Some of the scenes were even filmed here!

Learn more about the LaLaurie Mansion in Episode 18: "An Even Worse Eyeball Story and the Adventures of Captain Midnight."

TRUE CRIME

THE AXEMAN OF NEW ORLEANS

On May 22, 1918, an unknown intruder entered the New Orleans home of Italian grocer Joseph Maggio and his wife, Katherine. The intruder approached the sleeping couple, slit their throats with a straight razor, then proceeded to bash their heads in with an axe. This gruesome killer was soon dubbed the "Axeman of New Orleans," and his MO was clear. In the dark of night, the killer would chisel a small panel in a family's back door, brutally bludgeon the residents with an axe he found on their property, then escape the way he'd entered—through the same small, chiseled panel. He never left a single fingerprint.

Several of the Axeman's victims were of Italian descent, leading many to believe the crimes were ethnically motivated, but others stuck to a more … supernatural theory. They believed the killer was perhaps a demon or a ghoul, a theory bolstered by a mysterious letter received by New Orleans newspapers in March of 1919. The sender? The Axeman. The return address? "Hottest Hell."

That night, New Orleans's dance clubs were filled to max capacity, and virtually every home played jazz well into the night. Some have called it the loudest night in New Orleans's history. Amazingly, the Axeman kept his promise. No one that night was killed.

ESTEEMED MORTAL OF NEW ORLEANS: THE AXEMAN

They have never caught me and they never will. They have never seen me, for I am invisible, even as the ether that surrounds your earth. I am not a human being, but a spirit and a demon from the hottest hell. I am what you Orleanians and your foolish police call the Axeman.

When I see fit, I shall come and claim other victims. I alone know whom they shall be. I shall leave no clue except my bloody axe, besmeared with blood and brains of he whom I have sent below to keep me company.

Now, to be exact, at 12:15 (earthly time) on next Tuesday night, I am going to pass over New Orleans. In my infinite mercy, I am going to make a little proposition to you people. Here it is: I am very fond of jazz music, and I swear by all the devils in the nether regions that every person shall be spared in whose home a jazz band is in full swing at the time I have just mentioned. If everyone has a jazz band going, well, then, so much the better for you people. One thing is certain and that is that some of your people who do not jazz it out on that specific Tuesday night (if there be any) will get the axe.

-The Axeman

As the hysteria waned, locals began to let their guard down. Unfortunately, the Axeman wasn't quite finished. He sporadically attacked several residents over the next few months, culminating in the murder of local shop-owner Mike Pepitone, whose wife entered their bedroom to find Mike dying of gruesome head wounds, his skull barely recognizable. The blood spatter was so extensive it reached their portrait of the Virgin Mary. And with that, the Axeman's sadistic reign of terror was over. After brutally murdering six individuals, viciously wounding six more, and sending the entire city of New Orleans into a state of panic, the Axeman of New Orleans was never heard from again.

Listen to Episode 39: "A Girl Named German and La La Land 1½" *for the full story, as well as the many theories surrounding the Axeman's true identity.*

TEAM WINE HAUNTS

LAFITTE'S BLACKSMITH SHOP BAR
Haunted. Considered by many to be the oldest bar in the nation, built between 1722 and 1733

PAT O'BRIEN'S
Known as the home of the original Hurricane cocktail

THE OLDE ABSINTHE BAR
Haunted. Jean Lafitte himself is one of the alleged spirits here, and people still hear him throwing parties. Patrons have also seen other ghosts including children, a bride, a "Lady in Red," and Marie Laveau.

TEAM MILKSHAKE HAUNTS

HANSEN'S SNO-BLIZ
Still operated by the original family with the original (and first ever) ice-shaving machine, one of Em's favorites!

CREOLE CREAMERY

ICE CREAM 504
Black-owned

HAUNTED HOTELS

HOTEL MONTELEONE

DAUPHINE ORLEANS HOTEL

THE HAUNTED HOTEL

BOURBON ORLEANS HOTEL

SPOOKY TOURS

NOLA GHOST ADVENTURES TOUR

FRENCH QUARTER PHANTOM TOURS

HAUNTED HISTORY TOURS

THE MUSEUM OF DEATH

MARIE LAVEAU'S HOUSE OF VOODOO

THE ZAK AND ADDIE HOUSE

ST. LOUIS CEMETERY NO. 1

OTHER WEIRD (WTF) PLACES TO CHECK OUT

AUDUBON PARK METEORITE
Allegedly a crash-landed meteor or a rock is still here from the 1884 World's Fair

MARDI GRAS WORLD FLOAT WAREHOUSE

THE CAROUSEL SPINNING BAR & LOUNGE

NOLA HISTORIC VOODOO MUSEUM

NOLA PHARMACY MUSEUM

NICOLAS CAGE'S PYRAMID TOMB

SWAMP TOURS

CAFÉ DU MONDE

NASHVILLE, TN

I think it's safe to say *And That's Why We Drink* will always have a soft spot for Nashville. It was where we went to Crime Con together and performed for the first time, and it's probably the city we've traveled together to the most for our live shows. The times we've performed there, we've had Hattie B's before the show and later stayed up unnecessarily late watching *Ghost Adventures*. The last time we went, Eva was really sick (the "Nash-ill" to Christine's "Wis-cough-sin" and my "Flu-rida" while on tour) and she ended up going to bed early. Christine and I lost track of time while binging Zak Bagans and coloring, and before we knew it, it was 7 a.m. I remember we chose to power through and, instead of going to sleep, went for a very slaphappy walk to a nearby coffee shop and ended up eating some pretty tasty breakfast sandwiches. This all-nighter we pulled and another one back when we were in Portland are two of my favorite memories I have touring with Christine, and they're the ones I'll probably cherish the longest.

It's true: Em loves me the most when I'm drunk, slaphappy, and watching Zak Bagans. Eva and I had spent that day exploring some of the local thrift shops before doing back-to-back shows at Zanies. We also had a few samplings of moonshine . . . you know, for educational purposes. As Em said, Nashville holds the record for most *ATWWD* live shows, so it holds a special spot in our hearts!

PARANORMAL

HERMITAGE MANSION AND HOTEL

4580 RACHELS LN • HERMITAGE, TN

The Hermitage Mansion is the former home of President Andrew Jackson. On 1,100 acres, the building looks as it did from 1837–1845. The Jacksons loved kids, and many children lived with them throughout their lives. The president and his wife, Rachel, even adopted Rachel's nephew named Andrew Jackson Jr. The night before they planned on moving into the White House, Rachel died in the house. Andrew Jackson died seventeen years later and they are both buried here in the cemetery. Andrew Jackson Jr. inherited the Hermitage, where he lived and raised his kids. One of his sons died in the Civil War and is thought to be one of the spirits currently haunting the mansion alongside his grandparents. (Multiple generations all haunting the same property together? Freeform, are you listening? I smell a special for 31 *Nights* of *Halloween*!)

In 1893, the mansion was being restored by the Ladies Hermitage Association. While under construction, many of the members were worried about a potential break-in. A few of the women volunteered to stay there, but on their first night they woke up to terrible sounds all over the house. One was the sound of a horse galloping between the rooms upstairs in the hall. (A true night-*mare*, no?) Another was the sound of chains dragging outside, then pots and pans being thrown around in the kitchen, and then dishes breaking inside the cabinets. The women went to see what was going on, but there was no horse, the doors and windows were locked, and everything in the house seemed to be intact. Just then, the mansion's door flew open on its own, and the late Andrew Jackson burst into the house, riding his horse as he screamed, "What are you doing in my home?" ("Shitting my pants, Mr. President." — Anyone in their right mind.)

He then disappeared as quickly as he had shown himself. Instead of the women leaving as fast as possible, these volunteers STAYED! For many more nights! And every night this series of events would play out! I'll give them an

A++ for their commitment to a task and an F for their survival instincts. Finally, they left the mansion, and although nobody has seen anything like that since, there have been other spirits that guests have witnessed. People hear gunshots and phantom horse carriages outside, as well as footsteps and furniture moving around in the house. One employee even heard a child giggling under one of the beds, which to me is so much worse than when the entire house was auditioning for *Poltergeist*. Guests report feeling touched or tickled by someone and hearing whispers that come with a warm breath they can smell (I'm having secondhand embarrassment for the ghost right now, oh my god). Others claim to see apparitions around the house and sometimes even standing behind you in mirrors.

As for the Hermitage Hotel, whose name was inspired by Jackson's mansion, it was opened in 1910 as Nashville's first five-star hotel and first million-dollar hotel. Nicknamed the "Great Dame" of hotels, several diplomats have stayed here, including JFK, who also used it as his presidential campaign's main office. Other notable guests include: Hank Williams, Johnny Cash, Charlie Chaplin, Babe Ruth, and John Dillinger. Notable *spirits* in the hotel include: a crying baby in Room 912 and a woman who appears out of nowhere to soothe the baby (which, by the way, does not soothe me). This woman is seen gliding through the halls and eventually vanishes. Another female spirit will stand in corners and is said to stare at you. She is also known to steal stuff from you, and it will appear later on housekeeping carts. People have woken up to knocking on their headboards, and a mirror in the lobby allegedly cracks and repairs itself. If the history and ghosts aren't enough reasons to check out the Hermitage Hotel, go for a photo op in "America's Best Restroom." The men's bathroom in the lobby, which dates back to 1939, is in the Best Restroom Hall of Fame and, when empty, is also available to women who want to look around.

FUN FACT

The grand ballroom was used in the music video
"Your Man" by Josh Turner.

TRUE CRIME

THE MURDER OF JANET MARCH

Let's travel back to the golden years of the 1990s, when a young woman named Janet March worked as a children's book illustrator in the lovely town of Nashville. Known for being forgetful and often late, Janet slept through her first date with future husband Perry March. (The date was a trip to the campus synagogue, so I don't totally blame her for hitting snooze.)

Despite the initial hiccup, Janet and Perry became inseparable and soon settled into their own home in Nashville, where her parents paid for Perry's tuition at Vanderbilt Law School. In 1987, Janet was tired of waiting for Perry to propose, so she got down on one knee and asked him. (Get it, girl!) Janet's parents bought the couple a new house in a nice neighborhood, while Perry took a job at a local law firm.

I wish I could end the story there, but we all know shit had to hit the fan eventually. And hit the fan it did. One day, a paralegal at Perry's office discovered an anonymous letter on her desk, written by a secret admirer and filled with sexually explicit messages. As more notes rolled in, the office hired a private investigator and set up a sort of sting operation.

One of the secret admirer's notes had instructed for the paralegal to leave a response in an obscure tax law book in the library. The PI set up a hidden camera and quickly caught none other than our pal Perry opening up that specific book. Perry was fired, but not before paying a settlement to avoid a lawsuit, thus leaving Janet none the wiser.

Pretty soon, Janet and Perry began to have marital problems. On August 15, 1996, Janet's family received a phone call from Perry claiming that Janet had left him and the children for a twelve-day vacation after packing several bags containing her passport, $1,500 in cash, and a bag of marijuana. As the days rolled by, Janet's parents grew increasingly worried, as it wasn't like Janet to leave the kids for so long without notice. When Janet didn't reappear for her son's sixth birthday party, her parents knew something was seriously wrong.

Local police retraced Janet's steps and found her Volvo backed into a parking spot at a nearby apartment complex, though friends and family insisted Janet never backed into parking spots. A layer of dust and pollen on the exterior suggested the car had been there for a while. Inside the car they found most of the items Perry had mentioned Janet packing for her trip, but what struck police most was what they *didn't* find. Despite having packed several sundresses and some toiletries, Janet had apparently forgotten to pack toothpaste, a hairbrush, or any bras.

When Perry took the kids out of town for a couple days, police searched the March house and found that the computer's hard drive had been forcibly removed. When they looked closer into Perry's recent activity, they noticed he had recently had the tires on his Jeep replaced, even though they were in excellent condition. After the search, Perry hightailed it to Chicago with his kids.

Janet's friends and family believed Perry was responsible for Janet's death, and despite having no body, police ruled her death a homicide with Perry as the main suspect. Janet's parents sought custody of their grandchildren and in 1999 received visitation rights. They traveled to Chicago to pick up the children, only to learn that Perry had moved them to his father's house—in Mexico.

Turns out Perry was living it up on the beach, running a café he had opened with his new wife, Carmen. Perry may have thought he'd gotten away with it, but back in the US, prosecutors had begun to secretly present evidence against him to a grand jury, who ultimately found him guilty of second-degree murder, tampering with evidence, and abuse of a corpse.

In August 2005, Perry was arrested at his charming beachside café and turned over to the FBI. On his first night in jail, Perry approached his cellmate, Russell Farris, and offered to post his bond if he had Janet's parents killed. He insisted he'd be receiving a large cash advance for a novel he'd written, in which a detective investigates the murder of a woman who looked suspiciously like Janet. Hmm...

Farris immediately told his attorney, and Perry was set up for yet another sting operation. Perry orchestrated a call between his father, Arthur March, and his cellmate, Farris. Unbeknownst to both him and his father, police recorded the call, during which Arthur described the details of the hit—where to go, what kind of gloves to wear, and how to get to Mexico afterward. Meanwhile, Perry couldn't keep his mouth shut, telling another inmate the details of Janet's murder. According to Perry, Janet found out he was cheating and demanded a divorce, threatening to "take everything." In response, Perry hit her over the head with a wrench and disposed of her body.

Two months later, almost ten years after Janet's disappearance, Perry's trial began. His fate was all but sealed when the prosecution presented a deposition given by Perry's own father, Arthur March, who had agreed to offer evidence against his son in exchange for a reduced sentence. Arthur confirmed that Perry had killed Janet that night and admitted he'd helped dispose of her body in some brush up in Bowling Green, Kentucky. He was unable to find the location of the body when prosecutors took him back to Bowling Green, but they nevertheless found his account credible.

The trial lasted a week, and Perry March was found guilty on all charges, receiving fifty-six years in prison. He will not be eligible for parole until 2038. Unfortunately, Janet's body has never been found, but according to online sources, her kids have become happy, successful adults.

TEAM WINE HAUNTS

ALLEY TAPS
Haunted

URBAN COWBOY PUBLIC HOUSE
Black-owned

ACME FEED AND SEED

BOURBON STREET BLUES AND BOOGIE BAR

TEAM MILKSHAKE HAUNTS

MIKE'S ICE CREAM

BOBBIE'S DAIRY DIP

LEGENDAIRY MILKSHAKE BAR

HAUNTED HOTELS

HERMITAGE HOTEL

GAYLORD OPRYLAND HOTEL

CONGRESS INN

SPOOKY TOURS

NIGHTLY SPIRITS TOURS

AMERIGHOST HAUNTED TOURS

NASHVILLE GHOSTS TOUR

GHOST CITY TOURS

OTHER WEIRD (WTF) PLACES TO CHECK OUT

DEAD PEOPLE'S THINGS SHOP

HAIL DARK AESTHETICS SHOP
Reptiles on display above urinals

VOICE-O-GRAPH BOOTH

LANE MOTOR MUSEUM

BLUEGRASS UNDERGROUND HALL, AKA "THE CAVERNS"

DYER'S HAMBURGERS
"Cooking with the same grease since 1912."

FUN FACTS

During Prohibition, print shops along Printer's Alley opened up not-so-secret bars in the area, and many of them are still running today.

Elvis Presley recorded a Christmas album at Nashville's RCA Studio B. To help get him in the Christmas spirit, staff put up string lights that are still hanging in the booth.

JACKSONVILLE, FL

Jacksonville was the tail end of our Flu-rida trip, my symptoms were finally fading, and I was slowly regaining awareness of my surroundings. And yet, I'm unsure if this really happened or if my mind is playing tricks on me: Christine, Eva, and I went into a gas station at some point and on display was a tank of live baby alligators. If this did really happen, it *feels* like some sort of code violation. Then again, we were in Florida and that whole place feels like it lives for risky business. I also remember Christine and Eva buying vintage gator- and shark-themed shirts from that same gas station (and when I say "vintage," I mean the shirts themselves had dust on them from hanging for so long). I think I need to go back to Jacksonville just to find out if this place was real or a fever dream. One thing I do remember clearly from Jacksonville was trying the ice cream at Mayday. I had the blackberry Earl Grey flavor and it tasted like a perfect, icy London fog.

I wish I could confirm that Em was hallucinating, but it's true—Eva and I spotted a billboard for "Live Gators," and I screeched our rental car off the freeway and into an unassuming gas station that *literally housed baby gators.* I wanted to set them free, but Em wouldn't let me. I guess if I'd gone to jail, I'd have missed our show that night.

PARANORMAL

ST. AUGUSTINE OLD JAIL

167 SAN MARCO AVE · ST. AUGUSTINE, FL

In the late 1800s, Henry Flagler was quite the popular guy. He was huge in the railroad industry, cofounded Standard Oil, was friends with the Rockefellers, and is known today as the "Father of Miami and Palm Beach." Henry moved to Jacksonville later in life when his wife fell ill, and they loved traveling to St. Augustine.

During his stays there, however, he thought the hotels weren't anything special, so he decided to build his own. He built the luxurious Ponce de León Hotel, which is now part of Flagler College.

My college is built on top of an old high school and an apartment building where a dead body was allegedly found in the walls, but nice flex, Flagler students.

Well, once he built the hotel, Henry took issue with some of the visitors having to see the "eyesore" from their window that was the St. John County Jail. Henry asked the city if they could relocate the jail so nobody would have to see it. (Breaking news: Rich, entitled white man has the audacity to ask a city to move a whole building because he thinks it looks gross.) Although the town first said no, they gave in when Henry "donated" $10,000 to city commissioners. (More breaking news: Rich, entitled white man uses his money to successfully inconvenience an entire town.)

The Pauly Jail Building Company took on the job, and they later went on to also build Alcatraz. Henry had the new jail painted dusty rose so it would blend in with the rest of the prominent homes in the area and look nice for visitors. (If painting the new jail dusty rose makes it more appealing to the eye, why didn't we just paint the original jail this color and be done with it, Henry?)

The jail was complete in 1891, and although it looked Flagler-approved on the outside, the inside's conditions were awful. The cells were tiny with no insulation, so the cells were just as hot as the outdoors in the Florida heat. The jail only had space for so many people, but the cells were quickly overpopulated. There was no running water for hygiene; instead of toilets there were buckets in each cell, and inmates were only fed grits and beans. Many died from the illnesses that quickly spread through the jail, especially dysentery. The beds were made with Spanish moss and riddled with chiggers, and many inmates were beaten and given severe punishments for small infractions.

Eight people here were sent to the gallows, but many more are said to have died in the walls of this jail. To this day, there are said to be spirits that walk the jail. In fact, the St. Augustine Old Jail has had so much activity that it is listed in the National Directory of Haunted Places. Some people have heard a woman laughing in her cell and a man laughing in the office. People have also heard a little girl, which could be the sheriff's daughter still running around. People say they have heard footsteps walking behind them, cell doors slamming, chains, shouting, whispering, and voices talking in the cells. Others have heard someone humming songs, including "Swing Low, Sweet Chariot." Some visitors report smelling something that is either sickeningly sweet or rotting. (Wide range there, but they also both describe the smell of death. Either way, no thanks.)

People also feel their clothes getting pulled, their arms and shoulders getting grabbed, and someone pushing, punching, or tripping them. The absolute worst to me is the claim that unseen, cold hands have been known to slide down your back. People see shadow figures, too, including ones that pace back and forth, sit in a chair, and crouch down low and hide in corners of rooms. One entity has been called the Crawler: a dark human-shaped shadow figure that crawls behind you and follows you from room to room. If you are the opposite of me and can't wait to meet the Crawler, the St. Augustine Old Jail offers an After Dark investigative tour where you can peruse the jail and talk to all the creepy shadow figures you desire.

Learn more about St. Augustine's Old Jail in Episode 113: "Millennial Pink and Spanish Moss Red Bug Crayons" *and Episode* 128: "A Lasagna House and Scrapbooks of Destruction."

TRUE CRIME

THE I-95 KILLER

What kind of road atlas would this be if I didn't warn you about the I-95 Killer?? Well, a normal one, I guess.

Gary Ray Bowles was born in West Virginia in 1962, suffering a childhood of abuse at the hands of his stepfather. He left home at thirteen, turning to sex work to survive and beginning what would be a life of crime and extreme violence.

Gary's twenties were marked by a string of arrests for a variety of crimes, including beating and sexually assaulting his girlfriend, as well as robbing an elderly woman. Unfortunately, this was only the beginning.

Gary's first known murder victim was John Hardy Roberts, a 59-year-old Daytona Beach resident who offered him a temporary place to live in March of 1994. Gary hit John over the head with the base of a lamp before beating and strangling him to death, then stealing his car and credit cards.

Gary must have gotten a taste for murder after this first kill because he killed four more men over the next six months. The victims were David Jarman, age 39, Alverson Carter Jr., age 47, Albert Morris, age 38, and Milton

Bradley, age 72 (who the internet aggressively tells me is NOT to be confused with the business magnate of Candy Land fame).

Although these murders were spread all over the place—from Nassau County, to Savannah, all the way to Maryland—the MO was the same across the board. Gary would pose as a sex worker to gain his victims' trust, then beat and strangle them before taking their credit cards. Most of these murders took place along the Interstate 95 highway, which you might be traveling right now! Hence, Gary's moniker as the "I-95 Killer."

Gary quickly made the FBI's Ten Most Wanted list, but he wouldn't be caught before taking the life of one more victim, that of Jamelle "Jay" Hinton in Jacksonville Beach. Gary smashed a forty-pound stepping-stone over Jay's head while he slept, then stuffed a towel down his throat during the struggle. Gary was arrested for Jay's murder and promptly confessed to all six of his murders thus far.

But don't worry—Gary had a perfectly reasonable explanation. You see, his girlfriend had become pregnant and had gotten an abortion once she learned her boyfriend was a sex worker. So, according to Gary, gay men were at fault for the death of his child.

Insert link to my favorite Facebook group, *"Are you a yoga teacher because, wow, what a stretch."*

Unsurprisingly, Gary Ray Bowles was found guilty on three counts of murder and sentenced to death. A two-page letter was released to the media as Gary's final statement. It read, in part, "I never wanted this to be my life. You don't wake up one day and decide to become a serial killer … I am so very sorry to all of the family and friends of Mr. Hinton. I never wanted to kill him and I'm sorry for all of the pain and suffering I have caused. I hope my death erases your pain." Gary Ray Bowles was executed by lethal injection at Florida State Prison in August of 2019. His last meal consisted of three cheeseburgers, french fries, and bacon.

TEAM WINE HAUNTS

 TACOLU BAJA MEXICANA
Haunted

THE VOLSTEAD
Features Sunday swing dancing!

SIDECAR

TEAM MILKSHAKE HAUNTS

MAYDAY ICE CREAM

DREAMETTE

FIVE FX ICE CREAM AND WAFFLES

HAUNTED HOTELS

ST. FRANCIS INN

CASA MARINA HOTEL AND
RESTAURANT

OUR HOUSE BED & BREAKFAST

SPOOKY TOURS
(most ghost tours are in St. Augustine)

THE DEVIL'S SCHOOL

OLD ST. LUKE'S HOSPITAL

THE RIVERSIDE HOUSE

SAN MARCO THEATRE

EVERGREEN CEMETERY

FLORIDA THEATRE

ST. AUGUSTINE OLD JAIL + TOUR

ST. AUGUSTINE "ORIGINAL"
HAUNTED PUB CRAWL

OTHER WEIRD (WTF) PLACES TO CHECK OUT

WALK-THROUGH HEAD STATUE

POTTER'S WAX MUSEUM

WORLD'S OLDEST RUG

COUNTRY'S OLDEST SCHOOLHOUSE

MEDIEVAL TORTURE MUSEUM

FUN FACTS

Jacksonville has Florida's oldest farmers market, founded in 1938.

Jacksonville resident George Frandsen owns the "world's largest collection of fossilized poop," which you can learn about at his website, the Poozeum.

ORLANDO, FL

Whew, I wish I could remember more of my time in Orlando, friends. But Orlando was one of the tougher days I had on tour, since it was during my bout of the flu, or what I have come to call it: Flu-rida. I came into Florida a few days early, and I had a cough but didn't think much of it. That night, I woke up with the worst symptoms I've ever had. I don't even know what to call it, but I was out-of-my-mind sick. I had two days before the show and slept for nearly all 48 hours. When I woke up that day, I was down to just normal cold symptoms but I took a lot of medication before going on for the show so I could be "at my best." If you were at the show and remember me looking confused at my notes, and announcing into the microphone that "the text is running away" . . . yeah. That was brought to you by my random loss of vision and sanity (and also an ant that really was crawling around on my notes, or at least I think so).

While most of my time in Orlando was spent making sure Em stayed upright, I had a great time! Eva and I were thoroughly amused at all the Mickey Mouses (Mice?) on the highway's power lines. And I have to back Em up on this one— their on-stage notes looked like they were crawling away . . . and lo and behold an ant was walking across the page.

PARANORMAL

TOWN OF CASSADAGA AND CASSADAGA HOTEL

355 CASSADAGA RD · LAKE HELEN, FL

Here it is, the Psychic Capital of the World! Unlike most towns, here you won't find the usual restaurants, movie theaters, and corporate buildings. Instead, you'll find all types of psychic, medium, and spiritual healing services to fit nearly any need. People have been coming here for their spiritualist needs for over a century, and because of this, Cassadaga has a lot of spooky energy floating about.

It's said to have started with medium George Colby. Born in New York, he first encountered the spirit of his uncle, who told George he was a medium (kind of redundant since he can literally SEE his ghost right now, but okay). His uncle also told George that he would one day found a successful spiritual center. Over the years, George's talents got stronger as he developed his crafts for trance-work, healing, and clairvoyance. In 1867, George began offering private readings and séance sessions wherever he traveled, and he gained so much popularity that he earned the nickname the "Seer of Spiritualism."

During his work, he got help from his spirit guides. One of them was named Seneca, and she told George he was about to go on a journey and while traveling he must find a man by the name of T.D. Giddings.

A moment of silence for every person who had to "find" people without 411 or Google.

As time went on, George ended up in Wisconsin, where he ran into spiritualist Theodore Giddings. George reached out to Seneca about what to do next.

(I'm sorry—she's been reachable this whole time, but she let you wander the earth to find a stranger and wouldn't even give you his full first name? Messy friend alert!!!!) Seneca told him now that George and Theodore found each other, they needed to move to Florida and build a spiritualist camp.

They did so in 1875 and named it Southern Cassadaga Spiritualist Camp. When the word got out that George Colby, the famed Seer of Spiritualism, had built a retreat for like-minded people, mediums came flooding into the town and ended up staying in the area permanently. By the 1920s, Cassadaga was the hot spot for spiritualists, and in 1922 the camp built the Cassadaga Hotel to house their constant stream of visitors. Although the hotel no longer belongs to the camp, it does warn the public of its friendly spirits.

The most popular of the spirits here is Arthur, who is known to drag chairs through the hallway and leave the smell of gin and cigars in the air. In the town of Cassadaga you might also see a ghostly tabby cat brush past you or coins that are often left by the spirit of a little girl. There is also the spirit of a woman in a 1950s hairdo, a fisherman, a woman in Victorian-era clothing, and many others. Worst of them all is the Devil's Chair out by the cemetery, where people say the devil will appear to anyone who sits there.

Why do I know someone out there is reading this and telling their friend, "Let's go sit in it!"?

Another legend is that if you leave a beer can on the seat, the can will be empty by morning (Wait . . . is the devil . . . cool?) People also report seeing shadow figures and apparitions sitting in the chair and hearing sinister laughing. People have felt their clothes getting touched and heard voices when nobody was there, and UFOs have also allegedly been seen in the area. There are ghost tours in the area, plus classes or services in nearly any part of spiritualism you might want. The whole town is made up of a couple hundred people who are all spiritually gifted and offer readings, sessions, and their own homes. Today the Cassadaga Spiritualist Camp is the largest and oldest spiritualist community in the southern US.

TRUE CRIME

THE STRANGE CASE OF LENA CLARKE

By all accounts, Lena Marietta Thankful Clarke had a normal upbringing in West Palm Beach. But that's where the normalcy ends. Her brother Paul had worked as the postmaster at the West Palm Beach Post Office but unfortunately met a rather strange and untimely death on Christmas Day of 1920 when he died of a coral snake bite. "There are snakes in Florida," I hear you thinking. "That's not *that* strange." But no! As it turns out, Paul wasn't bitten by a rogue serpent hiding in some Floridian underbrush. Instead, he was working as an amateur taxidermist and snake charmer, and one of his own snakes had turned on him.

Pretty sure "amateur snake charmer" is the world's most dangerous oxymoron.

After her brother's death, 35-year-old Lena petitioned the community to become the new postmistress. She succeeded and took on the role. At that time, post offices made a lot of money not only from the usual fare like stamps and shipments but also for money orders and war bonds. About a year and a half into her stint as postmistress, Lena sent two registered mail sacks to the Atlanta Federal Reserve Bank. The sacks contained $41,000 in cash.

Except . . . they didn't. When they arrived in Atlanta, the sacks were found to have been filled with mail order catalogs cut to the size of US currency. According to my trusty inflation calculator, $41,000 back then is about $531,000 today. In other words, more than half a million dollars had gone missing.

When a postal inspector questioned Lena, she claimed to know nothing. But the following week found her hiring a driver to take her to Orlando, where she checked into Room 87 of the San Juan Hotel in downtown Orlando under a false name.

Later that evening, she walked into the police station in downtown Orlando and told police that she knew who had stolen the money—it was a man named Fred Miltimore, and he could be found at the San Juan Hotel in downtown Orlando. The man she accused was actually a friend of hers. He was a former mail carrier she had worked with in the past who had moved to Orlando and was running a restaurant called the Arcade.

Police asked how she knew he was still there, and she said he couldn't have left because she had drugged him with a morphine pill. Once the chief of police confirmed with West Palm Beach that Lena was indeed the postmistress, not just a "hysterical woman" telling fantastical stories, they took her accusation more seriously and decided to go check out the hotel.

Authorities arrived at the San Juan Hotel expecting to find a drugged Fred Miltimore. Instead, they found a *dead* Fred Miltimore. Not only had he been drugged with morphine, but he'd also been shot in the chest, presumably with the gun that lay near the body. Along with the gun were two empty money bags that had seemingly been slashed open with a knife.

Meanwhile, Lena was chilling at the police office. At first she vehemently denied having any involvement in Fred's death, but pretty soon she fessed up, not only to the murder but also to the theft of the $41,000. Apparently, the embezzlement was an attempt to cover up her theft of registered bank money she had stolen three years earlier, back in 1918, while she was then the assistant postmistress. According to Lena, "I shot Miltimore—I did it after attempting to make him sign a statement that he had committed the robbery. He wouldn't sign and in desperation, I shot him."

Is it just me or does this woman have exactly zero percent follow-through?

Within days, Lena Clarke was indicted on charges of first-degree murder in Orange County. Word spread quickly that Lena and Fred had had an ongoing romantic affair and he had jilted her. It came as no surprise, then, that in the months before the trial, her story became sensationalized. Suddenly a celebrity of sorts, Lena began receiving fan mail and flowers. She even sent her admirers poetry and letters on a small typewriter she had been given by a friend.

If the fact that Lena was allowed a typewriter sounds strange, get this— she was also allowed to redecorate and paint her jail cell to her liking. (BRB calling HGTV—Jailhouse Hunters? Love It or Lockup? Stolen Property Brothers? Weird, they hung up on me.) She even wrote an autobiography of sorts from her jail cell, which was sold through local newspapers for twenty-five cents (the trusty inflation calculator says that's $3.56 in today's money). Lena, enjoying her new lifestyle, soon recanted her confession, claiming to have no recollection of having made it.

Meanwhile, police had investigated several prominent men from Florida to New York as possible accomplices but couldn't find any connection. They simply couldn't believe a woman could pull off a crime like this by herself. There had to have been a man helping her.

Speaking of sexism, here's a quote from a local paper of the time:

In personal appearance and dress [Lena Clarke] is far from attractive. Her figure is heavy and uncorseted and her clothes smack of the backwoods. Her shoes are generally without heels and her stockings of cotton. Her skin is very fine in texture but covered with large, disfiguring freckles. Miss Clarke's only assets in appearance are her hair, which is decidedly . . . wavy, and her eyes, deep blue in color and absolutely straight and unwavering in their gaze.

Um . . . yeah.

Lena hired two law firms to defend her. Both settled on arguing an insanity defense. To her credit, Lena played this off well: when called to the stand, she brought a crystal ball with her and gazed into it as she talked for hours about the twelve past lives she had lived.

She claimed that she'd been present for the Creation in the Garden of Eden, where she was blocked from leaving Eden with Adam and Eve; had been the goddess Isis in Egypt; then Berenice, the last queen of the Jews; then King Herod's wife; then she was eaten by lions. She had to wait several centuries for her next life, where she hung out with Bill Shakespeare and served as the muse for his character Ophelia. There was one constant throughout all of these lives, though—Fred Miltimore was also there, and he was always persecuting her in various ways.

As she gazed into her crystal ball on the stand, Lena made a prediction that she would be found innocent and would then serve as the vice president under the head of the Socialist Party, Eugene V. Debs. When he was assassinated, she would become president of the United States.

This may surprise you to hear, but Lena's predictions never came true. Instead, several psychiatrists testified as to her mental state, and the jury voted "not guilty by reason of insanity." The judge committed her to the Florida State Mental Hospital at Chattahoochee, which, according to Lena, was worse than if she'd been sent to the gallows.

Fortunately for Lena, her stay didn't last long. Less than one year after her sentencing, Lena Clarke returned to West Palm Beach and resumed her work with the church and the Red Cross, living with her sister Maude and her 88-year-old mother, Marietta. Her handwriting in the census is barely legible but appears to read, "Nurse."

By 1940, neither Lena nor Maude had ever married (god forbid!) and were considered spinsters. Lena passed away in 1967 and is buried in Woodlawn Cemetery in West Palm Beach. Her final census occupation is listed as "Writer."

To hear Em roll their eyes at Lena's antics, listen to Episode 234: "An Anxious Tooth Mouse and an Amateur Alligator Charmer."

FUN FACTS

"Going postal" is an American English slang phrase referring to becoming extremely and uncontrollably angry, often to the point of violence, and usually in a workplace environment. The expression derives from a series of incidents from 1986 onward in which United States Postal Service (USPS) workers shot and killed managers, fellow workers, and members of the police or general public in acts of mass murder. Between 1970 and 1997, more than forty people were killed by current or former employees in at least twenty incidents of workplace rage. Between 1986 and 2011, workplace shootings happened at a rate of roughly two per year, with an average of twelve people killed per year.

At the time, psychiatrists were referred to as "alienists."

TEAM WINE HAUNTS

 HAMBURGER MARY'S
Haunted

THE DISTRICT GASTROBAR
Black-owned

 ASHLEY'S OF ROCKLEDGE
Haunted. Ashley's is outside of Orlando on the coast, but the cool setting and creepy backstory make it worth the drive!

TEAM MILKSHAKE HAUNTS

KELLY'S HOMEMADE ICE CREAM
Woman-owned

THE GREENERY CREAMERY

GINTHER'S SWIRLS ICE CREAM

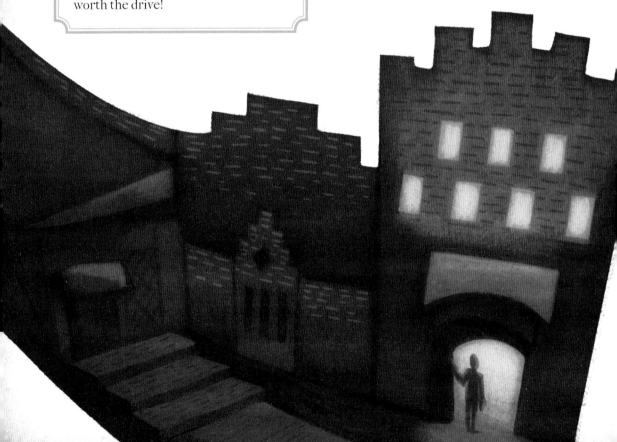

HAUNTED HOTELS

ANGEBILT HOTEL

PEABODY HOTEL

SUPER 8 ON INTERNATIONAL DRIVE

SPOOKY TOURS

AMERICAN GHOST TOURS

ORLANDO HAUNTS

AMERIGHOST TOUR

OTHER WEIRD (WTF) PLACES TO CHECK OUT

MUSEUM OF OSTEOLOGY

CARMINE ODDITIES BOUTIQUE

WONDERWORKS FUNDUCATIONAL AMUSEMENT PARK

PROMETHEUS ESOTERICA SHOP

TUPPERWARE MUSEUM

CHOCOLATE MUSEUM

COCKTAILS & SCREAMS BAR

MONSTERS' CAFE

GATORLAND

CHOCOLATE MUSEUM AND CAFÉ

FUN FACTS

The city's original name was "Jernigan."

The first waterpark opened here in 1977, called Wet 'n Wild.

MIAMI, FL

Although I've passed through Miami several times, I've never stopped in the town long enough to see the sights. Once I get the chance to hang out for a few days, my first stops are the Artem Mortis oddity shop, the Monkey Jungle zoological park, and obviously the burger museum. I would even have to drive the hour to see this bulk candy store, where I would obviously have to stock up for my road trip back. Just to creep myself out, I don't think I could leave Florida without checking Old Ghosts Odditorium, which, according to its pictures online, offers quite a few clown-themed items that even Ol' Sassy can't refuse. Fingers crossed we get to perform in Miami in the future so I can secretly purchase several clown toys for Christine and hide them all over her hotel room when she isn't around (but that will just be our little secret for now).

Unfortunately, I've also never spent time in Miami, though I'm currently manifesting a future live show there. While Em explores the oddities and candy shops, you will most likely find me drinking a Cuban coffee at the beach, counting down the minutes till happy hour. Oh, and re: Em's little secret—once again, they'll be foiled by their own plot when I become attached to the clown toys and insist we travel with them for the rest of the tour.

PARANORMAL

BILTMORE HOTEL OF CORAL GABLES

1200 ANASTASIA AVE · CORAL GABLES, FL

Construction for the Biltmore began on March, Friday the 13 (excellent start), 1925. Like every future haunted hotel, this space was meant to bring in wealthy businesspeople and social elites. It was designed as a combination country club, casino, and resort, with a custom golf course, ballrooms, tennis courts, and fashion and horseback riding events. When it opened in 1926, the hotel was the tallest building in Florida at 315 feet and had the largest swimming pool in the world at 2,300 square feet. The Biltmore used this pool for aquatic shows, which brought in upward of 3,000 people at a time. Politicians and celebrities came from all over the world, including the British royal family, Babe Ruth, Bing Crosby, Robert Redford, several presidents, the Vanderbilts (of famed namefellow, the Biltmore Estate, seen in our North Carolina pages), and Judy Garland (who now spends her time haunting the Palace Theatre, as seen in our New York pages).

The casino business brought in several mob men from the area, who during Prohibition repurposed the thirteenth floor's tower into a speakeasy and gambling hall. In 1929, gangster Thomas "Fatty" (yikes, of all nicknames?) Walsh was shot during a gambling dispute, and to this day he is known to haunt the thirteenth floor.

The hotel suffered after the Great Depression and became a few military hospitals, with the lobby becoming a medical school morgue (meaning: in this hotel, you check out where others have really *checked out*). By the 1970s the property was abandoned and gained a reputation for being haunted. In 1978, one group of investigators held a séance on the thirteenth floor tower, and their mediums saw people dancing, heard sounds of gambling, and spoke to spirits who said someone had been shot there.

By 1983, the Biltmore was being renovated, and during that time, construction workers' tools would go missing, and they allegedly found bloody weapons in the hotel's walls from its gangster heydays. People also heard music playing from empty rooms and saw weird flashes of light, shadow figures, and windows opening themselves. The hotel has been in full operation since the 1990s when it became a National Historic Landmark.

The Biltmore's ghost stories have only grown with time, and the hotel is one of the most haunted places in Miami. People hear phantom bands playing at 2 a.m., babies crying in empty rooms, and Fatty Walsh breathing heavily and laughing on the thirteenth floor. Apparitions are seen waving from the windows, blinds move on their own, and people have been tapped on the shoulder by phantom army soldiers. There is also a dancing couple in the ballroom, a man in the elevators, and someone who approaches the concierge—all who vanish in front your eyes. Light fixtures unplug themselves, people smell cigar smoke, Fatty Walsh is said to appear behind you in mirrors, and people feel things touch them. The elevators will go to the thirteenth floor on their own, and for those who dare to go up themselves, apparitions have been seen and voices say "hello" to you.

Sometimes when you aren't even trying to go to the thirteenth floor, the elevator will ignore the button you pressed and send you up. Other than Fatty Walsh, another popular spirit is the Lady in White, who fell to her death trying to save her son, who climbed over their balcony. She has been seen throughout the halls, floating a few inches in the air. The worst experience of them all is when guests wake up to men in hospital gowns staring at them.

That being said, most encounters here are very kind. In fact, several staff have reported an unknown force holding doors open for them when their hands were full. It's rumored that some housekeepers pin sage to their uniforms to keep negative energy away—just in case. (Wait, why isn't this the employee standard at all haunted hotels?!) So if you're someone who says, "I want to have a spooky experience . . . but only if it's a nice ghost," then the Biltmore Hotel of Coral Gables is for you. And in the off chance you run into a not-so-friendly spirit, the housekeepers might have some extra sage in the back.

FUN FACT

Johnny Weissmuller, five-time Olympic gold medalist and future star of *Tarzan*, was the swimming instructor here and even broke a swimming world record in the Biltmore pool.

TRUE CRIME

LIQUID MATTHEW

I like my crime stories like I like my martinis—with a twist. And while I do wholeheartedly regret that joke, the statement holds true. So let's crack into the mysterious "Liquid Matthew" case of the 1980s, which led Miami PD on a wild goose chase with an unexpected ending.

On the morning of December 6, 1983, two joggers in the Hialeah neighborhood of Miami stumbled upon the body of a man who had been dismembered and wrapped in plastic before being dumped in a parking lot near a "No Dumping" sign. (Seriously? There was ONE RULE!) Authorities arrived on-scene and determined that the man had been strangled to death.

Police initially suspected the murder to have been drug related . . . that is, until a police technician named Terry Anderson spotted a clue. Taped to the nearby "No Dumping" sign was a mysterious note in a plastic bag, which had protected it from the previous evening's rainstorm.

```
Once you're back on the track you'll travel in night. So prepare
your old self for a terrible fright. . . . Now the motive is
clear and victim is, too. You've got all the answers. Just follow
the clues.
```

Detectives were stunned. The killer appeared to be leading them on some sort of morbid scavenger hunt. Following the clue's orders, a sergeant named David Miller decoded the riddle within an hour and followed the riddle to the second clue, which was taped to the back of a speed limit sign.

```
Yes, Matthew is dead, but his body not felt. Those brains were
not Matt's because his body did melt. For Billy threw Matt in
some hot, boiling oil. To confuse the police for the mystery they
did toil.
```

Police were confounded. Who was taunting them? Was their victim named Matthew? And what the hell did boiling oil have to do with any of it? Their initial instinct was to treat this as a serial killer case, and detectives wondered whether there might be more victims to be found.

Miller grew frustrated at his inability to solve the second clue. Much like the Zodiac cipher a few decades earlier, the "Liquid Matthew" clues were released to the public. Miller hoped this appeal would lead to some answers. He was in luck. After reading that Sunday's *Miami Herald*, two Miami citizens stepped forward with a tip that would turn the case on its head.

It turns out the clues were not the work of a deranged, body-melting serial killer, but rather the playful antics of a local church group. The two callers explained that back in October their church had set up a Halloween murder-mystery scavenger hunt for their youth group. After the evening's activities had been called off due to rain, the clues were left out in their plastic coating and remained there until a body had been dumped nearby, leading police to the scene.

Fortunately, police didn't end up needing any more clues to get to the bottom of what was now dubbed the "Liquid Matthew" case. DNA had identified the victim as 28-year-old Colombian national Francisco Patino

Gutierrez. He worked as a seaman and had traveled to Miami aboard a cargo ship two weeks earlier.

Confirming investigators' initial suspicions, it was determined that Gutierrez had indeed been killed for drug-related reasons. It turns out he had smuggled eleven pounds of cocaine on board the cargo ship, prompting an immediate seizure of the drugs. According to police, the confiscation had gotten Gutierrez in trouble with someone who was angry enough to strangle him and leave his body in the parking lot.

Gutierrez's death was certainly tragic, but not quite as melodramatic as police had initially thought. I like to think the police were a little bummed about not getting to participate in a real-life mystery, but fortunately the case was closed on December 19, 1983.

TEAM WINE HAUNTS

THE BILTMORE BAR
Haunted

BAR ONE MIAMI BEACH
Black-owned

BLUE ANCHOR
Haunted. About an hour north of Miami but is haunted by a ghost named Bertha!

TEAM MILKSHAKE HAUNTS

AZUCAR ICE CREAM COMPANY
Cuban- and woman-owned

DASHER & CRANK

CREAM PARLOR
Woman-owned

HAUNTED HOTELS

THE BILTMORE HOTEL

THE DEERING ESTATE

MIAMI RIVER INN

SPOOKY TOURS

MIAMI HAUNTS

MIAMI GHOULISH GHOST TOURS

COCONUT GROVE GHOST TOUR

DEERING ESTATE HISTORIC
GHOST TOUR

MIAMI'S GHOSTLY, GHASTLY,
VICE AND CRIME COACH TOUR

MIAMI CEMETERY TOUR

FLORIDA CRIME TOURS AND
GALLERY

OTHER WEIRD (WTF) PLACES TO CHECK OUT

BULK CANDY STORE TOUR

BURGER BEAST'S BURGER MUSEUM

WORLD EROTIC MUSEUM

MONKEY JUNGLE PARK AND
HABITATS

ARTEM MORTIS—ODDITIES,
CURIOSITIES, & MURDERABILIA

OLD GHOSTS ODDITORIUM SHOP

PINEWOOD CEMETERY

FUN FACTS

Miami is home of the first Burger King.

January 19, 1997, was the only snowfall recorded in the city.

ATLANTA, GA

Once we got to Atlanta, our first stop after the show was Waffle House. It simply wasn't up for debate, especially since we left the venue so late at night, and it couldn't have been more appropriate timing. I stayed a few extra days with a friend who took me all around town, including stops at Junkman's Daughter, the Rainbow Crosswalks, and Doll Head Trail (although we got creeped out and left pretty quickly). On my last day here, I made last-minute pitstops to the 54 Columns installation, the SkyView Atlanta Ferris wheel, and the World of Coca-Cola Museum, where I tried about fifty different flavors of soda. Next time I go, though, I'm definitely going on the Superhero Tour, which takes you through all of the local filming locations for the Marvel Universe. See ya there!

As usual, Em fully outdid me on the tourist front when we visited Atlanta. That being said, seeing Eva eat Waffle House for the first time was more than enough of an experience for me!

PARANORMAL

FOX THEATRE

660 PEACHTREE ST NE • ATLANTA, GA

This paranormal hot spot happens to be one of Atlanta's most iconic landmarks, the Fox Theatre. This property originally belonged to the Kimball family and was used during the Civil War. The Freemason Shriners later bought this land to build a Masonic lodge but ended up not having enough funding to complete it. Well, in comes *Fantastic Mr. Fox* (except instead of a weirdly attractive fox puppet with George Clooney's voice, it was a guy named Will).

Mr. Fox offered to pay for the rest of the building's construction if the Shriners would let him use part of the building to show movies. They agreed, and on New Year's Eve of 1929, the 250,000-square-foot facility opened and premiered Disney's *Steamboat Willie* to a sold-out audience. The Fox Theatre's opening also introduced audiences to a ceiling that gives the illusion of a real, open sky and their 3,622-pipe organ "Mighty Mo," which is still the world's largest Möller theater organ. In the 1970s, the theater became a National Historic Landmark, and to this day, it offers live comedy performances and Broadway musicals.

Since 2012, the Fox Theatre has been offering annual Halloween ghost tours that allow visitors to see different parts of the building. They've ranged from backstage, on stage, the subbasement, electrical room, elevator, and "hospital" (a wildly loose exaggeration for a "nurse's room"). Since there were limited ambulances at the time, state-of-the-art buildings like the Fox had their own licensed nurses in case of illness or injury. But for the Fox Theatre, once nurses were no longer necessary, nothing was cleared out of the room, and all of the 1920s medical tools, equipment, and furniture still sit there.

There is said to be a woman who haunts this room named Mary, and while she keeps things spooky in the hospital, another spirit named Roosevelt haunts the old boiler room known as the "subbasement." Roosevelt was an employee back when the Fox was coal powered, and he ran the boiler room for sixteen years until his passing in 1945. He is said to still work down here, stoking coals to keep them warm.

"It ain't much, but it's honest work." —Roosevelt's ghost, as the HVAC unit runs behind him.

Staff members claim to bump into Roosevelt throughout the building. They hear him laughing in empty rooms, but he's also been known to slam doors, make banging sounds, and mess with the lights.

People also feel bursts of cold air, see shadow figures moving about, and hear humming, chains rattling, and footsteps up and down the audience aisles. Sometimes a dog is heard barking in one office that belonged to a former employee who brought their pet in to work. (Note to self: If I ever go ghost-hunting here, bring peanut butter treats.) Other spooky reports say that a massive steel door in the back will open on its own even though its heavy latch would prevent it from doing so, and the freight elevator will go up to the fourth floor on its own, where a former manager's girlfriend died. Staff also hear a little girl running around, who might be one of the Kimballs' children when they lived on the property, and each night after closing, employees turn on a "ghost light" before going home. This is a lamp that sits lit on stage so the spirits can perform while everyone is gone. If the staff forget to do this, the spirits get upset and are more active the next day (apparently every ghost at the Fox Theatre is a Gemini). Finally, the organ Mighty Mo itself is haunted by its previous organists, Bob Van Camp and Larry-Douglas Embury. We know it's them because both of them are interred *inside* of the organ!!! Larry-Douglas's ashes are in a pipe chamber on the left, and Bob's are on the right, making this the only musical instrument to have two bodies buried inside (at least, that authorities are aware of ...). Sometimes the staff allegedly hear the organ playing even though nobody is there, and when a part of Mighty Mo is acting up, they say Bob or Larry-Douglas is letting you know that they're around (or they're screaming "Get me out of here!"—it could be a lot of things).

TRUE CRIME

ATLANTA RIPPER

There are few things America loves more than copying another country's specialty and claiming it as our own. Usually this refers to food (Freedom Fries, anyone?), but I guess every now and then we need to up the ante. Enter: the Atlanta Ripper. Only twenty years after Jack the Ripper's spree of terror in London, a killer with a similar MO haunted the streets of Atlanta, leaving the city in fear and mourning.

It started in early 1911, when the bodies of young women began to appear throughout the Atlanta area. The victims had two things in common: they had been brutally murdered, and they were all Black. We can't be sure who the first Ripper victim was, but some speculate it was Rosa Trice, whose head had been crushed and whose throat was cut so deeply that she'd nearly been decapitated.

Unfortunately, despite a growing body count, the case was all but ignored by the press. Atlanta was steeped in racial unrest, and attacks on Black women simply weren't considered newsworthy. That is, until the death of Belle Walker.

On May 28, 1911, the body of a young cook named Belle Walker was found just twenty-five yards from her home on Garibaldi Street. Belle's sister had come by to check on her when Belle didn't arrive for work, and her worst fears were confirmed when she found Belle in a nearby field with her head nearly severed by a jagged cut across her throat.

Although the largely white-owned newspapers finally picked up the story, it still wasn't worthy of the front page. In fact, the *Atlanta Constitution* buried the story on page 7, underneath the headline "Negro Woman Killed; No Clew to Slayer."

The word "clew" is making my eye twitch, but apparently it's technically an acceptable spelling.

But even white journalists couldn't ignore the rising death toll when Addie Watts was killed only six weeks later. Addie's head had been bashed in by a coupling pin from a train before her throat was cut. The *Constitution* speculated that the recent deaths seemed to have been the work of one perpetrator, a sort of "Jack the Ripper" character who targeted young Black women. After a few attempts at a moniker, which included the "Black Butcher," ultimately one stuck: the "Atlanta Ripper."

Tragically but unsurprisingly, the papers were more concerned with the sensational story line than the victims themselves. For this reason, many of the victims went unnamed and are subsequently lost to history. What we do know is that the Atlanta Ripper claimed about *two dozen* women between 1911 and 1915, a horrifyingly high victim count that puts even his namesake's attacks to shame. All the victims were described as Black or dark-skinned, in their early twenties, "good looking" and "neatly dressed," some educated, all having been murdered in an equally gruesome manner, usually with a knife or other sharp object.

To give you an idea of just how uninterested the media was in this case, here's a very un-fun fact: the first victim to make the front page of the Atlanta papers was actually the *eighth* of the Ripper's victims. Sadie Holley's throat had been slashed ear to ear, and someone had bashed her head in with a large rock. Despite being far from the killer's first victim, she was also far from the last.

While all of the Ripper's murders were tragically barbaric, the death of Mary Putnam was perhaps the most shocking. Mary's body was still warm when it was discovered at 7 a.m. on November 21, 1911. Her throat and breast had been slashed, and her heart was found nearby her body. The killer had literally ripped out Mary's heart and disemboweled her before leaving the scene.

The only description we have of the attacker came from one of his only known survivors, 20-year-old Emma Lou Sharpe. When her mother, Lena, had failed to return home from a shopping trip, Emma Lou retraced her steps, soon encountering a man she later described as "tall, Black, broad-shouldered, and wearing a broad-brimmed black hat." Lena attempted to skirt the man's path, but he blocked her, saying, "Don't be 'fraid. I never hurt girls like you."

He promptly broke his own rule and stabbed her in the back. Fortunately, Lena was able to rip herself away from her attacker, who laughed and fled down a nearby alley. As Lena called for help, she didn't realize that she was only feet away from the body of her mother, who had been murdered by the Ripper only hours earlier. Lena's body was found soon after by a search party. She had been nearly beheaded by a large cut to the throat, which left her in a pool of blood.

One of the few clues the Ripper let slip was his seeming obsession with shoes. Several of his victims had their shoes cut from their bodies. Occasionally, they were found nearby, but sometimes they were never found.

Despite the high victim count, the Atlanta Ripper crimes remain unsolved to this day. No one has ever been convicted of the serial crimes, and over time the story has faded into nothing but a dark part of Atlanta history.

TEAM WINE HAUNTS

 SHAKESPEARE TAVERN PLAYHOUSE
Haunted. Watch a play while you have a drink!

9 MILE STATION
Black-owned

 KIMBALL HOUSE
Haunted

TOM, DICK, & HANK
Black-owned. BBQ and craft cocktails!

TEAM MILKSHAKE HAUNTS

BUTTER & CREAM

MORELLI'S GOURMET ICE CREAM

JAKE'S ICE CREAM

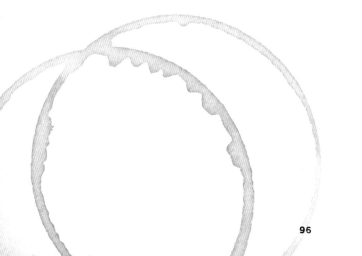

HAUNTED HOTELS

ELLIS HOTEL

HIGHLAND INN

SPOOKY TOURS

OAKLAND CEMETERY

FOX THEATRE TOUR

DECATUR GHOST TOURS

ROSWELL GHOST TOUR

MARIETTA GHOST TOUR

OTHER WEIRD (WTF) PLACES TO CHECK OUT

ATLANTA GLASS TREEHOUSE

747 EXPERIENCE AT THE DELTA FLIGHT MUSEUM

RAINY DAY REVIVAL, ATLANTA'S ODDITIES STORE & PROP HOUSE

THE ODD'S END SHOP

MODERN MYSTIC SHOP

WAFFLE HOUSE MUSEUM

GBI CRIME LAB MUSEUM

SISTER LOUISA'S CHURCH OF THE LIVING ROOM AND PING PONG EMPORIUM

THE SIDEWAYS GRAVE OF SIDEWAYS THE DOG

FUN FACTS

Atlanta was originally named Terminus and Marthasville.

There are over fifty-five streets with the name "Peachtree."

CHARLOTTE, NC

The day we had our show in Charlotte was a big day! First off, that morning we found out we won our first Webby! We were all over the moon and so stoked that so many people had helped us get to that point, and we're still beyond grateful for all of you. Then that afternoon before our show, I had lunch at the 7th Street Market with my girlfriend, Allison's, sister, and that night I had some of my family and Allison's family from the area in the audience. My favorite part of the meet and greet was when one of our listeners gifted us Funko Pops of ourselves! Apparently they made mine on top of a Captain America Funko Pop bobblehead, and to this day it's one of my prized possessions. After the show, I snuck away to McKoy's Smokehouse and had a pulled pork sandwich, mac and cheese, and fried okra at 2 a.m. For the middle of the night, that was some solid barbecue.

Em's right. Finding out we won a Webby really solidified the good time we had in Charlotte! While Em was busy being social with family, I decided to explore on my own. Anyone who knows me knows that was a huge mistake. I got hopelessly lost, probably because there was a different bank on every street corner (apparently, Charlotte is the banking capital of the US). Fortunately, Charlotte is a fun place to wander! I found a burrito place and a candy shop, and that night's show featuring Em's and Allison's families was a riot.

PARANORMAL

BILTMORE ESTATE

1 LODGE ST · ASHEVILLE, NC

The country's largest home? Built in Asheville, a massive spiritual vortex? Sounds like a perfect combo for some spooky tales! Built by the Vanderbilts in 1895, the Biltmore Estate is now one of North Carolina's biggest attractions, with over one million visitors each year.

Cornelius Vanderbilt was an incredibly wealthy man. Like, "by the time he died he had more money than the US Treasury" wealthy. He was also a dick. He was disrespectful to women, had no manners, all that jazz. He did have one son, William, who actually doubled the family fortune. William had many sons, and the youngest was George.

In the 1860s, George inherited $13 million from his family and decided to build a vacation home in Asheville. The mansion would be so big that it had to be measured in acres. By the turn of the century, the home was over 175,000 square feet, with 250 rooms, 65 fireplaces, 3 kitchens, an art gallery, and a two-story library with thousands of books. George loved the library and would hide there from people during parties, and his wife would have to remind him to come out and mingle. The property also had a gym, a heated and illuminated swimming pool, one of the first private bowling alleys, an underground tunnel leading to the dairy barn, secret passageways, and a private railway line to bring visitors onto the property. The Biltmore Estate was also one of the first to have modern fire alarms, intercoms, electricity, plumbing, hot water, refrigeration, and forced heat and air.

When George died in 1914, his wife believed he was still there in spirit and would sit in the library and talk to him. Their daughter inherited the estate and then her sons after that. During the Great Depression, it was opened to the public to help the town make money, and in 1964 it became a historic landmark. The Biltmore Estate is still owned and operated by a Vanderbilt descendant, William. As for the ghosts, George has been around since his wife, Edith, used to talk to his spirit in the library. In fact, once Edith also passed, staff reported hearing two voices talking to each other in the library, finally together again. I'm sorry, but that's the most romantic ending to a paranormal story I've ever heard. Stephanie Meyer could never!!!

Guests and staff say they see shadow figures walking through the library, especially during storms or parties, when George was most often in the library when alive. People still also hear Edith whisper George's name as if calling him back to his own party.

Edith, take a hint—he's pulled off an Irish goodbye that only you won't let go!!

There have also been reports of an apparition of a man in a striped suit in the sitting room, apparitions walking near the pool, and a crying shadow figure who glides faster than people can run (firm pass). People have heard unexplained sounds, such as laughter, music, splashing in the pool, glasses clinking, footsteps, furniture dragging, and book pages turning. Folks smell cigar smoke, and they feel someone bump into them on the stairs, water drip on their arms, gusts of wind, their clothes getting tugged on, and nausea or dread when they get near the pool. And last but certainly not least, the Biltmore's gardens are allegedly haunted by apparitions of headless cats. *sigh* I hope that's not true because it would freak me-owt. If I ever witnessed that, I would paw-sitively . . . lose my mind. I'm so sorry. I'll head out—I mean go!!

FUN FACTS

One of the priceless rare works in the library is a first edition of *On the Origin of Species* by Charles Darwin.

The estate has been in many films, including *Forrest Gump* and *Patch Adams*!

TRUE CRIME

HENRY LOUIS WALLACE— THE TACO BELL STRANGLER

Henry Louis Wallace's childhood in Barnwell, South Carolina, was somewhat of a mixed bag. On the one hand, he suffered the abuse we so often see in the backgrounds of serial rapists and killers, but meanwhile he served on the student council and enjoyed spending time with his classmates. His mother, a harsh disciplinarian, forbade him from playing football, so he joined the cheerleading squad instead, where he thrived.

Things were looking up for Henry as he graduated high school and enrolled at South Carolina State College. I'm beginning to sound like a broken record in this book, but I can't help but think how different things would have been if he'd stuck to this path. Instead, after being caught stealing CDs from his radio station job, Henry dropped out of school and things, well, spiraled.

After joining the navy and marrying his high school sweetheart in 1985 (again—this story had such wholesome potential!), Henry began using drugs. More specifically, crack cocaine. To pay for his habit, he began burglarizing homes and local businesses. After his arrest in 1992, Henry's wife left him, and he changed course, moving to Charlotte.

Charlotte, you know I love you . . . but it seems as though his move served as a sort of springboard for Henry's crime spree. To be fair, it would be learned later that Henry's first murder occurred before he ever left South Carolina, when he had murdered Barnwell High School student Tashanda Bethea in 1990 before dumping her body in a local lake. But the remainder of his crimes took place in Charlotte, where he would develop his MO and ultimately earn his moniker.

In May 1992, Henry picked up sex worker Sharon Nance, whom he beat to death when she requested payment for her services. The following month, Henry raped and strangled his girlfriend's friend, Caroline Love, before dumping her body in the woods. In a sick twist, he helped her sister file a missing persons report.

Henry lay dormant for more than half a year, until February of 1993, when he strangled Shawna Hawk at her home in Charlotte. If you've been wondering where and when he earned his moniker, you're about to find out. Shawna was his supervisor at his current workplace: Taco Bell. In a sick twist that would soon become a pattern, Henry went to Shawna's funeral to pay his respects.

On June 22, Henry strangled another Taco Bell employee, his coworker Audrey Spain, and in August he raped and strangled another of his sister's friends, Valencia M. Jumper. This time he changed his MO and set fire to the body in an attempt to cover his tracks. He took his sister to Valencia's funeral and even sent her family condolences. (There better be a special place in hell for folks who prey on their victims' vulnerable families.)

Only a month later, Henry attacked Michelle Stinson, a struggling college student and single mother of two small children. Most sources describe her as his "friend" from work, but I'm going to change that to acquaintance. He raped Michelle before strangling and stabbing her.

In February of 1994, Henry was arrested for shoplifting, but the connection between him and his murders hadn't yet been established by police. Only two weeks later, he strangled *another* Taco Bell coworker, Vanessa Little Mack, in her apartment. It's at this point in the story you'll find me pulling my hair out in frustration; despite four murders linked to the same Taco Bell location, it would take three more murders for police to even consider this the work of a serial killer.

On March 8, 1994, Henry strangled his girlfriend's coworker, Betty Jean Baucom, before robbing her of her valuables, which he later pawned. In a chilling turn, Henry returned to Betty's complex that night, knowing that her neighbor Berness Woods would be at work, so he could murder his girlfriend, Brandi June Henderson. He raped Brandi and strangled her before strangling her young son. Fortunately, the boy survived.

After two murders at the same apartment complex, police allegedly amplified their presence in East Charlotte. Despite this increased security presence, Henry managed to sneak in and murder yet another resident of the complex,

Deborah Ann Slaughter, another of his girlfriend's coworkers. After strangling Deborah, he stabbed her thirty-eight times.

Shortly after his last murder, Henry was finally arrested on March 13, 1994. He spent the next twelve hours confessing to the murders of ten women in Charlotte, describing the crimes in vivid detail and proving he was the perpetrator.

Henry was ultimately found guilty of nine murders and subsequently sentenced to death nine times over. Henry's time on death row was far from uneventful. Not only did he pull a 180 and claim his confessions had been coerced (don't worry, the North Carolina Supreme Court upheld his sentences), but he also got married. On June 5, 1998, Henry married a former prison nurse, Rebecca Torrijas, in a somewhat morbid ceremony next to his future execution chamber.

Charlotte's police chief celebrated the arrest, reassuring East Charlotte that its residents were now safe. But many in the community criticized the force's approach to the crimes, claiming the case had been neglected due to the race and socioeconomic status of the victims. According to Shawna Hawk's mother, "The victims weren't prominent people with social-economic status. They weren't special. And they were Black."

For what it's worth, police apologized to residents for not spotting a link between the murders sooner. But, they said, the cases were varied and sporadic enough to throw them off Henry Wallace's trail.

My friends, this is what we call a "fauxpology."

Unsurprisingly, this defense served as little comfort to the families of the victims.

Henry Wallace is currently awaiting execution at Central Prison in Raleigh.

TEAM WINE HAUNTS

RÍ RÁ IRISH PUB
Haunted

ALEXANDER MICHAEL'S
Haunted

CASWELL STATION
Haunted

KENNEDY'S PREMIUM BAR AND GRILL

TEAM MILKSHAKE HAUNTS

POPBAR
Black-owned. Customize your own popsicles!

THE LOCAL SCOOP

TWO SCOOPS CREAMERY
Black co-owned

NINETY'S SANDWICHES & ICE CREAM

HAUNTED HOTELS

BILTMORE — ASHEVILLE

DUNHILL HOTEL

SPOOKY TOURS

NIGHTLY SPIRITS CHARLOTTE
GHOST TOUR

CAROLINA HISTORY & HAUNTS
CHARLOTTE

CHARLOTTE NC GHOST TOURS

CHARLOTTE BEYON

OTHER WEIRD (WTF) PLACES TO CHECK OUT

TREEHOUSE VINEYARDS

SLEEPY POET ANTIQUES MALL

BENNY'S YARD ART AND WELDING

MUSICAL PARKING GARAGE

WORLD'S LARGEST DRESSER

THE CAROLINA MALL IN CONCORD
A parking lot with a cemetery inside

FUN FACTS

Charlotte is the largest US metropolitan city without a zoo.

Charlotte's downtown is called Uptown.

No wonder I got lost.

CHARLESTON, SC

I have yet to explore Charleston, but it is one of the cities highest on my bucket list! I will obviously have to check out Poogan's Porch (Episode 186) and stop at Carmella's for dessert. I have also heard great things about the Bulldog Tours, and we know I love a good teatime, so the Charleston Tea Garden sounds right up my alley. It may surprise a few people, but Allison and I love doing (and barely accomplishing) ropes courses, so you can be sure to find me at the Wild Blue Ropes Park, probably screaming from the treetops with regret once I'm up there. I have also heard Charleston is not only one of the most haunted cities but one of the prettiest cities. My ideal day in Charleston would be checking out the city as I walk from restaurant to restaurant and try just about every plate of comfort food I could find.

Yet another city we haven't toured! When we do go, I plan on joining Em at Poogan's Porch in hopes of spotting a little ghost puppy. And this will surprise absolutely no one, but unlike Em, I am wholeheartedly opposed to ropes courses. Instead, I will most likely be found standing at the bottom taking pictures of Em screaming to post on Instagram later.

PARANORMAL

CHARLESTON OLD CITY JAIL

21 MAGAZINE ST · CHARLESTON, SC

Charleston is one of the most haunted cities in the United States. One of the spooky buildings here happens to be the Old City Jail, the most haunted location in all of South Carolina. Constructed as early as 1738, the Old City Jail opened in 1802 as both a jail and an asylum. The jail was used as a POW camp during the Civil War and quickly became overcrowded. Disease was rampant in the jail during this time and thousands of prisoners died here. The abuse guards used on inmates got significantly worse over time. Prisoners were whipped, deprived of food, and eventually had limbs hacked off—and were burned at the stake, branded, and drawn and quartered.

One of the most famous inmates here was Lavinia Fisher, the country's first female serial killer. Around 1819, Lavinia's husband, John, ran a hotel called the Six Mile House, where Lavinia would lure rich men in and John would rob and kill them. Their rumored MO is that Lavinia would lace their tea then drop them through a trapdoor onto a pit of spikes (okay, girl, dramatic).

When caught, they were estimated to have killed 20 to 120 men. Before she was hanged, Lavinia said, "If any of you has a message for the devil, tell me now—for I will be seeing him in a moment," and then jumped from the gallows herself.

OKAY, GIRL, DRAMATIC.

The last execution here was in 1911, and by 1939 the jail closed after 137 years. In 2000 it became a trade school until 2016. Today, paranormal tours and investigations still take place. Lavinia is one of the more popular spirits here.

She will stare at you from the third-floor window, steal your jewelry, scratch people, and scream in empty rooms. (Even in death, she's loving the theatrics.)

There are also spirits here who will reportedly make you feel like you're being held down or you're choking; they will shove people and leave rope-burn marks around people's necks. Phones will malfunction, an old wheelchair will roll around and bump into people, and people see a black mass outside of doorways in the halls. People see apparitions wandering the cells, a guard that will charge at you, and a little boy who likes to hold visitors' hands (that last ghost I can get behind, but nothing else). The little boy will also sometimes throw rocks at bigger groups of people (Jesus, never mind), and during one tour a heavy iron door fell off its hinges for no reason.

Sometimes ropes in the cells will be tied together without explanation, and people frequently hear the sounds of chains, thuds, door slams, whistles, crashes, whispers, their name being called, crunching footsteps, and the out-of-order dumbwaiter moving. Bare footprints have been found in dust, and many people (especially those who work in corrections) report feeling nauseous and smelling a "foul odor." There are also some solid EVPs that have been picked up, including spirits of soldiers asking for morphine and someone telling Zak Bagans, "You make me mad." Zak also asked Lavinia about her last words and if she could finish the sentence. When Zak said, "If any of you has a message for . . . ," a female voice came through and said, "The devil." And just to add to the anxiety: in the "torture room" of the jail, so many people have used it for Ouija board sessions that some say the room has additionally become a demonic portal. Simply put, I'm never coming here.

What Does "Drawn and Quartered" Mean?

It was a series of punishments that began in fourteenth-century England for those guilty of treason.

1. Very Unlucky Person (aka the "VUP") would be hanged until they almost couldn't breathe anymore.
2. VUP was then pulled behind a horse with their intestines "drawn" and hanging out of their body.
3. Once at their execution site, the VUP's intestines and genitals would be sliced off and thrown in a fire so victims could watch them burn.
4. VUP was then beheaded, and the head was further "quartered" into four pieces.

Note: Sometimes the quartering wasn't the VUP's head but their whole body, and it was done by tying each limb to a different animal that walked in a different direction.

Zak Bagan's best line:
"I somehow seem to attract psychotic, evil women."

Hey!

TRUE CRIME

LAVINIA FISHER— AMERICA'S FIRST FEMALE SERIAL KILLER

Congrats, South Carolina! You're the home of America's first-known female serial killer, Lavinia Fisher. In the early nineteenth century, Lavinia and her husband, John Fisher, owned and operated an inn called the Six Mile House, located six miles north of Charleston. Lone travelers were invited for dinner, where Lavinia and her husband would make small talk about their occupations to determine whether they had any money to their names. If the men were determined to have anything worth stealing, they'd be sent up to bed with a cup of poisoned tea, after which John would kill them.

Because this story has become more lore than fact, a lot of its details can't be verified. For example, some say the tea would put the men to sleep for a few hours, after which Lavinia pulled a lever that would drop the victim into a very medieval-sounding pit of spikes.

While many details of Lavinia's life are contested to this day, contemporary accounts in the *Charleston Post and Courier* tell the story of a vigilante gang that went to Lavinia's neighborhood in 1819 in an attempt to put an end to gang-related crime in the area. On their way out of town, the vigilantes left a man named David Ross to stand watch in their stead.

When Ross was attacked by gang members in town, he looked to Lavinia, begging for help. Rather than help him, she choked him and smashed his head through a window. Thankfully, Ross survived, but this just goes to show how ruthless Lavinia could be, with or without her spikey pit.

Perhaps my favorite tale from Lavinia's life involves John Peeples, a traveler who stopped by the Six Mile House seeking lodging. Lavinia told him they were fully occupied but nevertheless invited him in for tea. Peeples wasn't a fan of tea, a dislike that ultimately saved his life. Not wanting to seem rude,

Peeples dumped the tea when Lavinia wasn't looking, not realizing he had just dumped out the poison that would have led to his death. Lavinia, none the wiser, interrogated Peeples for hours and eventually offered him a room that just happened to open up in the inn.

Peeples went to bed but felt something about Lavinia was off. (Trust your gut, John!) Instead of sleeping in the bed, John slept in a wooden chair by the door, where he was later awoken by the sound of a large collapse from the middle of the room. Aghast at the pit that had opened up in the middle of the room, presumably meant to capture and kill him, Peeples leapt out the window and rode to Charleston to alert authorities.

Lavinia and John were ultimately arrested, but both claimed innocence. Good luck explaining away your Pit of Spikes,™ Lavinia. The jury convicted the couple of highway robbery, which was not just an idiom, but an actual capital offense back then. Despite their attempts to escape the "Old City Jail" (see Em's story), the rope they'd made out of prison linens broke, foiling their plot.

Both Lavinia and John were hanged in 1820. According to legend, Lavinia stood on the gallows and screamed, "If any of you have a message for the devil, tell me now, for I shall be seeing him shortly," before jumping to her death. See Em's story of the jail for details of Lavinia's ghost, which can still be seen at the Old City Jail.

FUN FACT

Although the Six Mile House is no longer standing, you can visit the site of its former location at the corner of Rivers Avenue and Dorchester Road.

TEAM WINE HAUNTS

POOGAN'S PORCH
Haunted. Featured in Episode 186!

BLIND TIGER PUB
Haunted

REPUBLIC GARDEN & LOUNGE
Black-owned

TEAM MILKSHAKE HAUNTS

YE OLE FASHIONED ICE CREAM

PARK CIRCLE CREAMERY
Black-owned

CARMELLA'S

HAUNTED HOTELS

BATTERY CARRIAGE HOUSE INN

MEETING STREET INN

THE OLD CITADEL

1837 B&B

THE MILLS HOUSE HOTEL

RUTLEDGE VICTORIAN GUESTHOUSE

FRANCIS MARION HOTEL

SPOOKY TOURS

BULLDOG TOURS

OLD CHARLESTON WALKING TOURS

GHOST OF CHARLESTON TOUR

BUXTON BOOKS GHOSTS OF
CHARLESTON TOUR

OTHER WEIRD (WTF) PLACES TO CHECK OUT

WILD BLUE ROPES PARK

BLACK FEDORA COMEDY MYSTERY
THEATRE

MACAULAY MUSEUM OF DENTAL
HISTORY

CHARLESTON TEA GARDEN AND TEA
FACTORY TOUR

SALTWATER CYCLE PARTY BOAT

ALLIGATOR ADVENTURE

TUNNELVISION ILLUSION MURAL

PROVOST DUNGEON

FUN FACTS

Charleston is home to the country's first theater, the Dock Street Theatre, and golf club, Harleston Green.

The city's minor league baseball team is partially owned by "Director of Fun," Bill Murray.

MIDWEST

MINNEAPOLIS, MN

What a time I had in Minneapolis. Unfortunately, Christine was dealing with a gnarly cold during this leg of the tour, so I personally spent most of my time with the lovely ladies of the podcast *Wine & Crime*. Amanda and I went to lunch and a bunch of thrift shops the afternoon before our first show that weekend. While there, we found several horrific and absolutely haunted-looking teddy bears. We decided I would have to gift them to Christine on stage that night in front of everyone, and lo and behold, Christine got emotionally attached to the bears, just as anticipated. The next night after our second show, I saw Amanda and Lucy from *Wine & Crime* again and hung out with them at the Bulldog (Uptown) until about 4 a.m. Wonderful bar if you're looking for poutine, fried pickles, and darts!

Home to our *Wine & Crime* pals, Minneapolis was just as fun as anticipated. Although I was still recovering from Wis-cough-sin, I loved exploring the area and making long-lasting friendships with the trio of haunted teddy bears Em gifted me on stage. I did manage to get lost in the town's famed Skyway System, but maybe that's a me-problem . . .

PARANORMAL

WABASHA STREET CAVES

215 WABASHA ST S • MINNEAPOLIS, MN

When you come to Minneapolis, do you ever think, "Man, I really wish I knew more about their local caves?" Well look no further! Here's the history on the city's man-made and only privately owned sandstone caves. At 12,000 square feet, these seven caves were originally mines in the 1840s where workers extracted silica, which was later used for glass making. By the 1900s, the mines were abandoned and a local family used the space to cultivate mushrooms to sell to nearby restaurants. The daughter of the family later turned the cave into St. Paul's first speakeasy (with its own whiskey still). It was a popular watering hole for the local gangsters, who made a deal with the chief of police that if they kept crime outside of St. Paul, the cops would leave them alone.

This made the Wabasha Street Speakeasy an easy hangout choice for gangsters in town, including the Barker-Karpis gang, "Pretty Boy" Floyd, and John Dillinger. After Prohibition, the speakeasy became a restaurant/nightclub called Casino Royale. Although the mob were mostly well-behaved with the general public, they did conduct business in the caves' "Fireside Room," the room where many gang-related murders were allegedly committed. Since unused parts of the tunnels had such loose soil, victims who died in the Fireside Room are rumored to still be buried in these cave walls.

By the 1930s, Casino Royale was shut down, and the family went back to using it to cultivate mushrooms, while other companies rented parts of the caves for cultivating cheese. In the 1970s, the caves were temporarily turned into a disco hall called Casino Royale 2, and in 1991 they were reopened as the Wabasha Street Caves, an event space decorated as it was in the 1930s (think of the murder mystery themes you could host here). The owners also host the Tommy Gun Trouble tour, Lost Souls tour, and Caves and Graves tour, and they also host a swing dance night every week. Sometimes they still use the space as a speakeasy too. (Note: the password to get in is "Gus sent me.")

As for the cave's ghostly activity, psychics have said up to thirty spirits hang around here. People report feeling someone tugging on their clothes and hair, smelling smoke and alcohol, and hearing cries, screams, glasses clinking, poker chips shuffling, and a disembodied jazz band. People also see apparitions in "gangster attire," some pacing the tunnels, others looking for something, some even talking at the bar at 3 a.m. There have been reports of these spirits angrily walking past you and into walls or vanishing in front of your eyes. They seem to come out when music is playing; however, when the caves were a disco hall, there were many sightings of "old-fashioned men" scowling in the corners of the space. They allegedly also like throwing things around the caves and have been known to interact with children. One boy even walked into a bathroom and saw the spirit of a man straighten his tie, wink at him, and then fade away. Another boy at a wedding told his parents he had fun playing with "those men." When the wedding photos developed later, pictures of the boy showed him surrounded by misty apparitions.

TRUE CRIME

HARRY HAYWARD AND THE MURDER OF KITTIE GING

There's not much to say about Harry Hayward's childhood in the late 1800s except that he was a problem child—times a thousand. He violently bullied his classmates, seemingly having no conscience. The priest at his elementary school even described Harry's time there as "vague and shadowy."

I'm not saying that's how I describe many of my own Catholic school years, but I'm not *not* saying that . . .

The 1890s marked a Minneapolis that was booming, with a population that had tripled over the past decade. Harry spent his thirties living in a downtown apartment with a Swedish neighbor named Claus Blixt. Though I'm sure Claus was charming in his own right, Harry set his sights on another neighbor—29-year-old dressmaker Catherine "Kittie" Ging.

A talented con artist, Harry seduced Kittie and conned her into loaning him $10,000, which he repaid in counterfeit money. He also convinced her to take out two life insurance policies with him as the beneficiary (red flag central), before asking his older brother, Aldry, to kill her for him. Understandably, Aldry was like...no thanks?

Harry shrugged off the rejection and turned to his Swedish neighbor, Claus. Through a combination of threats and bribes, Harry convinced Claus that he had to kill Kittie. He told Claus she had to die, because (*horrific language alert*) "Every time I go up to her room she puts her arms around me and I would like to put a knife in the God damned bitch...if there was a dog and her I would rather shoot her and let the dog go." Although Claus wasn't immediately won over by Harry's attitude, once Harry threatened to murder Claus's own wife, he agreed to the plan.

Harry instructed Claus to pick Kittie up in a horse and buggy on December 3, 1894. He gave Claus a gun and a bottle of whiskey, instructing him to drink it all. Meanwhile, he told Kittie he would rendezvous with her later near Lake Calhoun (now called its original Dakota name, Bde Maka Ska). Meanwhile, he headed to the opera with another lady friend. What a snake!

As Claus and Kittie drove down the road, Claus, indeed having drunk all the whiskey, pulled out the gun, pressed it behind Kittie's ear, and fired. He pushed Kittie's body out of the carriage and sped away.

Harry got home from the opera to find his apartment building crawling with cops. You see, Harry had such a bad reputation in town that he was almost immediately singled out as a suspect. Even the mayor of

Minneapolis demanded he be questioned. Unfortunately, Harry had an air-tight alibi, as many people had spotted him at the opera that evening.

Harry thought he was in the clear, but his brother Aldry had other plans. After he'd refused to be his brother's hitman, Aldry informed his lawyer of his brother's intent to kill Kittie. With this information, police were able to put Harry on trial for her murder.

The massively sensational trial lasted forty-six days and culminated in Harry's being sentenced to death by hanging. Claus himself received a life sentence, despite trying to convince the jury he had been hypnotized by Harry.

Harry maintained his innocence until the evening before his execution, when he gave a complete confession. In a shocking twist, Harry confessed not only to Kittie's murder, but to three more murders as well.

The first of Harry's victims was a sex worker from Pasadena, California, whom he had lured into the mountains before shooting her and stealing her wallet. He also claimed to have fatally shot a man with consumption near Long Branch, New Jersey, robbed him of $2,000, and disposed of his body in the river.

And, finally, perhaps his most brutal murder took place at a gambling joint in New York. Harry had gotten into an altercation with another card player, knocking him down and kicking him in the stomach. He then (brace yourself) picked up a wooden chair and jabbed the leg through the man's eye, before sitting on the chair and killing him. Harry would later say with a chuckle, "His skull was kind of thin." I know, I know. Vomitous beyond belief.

Harry also admitted that he'd plotted to kill several people, including his father, his brother Aldry, and countless "unpleasant women" he had encountered. While on death row, Harry even attempted to hire a hit man to kill a journalist who wrote negatively about him. In fairness, I'd probably be mad, too, if the media referred to me as "the most bloodthirsty soul ever to usurp the human frame" and "the most cold-blooded murderer that ever walked God's footstool."

During his time on death row, Harry seduced a woman through the mail and was able to finagle conjugal visits with her. He even filed for the insurance claims on Kittie's life *after having just been convicted of her murder.* Unsurprisingly, that didn't work.

On the evening of his execution, Harry cheerfully walked toward the scaffold shouting, "Good evening!" to the spectators. He requested three cheers before beginning a long and rambling speech filled with jokes about his impending death. Finally, the sheriff cut him off and ordered him to "die like a man."

Executioners placed the noose around Harry's neck as he spoke his last words: "Pull her tight; I'll stand pat." The trap swung open at 2:12 a.m., but they had mismeasured the height; Harry wasn't pronounced dead until 2:25 a.m., thirteen minutes later.

Kittie doesn't get nearly enough airtime in the story of Harry's life, but for what it's worth, she was a badass. A single, independent business owner in her late twenties, Kittie was an anomaly among women of her time. After her death, her parish priest used her story as a cautionary tale, warning young women of the dangers of "rejecting the domestic sphere, where they properly belonged." Yikes™.

Fortunately, Kittie's memory lived on after death. Her twin sister moved to Minneapolis to take over the dressmaking business, successfully running it for decades, and in 2002 a Minneapolis soccer field was named "Kittie Ging Green" in her honor.

As for Harry Hayward, I think it's best expressed by his jailer, John West, who said, "All that remains of Harry Hayward, the Minneapolis murderer, is a handful of ashes. And that is enough."

FUN FACTS

"Stand pat" is a poker term—it means to play the cards you were dealt without drawing any new cards.

Harry Hayward's brain weighed in at 3.4 pounds (or 55 ounces). Back then, some criminologists believed criminals had a distinctive skull shape compared to the average human. Doctors ruled that Hayward's skull proved him to be "a degenerate biological phenomenon somewhat below the savage and above the lunatic." Maybe they were onto something.

To hear me tell this story live in Minneapolis, check out Episode 174: "A Vegetarian Lake Monster and a Proud Consumptive."

TEAM WINE HAUNTS

CUZZY'S BAR AND GRILL
Haunted

DU NORD'S CRAFT SPIRITS DISTILLERY
Black-owned

PALMER'S BAR
Black-owned

MERLINS REST PUB

TEAM MILKSHAKE HAUNTS

MILKJAM

SEBASTIAN JOE'S

2 SCOOPS ICE CREAM EATERY
Black-owned

HAUNTED HOTELS AND BARS

ST. JAMES HOTEL

PALMER HOUSE HOTEL

THAYER'S B&B

SPOOKY TOURS

AMERICAN GHOST WALKS

REAL GHOST TOURS

WABASHA STREET CAVES
GANGSTER TOUR

OTHER WEIRD (WTF) PLACES TO CHECK OUT

WORLD'S OLDEST ROCK

MINNESOTA'S LARGEST CANDY
STORE

DRIVE A TANK

SPAM MUSEUM

JOLLY GREEN GIANT MUSEUM

ORFIELD LABS ANECHOIC CHAMBER
"The Quietest Place on Earth"

FIRST PLACE TO HOST TURTLE
RACES

SANDPAPER MUSEUM

INTERNATIONAL WOLF CENTER

THE ABANDONED FERGUS FALLS
STATE MENTAL HOSPITAL

HORSE AND HUMAN DRINKING
FOUNTAIN

ED'S MUSEUM
(of his personal collection)

JAIL HAUS BED & BREAKFAST

FUN FACTS

Here, many streets are named after US presidents in order to help immigrants prepare for their citizenship tests.

Minneapolis is home of the Honeycrisp apple.

MILWAUKEE, WI

In Milwaukee, I learned what true happiness looks like when Christine and Eva realized how readily accessible cheese curds could be. I, on the other hand, could not have been more excited about the amount of Cheesehead hat and tie options in the airport. I plan on collecting all of them over time so that eventually my closet looks like a wall of cheese. Milwaukee also did not disappoint in the steak department. Christine, Eva, and I stayed at the Pfister and treated ourselves to one of the tastiest and swankiest dinners we've had together, down in the hotel lobby. I had a filet mignon and some of the best mashed potatoes out there. I have no idea what the others ordered because I was in steak heaven, but I do remember seeing a lot of cocktails on our table, so I'm going to guess they also had an amazing time! Knowing the two of them, I would bet there was a platter of cheese there too.

Em's right—most of my Milwaukee memories revolve around cheese curds. I do, however, remember Em's face when I told them we'd be staying at the haunted AF Pfister Hotel during our stay. The steak dinner was my attempt to make it up to them. While Em devoured their steak, Eva and I indulged in one (or five) vodka martinis.

PARANORMAL

PFISTER HOTEL

424 E WISCONSIN AVE · MILWAUKEE, WI

As someone who has stayed here, I can assure you this place is haunted (it also has incredible steak). The Pfister was built in 1893 and is known as the "Grand Hotel of the West." When it was conceptualized, founders Guido and son Charles Pfister wanted the hotel to be a "People's Palace."

Although Guido passed before he could see the hotel come to life, Charles spent $1.5 million ($44 million today) and created an eight-story hotel made of marble, limestone, granite. Three of those eight stories are the lobby alone, and the hotel offered a list of high-end amenities and shops, including a hair salon, soda fountain, clothing store, and restaurants. Many famous dignitaries, celebrities, and athletes have stayed here, and it is even the official hotel for the visiting sports teams, especially baseball. The Pfister is not only a historical landmark, but it's also been put on Travelocity's top ten list for the "Country's Most Haunted Hotels."

That being said, the hotel claims it is not haunted. I tried asking the concierge for spooky stories, and they "could neither confirm nor deny" any alleged paranormal activity. I asked two other employees, and they said the same thing, which felt entirely too fishy to me. But fret not, because I found out the hard way for all of us that the hotel is in fact haunted. While in my room, I heard footsteps pacing the perimeter of my bed for a solid hour—from one side of my bed, down to the foot of my bed, and up the other side. I told "whoever" was with me to just not touch me, although I was convinced I would be tackled by an invisible person at any moment. The next morning I woke up and saw that the other bed next to me had been messed with, and the indent in the linens from someone sitting on the bed was still there.

This is apparently very common here. People report something sitting on their beds or standing at the foot of their bed, staring at them. Guests have seen items get thrown or knocked over by themselves; they've seen lights and electronics turn on and off at random; they've gotten locked in their rooms or bathrooms even though the door is unlocked; people hear animals running and scratching in their rooms and witness a shadow figure that has pushed or grabbed people. Phones will get disconnected or have staticky connections, there will be knocks on the door but nobody is there, they wake up to something banging on their headboard, and curtains will open and close by themselves. Guests have also reported seeing shadow figures in reflections of their rooms' mirrors and the TV.

Many visitors report seeing Charles Pfister himself all over the hotel, especially on the stairs and in the lobby. Some will even think he's alive and realize later he was a ghost after seeing his portraits around the hotel. If you bring your family here, beware! There is allegedly a spirit of a pregnant woman who will interact with kids by making their toys turn on and off all night long. Since the Pfister houses visiting sports teams, a lot of the reports come from athletes, and most of them are baseball players. Some think this is because Charles Pfister was a fan of the Milwaukee Brewers, and he might be trying to freak out opposing teams so they won't sleep well the night before a game. Many athletes choose to bunk together when they stay here, and some refuse to even spend the night. So if you ever want to become friends with a baseball player and a ghost at the same time, might I suggest staying at the Pfister the night before a game and forming an alliance with the jocks across the hall?

FUN FACT

When I checked in to the hotel, my phone got a text from the "Digital Pfister Butler," whom I texted back asking for chocolate cake, and sure enough cake came to my room. Hats off to the butler!

Learn more about the Pfister Hotel in Episode 115: "A Digital Butler and Walls Full of Secrets."

TRUE CRIME

THE NORTH MILWAUKEE STRANGLER

I know, I know . . . You're expecting me to cover Jeffrey Dahmer. But to be honest, I thought that'd be too obvious, so I went with a more obscure pick: Walter Ellis, also known as the North Milwaukee Strangler. He was born the same year as Dahmer, so . . . close enough?

Walter Ellis was born in 1960 in Holmes County, Mississippi, but moved to Milwaukee at the age of six. Walter showed signs of antisocial behavior from a young age, often assaulting classmates and earning a reputation as a bully. His bullying escalated to a career in crime when he dropped out of school at age fourteen.

The next several years saw Walter frequently getting arrested for various crimes, including robbery, assault, and drug possession. Let's just say I'd run way over my word count if I listed all his offenses here. Walter was eerily good at talking his way out of jail time, often simply paying a fine before being set free. (There's that good ol' psychopathic charm come to play!)

After quite a career journey from pimp, to day laborer, to drug trafficker, Walter made the unlikely career move of becoming a police informant. After his extensive rap sheet had sent him to federal prison, Walter was staying at a halfway house when he was caught leaving the premises without permission. His slick talking once again saved his bacon. He ratted out the halfway house officials who regularly took bribes from prisoners in exchange for letting them leave, and police took him on board as an informant.

While I'm sure becoming a police informant wasn't part of Walter's five-year plan, he sure took advantage of his newfound status. Any time he violated parole (which was a lot), he'd avoid criminal liability by standing behind this role. And these weren't small offenses either—between 1994 and 1995 Walter was arrested numerous times for assaulting his girlfriends, once with a screwdriver. It took several more offenses before police stripped him of his informant role, and after three more years in prison he wound up back in Milwaukee.

I wish that were the end of the story, but unfortunately the worst is yet to come. In May 2009, Milwaukee police were reexamining a cold case involving the murders of seven local sex workers. The crimes had been connected via a recent DNA analysis. After analyzing samples of prisoners throughout the state, authorities realized that inmate Walter Ellis's DNA sample had apparently gotten lost on its way to the labs many years earlier. (I'm sorry, what?!)

After a search warrant was issued, police obtained Walter's DNA from a toothbrush in his apartment. Lo and behold, his DNA could be linked to *nine murders* of sex workers within a three-mile area of northern Milwaukee between 1986 and 2007.

A warrant was issued for Ellis's arrest, and his car was soon spotted outside a motel in nearby Franklin, where he was staying with his girlfriend. Walter Ellis was charged with the murders of seven women: 31-year-old Deborah L. Harris; 19-year-old Tanya L. Miller; 25-year-old Irene Smith; 28-year-old

Florence McCormick; 37-year-old Sheila Farrior; 41-year-old Joyce Ann Mims; and 28-year-old Ouithreaun C. Stokes.

Walter was also suspected in the murder of 32-year-old Carron D. Kilpatrick in 1994. Horrifyingly, another man had already been charged with her murder but was later acquitted. Walter was also a suspect in the murder of 16-year-old Jessica Payne in 1995. Another man had also been charged with Jessica's murder and had wound up in prison for fourteen years based solely on witness testimony. All charges against him were dropped and he was released in 2009.

Meanwhile, Walter Ellis was sentenced to seven consecutive life sentences without the chance of parole. He died of complications from diabetes in 2013, at the age of fifty-three.

Need a silver lining? Me too. The discovery of Walter Ellis's missing DNA prompted a statewide audit, which found that nearly 17,700 offender samples were missing from the crime lab's database. Though this exposed massive flaws on the part of state law enforcement, it also led to more stringent policies in gathering such evidence, hopefully closing more cold cases in the future.

FUN FACT

Colin Pitchfork was the first killer to be caught using DNA testing. He was arrested and sentenced to life in prison in 1987.

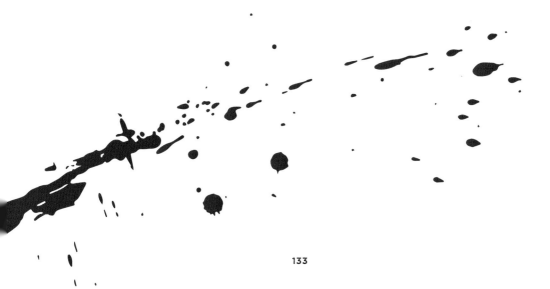

TEAM WINE HAUNTS

TEAM MILKSHAKE HAUNTS

MILLER BREWERY AND CAVES
Haunted. Take a tour of the brewery and maybe you'll spot a ghost!

WHITETAIL MKE
Black-owned

SHAKER'S CIGAR BAR
Haunted

SWISS STREET PUB & GRILLE
Haunted

PURPLE DOOR

LEON'S FROZEN CUSTARD

GILLES FROZEN CUSTARD

HAUNTED HOTELS

BRUMDER MANSION B&B

HILTON GARDEN INN

AMBASSADOR HOTEL

SPOOKY TOURS

AMERICAN GHOST WALKS

HANGMAN TOURS

GOTHIC MILWAUKEE TOUR

HAUNTED HISTORY TOUR PUB CRAWL

OTHER WEIRD (WTF) PLACES TO CHECK OUT

HARRY HOUDINI HISTORICAL CENTER

CIRCUS WORLD MUSEUM

ORGAN PIPER PIZZA
Pizza parlor with a live organist

DEVIL'S PUNCHBOWL
Part of the woods in Menomonie where ghosts, fairies, and trolls have all been reported

CHEESEHEAD FACTORY TOUR

NATIONAL BOBBLEHEAD HALL OF FAME AND MUSEUM

SAFEHOUSE
Spy-themed bar

ED GEIN'S GRAVE AND MURDER HOUSE

UFO LANDING PORT AT TOHAK WELDING
Exact center of the northern half of Western Hemisphere

MUSEUM OF HISTORIC TORTURE DEVICES

FUN FACTS

Their downtown ice rink is bigger than Times Square.

Milwaukee has three of the top five oldest breweries in the US: Pabst (1844), Blatz (1846), and Old Milwaukee (1849).

CHICAGO, IL

Chicago was so much fun. It was one of the first times I stayed behind after a leg of the tour so I could just explore for as long as I wanted. I had a blast doing all of the traditionally touristy things like see the Bean and eat deep-dish pizza (not a fan, but I do love Chicago dogs). I also discovered the Shit Fountain and that Portillo's cake shakes are hands down the best milkshake I've ever had. While on my adventures, I met a father and daughter, Loren and Hannah, waiting in line for the Skydeck. When they found out I was alone, they took me in for the next couple of hours. They even had me join their only photo op on the Skydeck as one big, happy family. A few months later, I came back to Chicago with my mom, and we had a great time going on several of the ghost and gangster tours.

As a Midwesterner, I've always had a soft spot in my heart for Chicago. During our tour, my family drove up to see us there and got to watch the show from the Vic's balcony seats. I'm going to politely decline getting involved in the Great Pizza Debate™, but I will agree with Em that Portillo's makes a great shake.

PARANORMAL

THE OLD JOLIET PRISON

1125 COLLINS ST · JOLIET, IL

The Old Joliet Prison is one of the oldest prisons in Illinois, one of the largest prisons in the country (when constructed), and has been called the "last of the Illinois medieval prisons." It officially broke ground in 1858, and its first handful of inmates were used as free labor to build the jail themselves. They quarried local limestone, carried it to the prison property, and essentially built the prison around themselves. Old Joliet Prison was built to replace a jail in Alton, Ilinois, that had such poor conditions that even Dorothea Dix petitioned to build a new place entirely.

Ironically, this prison soon also had terrible conditions. The jail was over-populated with inmates as young as ten, and disease was rampant through the cellblocks. Before the 1920s, there were only fifteen tubs for bathing. Inmates showered once or twice a week and often had to share the tub with others. Buckets were used for toilets until the 1950s, there was minimal ventilation, and until 1917 prisoners weren't allowed to speak to each other during meals or work. Execution hangings were done in such a way that instead of dropping the inmate down in the noose, the prisoner was sitting and his noose was yanked up.

Early on, the prison offered tours to the public for a quarter—while it was still in operation.

> Imagine your in-laws coming into town and this is what you've planned for their visit.

Nearby is the Old Convict Cemetery, where hundreds of inmates are buried, along with single body parts from convicts. This includes arms and fingers of prisoners who cut them off with a buzzsaw to avoid working (I get not wanting to work, but Jesus), a prisoner who was dismembered and scattered over the cellblock, and an interred inmate whose head was removed as evidence during his murder trial (and later mysteriously vanished.

Another headless inmate buried here is George Chase, also known as the "Singing Ghost." He was the prison's first execution, and his brain was removed afterward for doctors to study. It's said that George can still be seen in the Old Convict Cemetery searching for his head. My personal favorite inmate here is a man named Kennedy, who once tried to escape the prison by stealing a corpse's coffin in the morgue. But after the funeral service, he lifted the lid for air, and the hearse driver thought a corpse had come back to life (maybe not as brilliant as a *Shawshank Redemption* escape, but definitely funnier). He was later executed at the prison and his head was removed for doctors to study his brain. It's said George can still be seen in the Old Convict Cemetery searching for his head. Other inmates at the prison were notorious criminals Leopold and Loeb, James Earl Ray, Baby Face Nelson, Richard Speck, and the "Sausage King" Adolf Luetgert (to be clear, the "sausage" did not come from animals . . .). John Wayne Gacy, aka Pogo the Clown, was processed here and stayed in the prison's hospital for a few months.

As early as 1905 there were people asking for Old Joliet to close its doors, but it remained open until 2002. Although abandoned for many years, in 2017 the Joliet Area Historical Museum helped create the Old Joliet Prison Preservation Coalition.

Today, they offer tours of the prison to fund further restorations. You can also catch glimpses of the prison in *The Blues Brothers*, *Saw II*, *Prison Break*, *Empire*, *Mindhunter*, and most importantly an episode of *Ghost Adventures* (where Zak literally holds a slice of John Wayne Gacy's brain, which was being stored this whole time in Tupperware). As for the spirits, people see shadow figures, orbs, and flashes of light. They have gotten photos of mist, felt cold spots out of nowhere, and heard the sounds of someone walking around, knocking, crying, screaming, and whistling.

Although most of the spirits here are of inmates, some believe another entity here is the warden's wife, who was bludgeoned and burned to death by an unknown assailant. Most of the paranormal activity is said to come from the hospital, where there is also an aggressive spirit. Ghosts here have scratched, groped, and shoved people. Spirits have followed people home, given people panic attacks and chest pains, and drained electronics' batteries. People also smell blood, feel irritable, and see solid black masses and apparitions in empty rooms. There have been EVPs of prisoners rioting and voices threatening you. When Zak's team investigated, his equipment was pulled up and out of his own pocket and thrown onto the floor (which I have to say was actually super creepy), and they caught it on camera. If you would also like to be pickpocketed by spirits, check out the Joliet Prison tour yourself!

FUN FACT

The same architect for the Old Joliet Prison also designed the Chicago Water Tower.

TRUE CRIME

H. H. HOLMES— THE BEAST OF CHICAGO

I still remember the first time I learned about H. H. Holmes. I was at my temp job in Los Angeles, reading Wikipedia instead of working, when I stumbled upon a story that seemed too outrageous to be true and too horrific to forget.

Born in 1861 with the unfortunate name of Herman Webster Mudgett, H. H. Holmes was a con artist and bigamist who is widely known as America's first serial killer.

Holmes dipped his toe into a life of crime at a young age, stealing cadavers to make fraudulent insurance claims while studying medicine at the University of Michigan. It wouldn't be long before he upped his game. Holmes moved to Chicago in 1886 to begin work at a pharmacy, whose original owner he is widely believed to have murdered.

Holmes settled in nicely, building himself a three-story home down the street that would ultimately become a hotel. The mansion featured trapdoors, secret passages, and dead ends. Sounds cool, right? Sure, if you want to check into your hotel and never leave, à la Hotel California.

Yep. Rather than focus on treating his guests to a five-star experience, Holmes had instead built himself an elaborate torture chamber that would later become known as his "Murder Castle."

If only Yelp had existed back then . . . I'd love to read the reviews.

In addition to an inescapable labyrinth of rooms, Holmes's hotel also featured soundproof walls, doors that could only be locked from the outside, gas chambers to suffocate his victims, and a kiln for cremating the bodies. Any bodies that weren't cremated would be sold to local medical schools.

The ever-so-generous Holmes even paid for his employees' life insurance policies, as long as they agreed to list him as the beneficiary. Red flag, anyone? In addition to targeting his employees, Holmes had a reputation for seducing women with his wealthy bachelor act before killing them and inheriting their life savings.

I know it seems impossible for Holmes to have escalated beyond this point, but trust me, he found a way. After taking advantage of the 1893 World's Fair by murdering a number of tourists visiting Chicago, Holmes took to the road with a business partner named Benjamin Pitezel. Their plan was to fake Pitezel's death and split the resulting life insurance money, but poor Pitezel didn't realize that he was the victim all along. Holmes killed him but told his widow that her husband was simply in hiding and would be back soon.

Apparently lying to this unsuspecting woman about her husband wasn't enough, because Holmes also found a way to convince her to let him take three of her five children on the road with him. I'm not sure what he told her, but it must have been hella convincing, because she agreed, and pretty soon the three children became his victims as well.

Holmes was eventually captured in November 1894, but not before out-running authorities for several weeks. An accurate body count of his victims couldn't be determined, as many of the victims' bodies couldn't be recovered. (Did I mention he also had an acid bath in his hotel as another body-disposal method?)

Although I trust Holmes as far as I can throw him, it's worth noting that he himself did confess to twenty-seven murders. That being said, he eventually increased the total to more than 130. Chillingly, some historians believe his victim count exceeded 200. Whatever the real total was, Holmes was undeniably guilty and was hanged in May 1896. His confession included the now-famous line:

> *"I was born with the devil in me. I could not help the fact that I was a murderer, no more than a poet can help the inspiration to sing."*

For those of you who are itching to check out the site of Holmes's original Murder Castle, I'm sorry to report that it burned to the ground shortly after Holmes's death. Considering its dark and twisted history, that's probably for the best.

To hear Em's reaction to H. H. Holmes's Murder Castle, listen to Episode 10: "Annabelle the Doll-y Parton Impersonator and the Tap Water Scammer."

TEAM WINE HAUNTS

THE LEAVITT STREET INN & TAVERN
Black-owned

 RED LION PUB
Haunted

 SIGNATURE ROOM
Haunted

 ADOBO GRILL
Haunted

TEAM MILKSHAKE HAUNTS

PORTILLO'S
The Cake Shake is Em's #1 favorite milkshake of all time!

BOMBOBAR

THE ORIGINAL RAINBOW CONE

HAUNTED HOTELS

DRAKE HOTEL

RUEBEL HOTEL

CAPITAL HOTEL

DESOTO HOTEL

SPOOKY TOURS

GANGSTERS AND GHOSTS TOUR

CHICAGO CRIME TOURS AND
EXPERIENCES

CHICAGO HAUNTED SEGWAY TOUR

CHICAGO HAUNTED BEER TOUR /
PUB CRAWL

OTHER WEIRD (WTF) PLACES TO CHECK OUT

HISTORIC MUSEUM OF TORTURE
DEVICES

GRANITE CITY'S TEN-PERSON
SWING

THE WORMHOLE—A TIME TRAVEL
COFFEEHOUSE

BIOGRAPH THEATER
Where John Dillinger died

H.H. HOLMES'S MURDER CASTLE
SITE

AL CAPONE'S GRAVE

WORLD'S FASTEST SODA MACHINE
IN LERNA, IL

DALLAS CO. CURIOSITY AND
MAGIC SHOP

AHLGRIM ACRES
Mini golf in a funeral parlor

GROUNDHOG DAY FILMING
LOCATIONS

POPEYE THE SAILOR MUSEUM

SCOTT'S VINTAGE AND ANTIQUES

FUN FACTS

In 1918, over 100 waiters in Chicago poisoned bad tippers.

The city is the home of spray paint, the Twinkie, and the first US blood bank.

CINCINNATI, OH

We only got to visit Cincinnati once on tour, but we had the best time hanging out at Christine's childhood home before the show. We actually recorded an entire episode for the podcast in Christine's bedroom (underneath a very old Fall Out Boy poster, of course) before heading out to the venue for our show that night. We didn't have microphones with us, so we used a handheld device and kept (very professionally) throwing it in front of each other's face to catch audio whenever one of us started talking. It was also Eva's first time at Christine's house, which meant I got to witness Eva witnessing the chaos that is the spooky handwriting upstairs on Christine's walls, the elevator that a priest built into their home, and the cemetery in their yard. It's like I became business partners with Wednesday Addams.

I wish I could say Em is exaggerating, but that's pretty much my childhood home to a T. (Once again, I'm amazed Eva has stuck around this long.) Now that I've moved back, I can't wait to drag both of them along for many more cemetery adventures in my hometown.

PARANORMAL

SEDAMSVILLE RECTORY

639 STEINER AVE • CINCINNATI, OH

Welcome to Cincinnati, home to Skyline Chili, the infamous cryptid known as America's Hircine Shifter, and a house so haunted that I advise you not to go if "potential demonic possession" doesn't sound appealing to you. Of all the haunted locations in this book, the Sedamsville Rectory is by far the scariest, complete with a dark entity that enjoys attaching to visitors at will.

The rectory itself was built in the 1800s and housed priests in the Cincinnati area. Although this was meant to be a devout home, dark secrets were later uncovered when one of these priests was caught and charged for abusing children throughout the 1950s and 1960s. When the rectory was abandoned around the 1980s, it was also discovered that the basement was used as a local dogfighting ring, with hundreds of scratch and bites marks covering the doors frames. Thanks to those two very dark stamps on the rectory's history, there is now an über-powerful negative energy that roams the halls.

Many believe the entity here is the priest's spirit in purgatory after having committed his crimes; others say the energy is purely demonic. This is because activity still occurs despite attempted blessings, a sulfuric burning smell comes and goes, and multiple people have been affected in the building. Past tenants say they would hear barking in the basement and see shadow figures. When another former tenant was being interviewed, an EVP was picked up of a voice saying, "This guy..."

How relatable that this demon is annoyed about running into his old roommate.

There have also been EVPs of a voice insulting women and one voice admitting it would scare the dogs before their fights. When investigators have spent the night, something will kick their bed, and people have seen a tall figure standing in an empty room. Pictures of the entity show it as a black mass, a thick purple mist, or sometimes as a horned reptilian figure. Guests have been scratched on either their back or face, sometimes in the shape of an upside-down cross. Children's voices and deep, guttural growls have been heard, unseen hands touch visitors, and from the basement it sometimes sounds like someone is kicking in the front door and breaking into the house. One woman even felt her legs being pushed together when sitting on a chair, as if a pro-purity-culture priest thought she was too spread-eagled.

Beyond the normal scary activity like being pushed or sensing an intimidating presence, the creepiest and seemingly most common thing to happen here is that people's behavior changes out of nowhere. There are multiple accounts of people coming into the rectory and getting uncharacteristically irritable and sick, then losing hours of time where they appeared catatonic to their cohorts. In one account, a person had to be informed later that while in a room by himself he was screaming at the top of his lungs.

The people most influenced by the spirit here are Tim and Terrie, who bought the building years ago. Both of them reported feeling addicted to the house, and when there, Tim's behavior would be incredibly hostile. During a blessing of the rectory (orchestrated by the fine people of *Ghost Adventures*), Tim and Terrie heard growling that nobody else could, another sign that they were more attached to the building than others. Tim has also been bitten by something and now won't go into the house alone.

One time when Tim did have to go alone, Terrie realized he went missing for four hours. She went over to check on him and found him sitting silently in the dark. Eventually, Tim got up, walked around, told Terrie to "get the fuck out," and woke up out of his trance. When Tim's brother passed, an EVP was also caught in the house saying one of their inside jokes, as if the demon was tricking a grieving Tim into thinking his brother was there. It's all bone-chilling, all terrifying, and yet (curveball of the century) all available to you soon on AirBnB! I'm not kidding: the Sedamsville Rectory is slowly being restored and is rumored to one day be available to rent for your very own twisted vacation. So if you're a ghost-busting thrill-seeker, check out the rectory and report back on any demonic activity, because as Zak says, "We want answers."

For more on America's Hircine Shifter, check out Episode 226: "Poisonous Sharks and the Patchsquatch."

TRUE CRIME

DONALD HARVEY— THE ANGEL OF DEATH

Sometimes called an "angel of mercy," an "angel of death" is a type of criminal offender, often serial, whose job is to care for the sick but instead intentionally harms or even kills the people under their care. Several killers have earned the moniker over the years, but Donald Harvey puts many of them to shame.

Born April 15, 1952, in Butler County, Ohio, Harvey not only suffered a severe head injury as a child but also endured abuse at the hands of several adults.

Fast-forward to 1970: Harvey was eighteen and began to regularly visit his ailing grandfather at Marymount Hospital in London, Kentucky. Harvey soon became a familiar face around the hospital, and both the nuns and nurses grew so accustomed to his presence that they offered him a job as an orderly.

So this guy just shows up and gets a job in the medical field . . . meanwhile, I had to write a cover letter to apply to IKEA, and I didn't even get an interview.

Harvey's position involved not only supervising patients on his own but also dispensing medication and inserting catheters. Only two months into his new job, one of Harvey's patients, a stroke victim named Logan Evans, grew angry with him and rubbed feces on his face. In return, Harvey grabbed a pillow and smothered him. He cleaned himself up and calmly announced Mr. Evans's death to the rest of the staff, obviously leaving out the whole smothering-him-with-a-pillow bit.

Over the next ten months, Donald Harvey killed fifteen more patients. Because most of them were old or in poor health, no one suspected him of murder. His mild-mannered temperament with coworkers also helped him cover his tracks.

Harvey's home life was no picnic either, as he was deeply depressed and often contemplated suicide. He was involved in two relationships at this point, the first of which was with James Peluso, an on-again-off-again boyfriend Harvey later killed when he became too ill to care for himself. Harvey's other relationship was with Vernon Midden, a married man with children who worked as—get this—an undertaker.

Harvey often asked Vernon super-duper-innocent questions about how the human body reacts to different trauma. He also later admitted that when their relationship went south, he entertained fantasies of embalming Vernon while he was still alive. *Cool-cool-cool-cool-cool.*

Vernon's talents extended beyond the mortuary sciences; he also taught Harvey all about our favorite subject, the occult. According to an article from Thoughtco.com, "This is where [Harvey] met his spiritual guide, 'Duncan,' who was at one time a doctor. Harvey attributes Duncan to helping him decide on who would be his next victim."

In March of 1971, Harvey was arrested for burglary. During the interrogation, he drunkenly confessed to his previous murders, but an extensive investigation failed to turn up any evidence, so he only faced the burglary charges.

After a brief stint in the US Air Force, Harvey landed a night position in the morgue at Cincinnati's Veterans Affairs Hospital. He began experimenting with cyanide, arsenic, and even rat poison, which he would put into patients' dinners, fruit juices, and pies. He even administered fluid tainted with hepatitis B and HIV. It is believed Harvey killed at least fifteen patients during this time.

Pretty soon, killing patients wasn't enough for Harvey. When he learned that his boyfriend Carl Hoeweler was cheating on him, Harvey began poisoning his food with arsenic as a way of keeping him at home. Harvey also went after his neighbor Helen Metzger, whom he felt was a threat to his and Carl's relationship. He laced Helen's jar of mayonnaise with arsenic. When that didn't work, he baked her a pie filled with arsenic, which killed her.

On April 25, 1983, following an argument with Carl's parents, Harvey started poisoning their food with arsenic. Four days after the initial poisoning, Carl's father, Henry Hoeweler, suffered a stroke and died. On the night of his death, Harvey visited him at the hospital and gave him arsenic-tainted pudding. Fortunately, Harvey's attempts to kill Carl's mother were not successful.

Despite his murderous home life, Harvey excelled at work, earning himself a promotion to morgue supervisor. His success didn't last long, though, as a few months later he was forced to resign when a gun was found in his gym bag. Unfortunately, the incident wasn't recorded, so Harvey was able to take his clean record and land a job at Cincinnati Drake Memorial Hospital.

In his own sick way, Harvey "thrived" here, as he had control over patients again. From April 1986 until March 1987, Donald Harvey killed twenty-six patients. The spree had to end somewhere, though, and indeed it did—with 44-year-old John Powell, Donald Harvey's last known victim. Powell had been in a motorcycle accident, and the forensic pathologist who performed the routine autopsy happened to catch a whiff of something strange—a distinct almond smell. Cyanide.

Harvey quickly became the lead suspect in the investigation of Powell's murder. Police had grown suspicious when they learned that Harvey had a super-fun nickname at work: *the Angel of Death*. His coworkers thought it was a funny coincidence that he always happened to be around when patients died. Oh, and patient deaths had more than doubled since he began working at the hospital. Fun coincidence, indeed.

Harvey accepted a plea deal to avoid the death penalty and was ultimately sentenced to eight life terms plus twenty years. On March 28, 2017, Harvey was beaten by a fellow inmate at the Toledo Correctional Institution and died shortly thereafter.

Donald Harvey ultimately confessed to eighty-seven murders. Not all of his claims could be verified, but if this count is accurate, that would make him one of the most prolific serial killers in US history.

FUN FACTS

Studies have shown that many mass murderers and serial killers have something in common: they suffered a head injury as a child. It's been theorized that brain injuries are linked to "acquired sociopathy."

Only 60 percent of people are able to detect the smell of cyanide.

To hear Em's reaction to Donald Harvey's heinous crimes, check out Episode 159: "A Sinister Vibe Check and the Governor of Noodletown."

TEAM WINE HAUNTS

OVERLOOK LODGE
Inspired by Stephen King's *The Shining*!

ARNOLD'S BAR AND GRILL
Haunted

BOBBY MACKEY'S MUSIC WORLD
Haunted. Featured in Episode 13

THE BLIND LEMON
Location of Christine's first (legal) drink

16-BIT BAR + ARCADE

ROSEDALE

TEAM MILKSHAKE HAUNTS

GRAETER'S ICE CREAM

AGLAMESIS BROS.

HELLO HONEY

UNITED DAIRY FARMERS
Christine's personal favorite. Try the Blue Moo Cookie Dough.

HAUNTED HOTELS

GOLDEN LAMB INN

BUXTON INN

HILTON NETHERLAND PLAZA
Location of Christine's rehearsal dinner and where Christine's stepmom hurled a glass at the wall … "It's tradition."

SPOOKY TOURS

MURDER MYSTERY WALKING TOUR

NEWPORT GANGSTER TOUR

AMERICAN LEGACY TOURS

SINISTER CINCINNATI TOUR

HAUNTED CINCY TOURS

MURDER ON THE MENU

CINCINNATI GHOST TOURS

HAUNTED CINCINNATI TOURS

GHOST TOURS OF MUSIC HALL

OTHER WEIRD (WTF) PLACES TO CHECK OUT

SPRING GROVE CEMETERY AND PARK

LOVELAND CASTLE

THE TROLL HOLE
World's Largest Troll Collection

PASSENGER PIGEON MEMORIAL HUT AT THE CINCINNATI ZOO

THE ABANDONED CINCINNATI SUBWAY TUNNELS

THE BETTS HOUSE

FUN FACTS

Home of Graeter's Ice Cream, Charles Manson, and Christine.

Jerry Springer was once mayor of Cincy.

Because of their love for chili, Cincinnatians consume more than two million pounds of their favorite food each year topped with 850,000 pounds of shredded cheddar cheese.

DETROIT, MI

Detroit was a quick stop for us, since it was sandwiched between our shows in Milwaukee and Chicago. There were a lot of things I wanted to see while I was there, but unfortunately the only "Detroit" experience I got was sampling some of their late-night food in the hotel. I heard about two 24-hour places called Duly's Place Coney Island and Telway Hamburgers, and since I had barely eaten all day, I went to both. Both were amazing—you have to try them next time you're here! The other highlight of our time here was during our meet and greet when two people asked if we could sign their copy of *I'll Be Gone in the Dark*, which had also been signed by Karen Kilgariff and Georgia Hardstark from the legendary podcast *My Favorite Murder*. I don't know if Christine was more honored or if I was, but to the folks who asked us to sign their book, you made our night.

I brought my groupies—er, family—to our Detroit show, and we had a blast. We spent the day exploring the Ford Factory up in Dearborn before heading to the venue. The show was delayed, but luckily there was a piano backstage so I could serenade everyone who was trapped in the greenroom with me.

PARANORMAL

ELOISE ASYLUM

30712 MICHIGAN AVE · WESTLAND, MI

Half an hour west of Detroit is the Eloise Asylum (not to be confused with the much happier *Eloise at the Plaza*). In 1839, Wayne County built the Wayne County Poorhouse, originally for vagrants and criminals, but soon the mentally ill also began getting transferred here. The poorhouse quickly became overcrowded, but after several expansions of the property, the massive asylum was running as its own city. It had its own bakeries, greenhouse, slaughterhouse, farms, police department, fire station, powerhouse, tobacco field, and zip code.

The facility was named the Eloise Asylum in 1894 after the daughter of the board president.

Thanks, Dad? —Eloise one day

The asylum was also known for having the most advanced modern treatments out there, which sounds great! But it's terrible. Because "modern treatment" meant hydrotherapy, electroshock, chemical burn experiments, and the first ever lobotomies! These lobotomies were performed at random and in the hospital's tunnels, where up until recently curious explorers were still finding vials of brain samples. (Okay, fine, the asylum also gave us the first diagnostic X-rays as well as occupational, recreational, and music therapies. But still, underground experimental lobotomies.)

There were insane levels of overpopulation, beatings, neglect, failed medical experiments, and a complete lack of sanitation. Not only was there an on-site morgue but also three cemeteries for the over 7,000 unclaimed or unidentified bodies left here. The hospital was completely closed by the 1980s.

In terms of hauntings, Eloise Asylum is known to be quite active. The second, third, and fifth floors are said to be the most haunted. People claim to hear footsteps, screaming, dragging, gurneys rolling down the halls, fire station bells, whispering, humming, doors slamming, someone following you, and someone calling out your name when nobody is there. Many have said you can feel someone staring at you in the dark and that the building is eerily quiet. Visitors say they have felt their clothes being tugged and their arms and backs being touched; some say they have even been pushed out of rooms. People have also reported seeing apparitions of patients eating in the cafeteria, people sitting in chairs in empty rooms when you walk by, a woman in white on the top floors, and a man walking up and down the stairs.

Personally, the scariest apparition people report seeing is a man wearing Bermuda shorts. Furniture and filing cabinets move around, papers shuffle themselves, and items are thrown around by unknown forces. Investigative teams coming in have captured some scary EVPs, including "Who are you?" "Don't say that," "Lost, bitch?" "Better get out of here," and "Lobotomy." One time a tour guide claims to have finished cleaning the hallway after guests left, then turned around and saw a walker sitting in the middle of the hall. If you would like to check out some of these claims yourself, the Eloise Asylum is being renovated into a "haunted attraction" and also a vintage bar for those of us who like to sleep at night.

TRUE CRIME

THE ST. AUBIN FAMILY MASSACRE

Sometimes called the "Detroit Occult Murders," the St. Aubin Family Massacre is the perfect blend of true crime and paranormal. On July 3, 1929, police

the midst of a horror scene. In the basement, they found the father, Benny Evangelista, seated behind his desk. His hands were neatly folded as though in prayer, his head casually resting on a chair nearby.

While I'm sure this was enough to make even the most seasoned detective queasy, things only got worse. Upstairs, they found Mrs. Evangelista dead as well, her head having been nearly severed. Nearby were the bodies of the couple's four children—Angeline, age 8; Margaret, age 5; Jeanne, age 4; and Mario, 18 months. All had had their skulls crushed.

Detroit at this time was home to a number of immigrants who had moved in with entrepreneurial hopes and dreams. Unfortunately, many of them arrived only to find atrocious working conditions, poverty, and even death. Italian immigrant Benny Evangelista was one of a few who managed to beat the odds and make a successful living. Having arrived in America in 1904, Benny invested in real estate and had soon become a prosperous realtor and landlord, supplementing his income with carpentry work.

Most men may have been satisfied with this setup, but Benny wasn't most men. The businessman soon began having what he called mystic visions, which went against the strict Catholic upbringing with which he'd been raised. Benny believed he was receiving divine messages about the creation of the world, which he compiled into a book called *The Oldest History of the World Discovered by Occult Science in Detroit, Michigan.* Imagine spotting someone reading that on the plane.

His obsession with the occult bothered some, but not the young Santina Evangelista, who sought his healing and ultimately became his wife. Although he had some followers who revered his mystic guidance, others understandably began referring to him as a cult leader. It didn't help that peeking into Benny's windows offered passersby a view of his "Great Celestial Planet Exhibition," which featured paper-mache planets and wax dolls hanging from the ceiling. Nearby sat an altar where Benny would practice rituals and mix potions.

Fast-forward to 1929—the spooky setting where Benny's decapitated body was found added a new layer (or ten) to the creep-factor of this murder. The first clue came in the form of a purchase Benny was meant to make the following morning. He had planned to purchase a large amount of lumber, yet no cash was found in the home. Even stranger, the lumber deliveryman never showed, as though he knew the transaction would never be completed. Police were never able to locate the delivery company itself, but money became a suspected motive.

Another potential motive was revenge. The brutal, hands-on nature of the slayings indicated the murder was personal. Perhaps, police thought, someone had felt duped by Benny's promises of "healing powers" and had returned to the home in search of revenge.

Although it was determined that the family had been killed by the same axe, the murder weapon was never found. Despite a $1000 reward offered by police (approximately $16,000 in today's currency), leads went nowhere. There wasn't much of an update in the case until 1930, when an article was released featuring the headline, "Eye Witness to Brutal Detroit Axe Slaying Finally Turns Up." Consider this old-fashioned "clickbait," because it turns out the eyewitness was none other than the family dog, who had disappeared sometime during the attack and didn't reappear until the following year, when he showed up on a woman's doorstep. Unfortunately, the dog's backstory kept the woman from adopting him, but I like to think another kind soul took him in instead.

St. Aubin Street still carries remnants of its dark past, with many locals considering the area haunted. People have reported seeing a headless man wandering around, as well as hearing disembodied voices and screams. The house itself was demolished, and all that remains is an empty lot.

To this day, the brutal slaying of the Evangelista family remains unsolved.

TEAM WINE HAUNTS

CADIEUX CAFE
Haunted

CENTRAL KITCHEN + BAR
Black-owned

THE GHOST BAR AT THE WHITNEY
Haunted

FENTON HOTEL
Haunted

BAD LUCK BAR

TEAM MILKSHAKE HAUNTS

DETROIT WATER ICE FACTORY

COLD TRUTH

CUSTARD HUT

HAUNTED HOTELS

TWO WAY INN

FORT SHELBY HOTEL

NATIONAL HOUSE INN

SPOOKY TOURS

HAUNTED DETROIT TOURS

NIGHT IN JAIL GHOST HUNT & TOUR

PARANORMAL DINNER TOUR

ELOISE HAUNTED TOURS

TRUE CRIME AND GHOST WALKING TOUR

NOTORIOUS 313 TOURS

OTHER WEIRD (WTF) PLACES TO CHECK OUT

NORTHVILLE PSYCHIATRIC HOSPITAL

ALLEGAN COUNTY OLD JAIL MUSEUM

JIFFY CORN MUFFIN MIX TOUR

ANATOMY OF DEATH MUSEUM

NUN DOLL MUSEUM

ICE MUSEUM

MUSEUM OF MAGIC
Car-themed diner where the booths are whole vintage cars

Detroit has its own pizza: it's chewier and baked in a square pan.

Home of the country's oldest soda: Vernor's ginger ale.

ST. LOUIS, MO

The day we performed in St. Louis for the first time was January 19, which was the anniversary of me asking Christine to start a podcast (also known as the podcast's date of conception). The sweetest part was that some of our listeners made us a sign to celebrate us performing two years after starting the show together. Before the show that night, Christine, Eva, and I all spent some time at Ozarkland, which I still consider one of my favorite shopping pit stops out there. Most of the items there blew my mind, especially this blue and green backpack that I ended up using for my laptop for the rest of the 2019 tour! Finally, St. Louis in 2019 marked the beginning of our on-the-road tradition: eating McDonald's for breakfast when we drive from one city to the next. Shoutout to my Hotcakes and Sausage platter lovers, because that meal has gotten me through some early mornings!

I've driven through St. Louis many times, but our 2019 show was the first time I'd ever really gotten to experience the city. I remember downtown St. Louis was bustling, and Em is right—our stop at Ozarkland on the way there was one for the books! Oh, and while we're sharing—my Mickey D's order is a hazelnut iced latte and an Egg McMuffin, no ham.

PARANORMAL

MINERAL SPRINGS HOTEL

301 E. BROADWAY • ALTON, IL

What would happen if an entire town was built out of rocks from the state's first prison where nearly 2,000 people died? You would get Alton, one of the most haunted small towns in the country!

One of the buildings made out of these rocks is the Mineral Springs Hotel, which is actually now an antique mall by the same name. Originally meant to be an ice plant, a natural spring was discovered under it during its construction in 1909, and the water was determined to have magical healing properties. The property owners decided to profit off of the "magic" and the building became a resort and spa, boasting the "largest swimming pool in Illinois" and my favorite—Alton's biggest table. In the 1970s it was fashioned into a shopping mall.

Well, although this location was known for its relaxation and peaceful aesthetic, it was also the site of many deaths. Two people have died by suicide and another man drowned during a swimming lesson. In the 1920s, a wife saw her husband flirting with another woman near the pool. Rumor has it, she took off her shoe, hit him with the heel, and he fell into the pool, where he drowned.

The most famous death here has been the "Jasmine Lady." While at the hotel, her husband walked in on her with another man, and he chased her down the hall. She ended up dying after falling down the stairs, and her husband then ended his own life. These are just some of the deaths at the Mineral Springs Hotel, although there are many more spirits than just these six (duh, the town built a spa out of haunted prison bricks). The reports of ghostly activity in this hotel run the gamut, from sweet spirits to angry demons. As the prince of paranormal Zak Bagans has said of Mineral Springs, "This is not a building; this is a beast."

Some of the less intense reports include unexplained sounds of music and laughter as well as smells of jasmine and liquor. People have also seen shadow figures, doors open, wet footprints by the pool, items fly off the table, and intense energy spikes on equipment. Most of the darker activity happens near the pool, where people used to hold séances (quelle surprise). People have been shoved, scratched, growled at, had rocks thrown at them, and have allegedly become fully possessed down here. The owner of the building even said, "They're here in this pool; there's not a doubt about it." People have been grabbed and heard someone say "get out" on multiple occasions.

People have also seen spirits down here, most often a little girl and a well-dressed man. The man is said to be a demon named William, who on *Ghost Adventures* was heard through spirit boxes saying charming words such as "demon," "unholy," and "Got him." Not only does Mineral Springs Hotel have pleasant spirits and evil spirits, but it also has asshole spirits. People have reported music playing just to irritate them and temporarily losing their items just to find them in random places later. A storekeeper here even watched a spirit knock over all of his Tupperware that he had just finished organizing. Whether you want to be haunted, possessed, or just mildly inconvenienced, check out Mineral Springs next time you're nearby!

TRUE CRIME

BERTHA GIFFORD— MISSOURI'S FIRST SERIAL KILLER

Folks, this one's an oldie but a goodie. I'm going to tell you the tale of Bertha Gifford, who not only holds the title of Missouri's first serial killer but also ranks as the country's fourth solo female serial killer. Buckle up!

Bertha Gifford was said to be one of the most beautiful women in all of Jefferson County. At the age of twenty-three she married a man named Henry Graham, who died suddenly of stomach cramps. Bertha went on to marry a man named Eugene Gifford, and the pair moved to Catawissa in Franklin County.

Side note: I looked up this town, and it's, well, tiny. According to TripAdvisor, there is one restaurant here called "Tavern," which is described as "Pub."

Neighbors described Bertha as not only an extraordinary cook but also a friendly, compassionate woman. She had adopted the role of "nurse," tending to sick people all over town and helping them recover from their ailments. Bertha was so well loved that she was nicknamed the "Good Samaritan" of Catawissa and would often jump out of her bed in the middle of the night, put on her white nurse's uniform, and drive her horse and buggy through any sort of weather, even blizzards, to make it to an ailing neighbor's home, oftentimes before the county doctor even arrived. I hope you see where this is going.

Bertha, though not a trained nurse, was considered a very competent volunteer whom the local doctors truly appreciated. Because she understood symptoms and drugs, she was given permission to administer medicines to patients. (Thank goddess for modern-day licensing boards.) According to witnesses, when she took a case, she would take command of the household, impressing the family with her superior knowledge and experience.

Unfortunately, there was one small problem with this arrangement. *Bertha's patients kept dying.* The typical order of events went as follows: Bertha would head to a person's bedside, tending to them throughout the night, then inform the family the following morning that their loved one had passed. Sometimes, a patient would seem to be on the road to recovery but would mysteriously take a turn for the worse once Bertha arrived. Upon her patients' deaths, Bertha would weep harder than anyone else, presumably in an attempt to mask her guilt.

Finally, people in town started to catch on, recognizing that whenever Bertha "plunks herself down in a sick-room, the patient never gets well." This incidentally super-sexist article, published in 1928, questioned whether "a lot of ignorant gossips [could] know more than the doctors." Yikes. The men laughed at the women's hysteria and let Bertha continue her prolific nursing career.

Infuriatingly, it wasn't until Bertha Gifford's seventeenth patient-victim passed away that the men in town began to take the women's concerns seriously. This victim's name was Ed Brinley, and his death finally prompted an investigation into Bertha Gifford's behavior. The way Bertha had defended herself in the past was by saying each of her patients' deaths were due to acute gastritis caused by the "rural habit of eating a heavy dinner at noon and then laboring on a full stomach." Somehow this worked every time, as each time a patient died, a death certificate had been issued without question.

But State Health Commissioner Dr. James Stewart began to dig deeper. He had the records of drugstores in neighboring towns examined and learned that Bertha had been a steady customer of arsenic rat poison, which produces symptoms quite similar to gastritis. In many cases, she had made her purchases just before the patients' deaths. Oddly enough, Bertha also attended virtually every single funeral in town over the span of eighteen years, often taking command and organizing the affair.

Bertha Gifford was arrested in Eureka, Missouri, and charged with three counts of murder. Despite her proclamations of innocence, prosecutors were able to prove that Bertha's murder streak stretched all the way back to 1909. Remember her first husband, poor old Henry Graham? Well, it turns out that the mysterious "stomach cramps" that killed him were inflicted by none other than Bertha herself.

Bertha's second known victim was her mother-in-law, who had died of food poisoning in 1913. An article published around this time claimed that Bertha's grief was "not so great but considered adequate for a mother-in-law." (Ouch.) A year later, her thirteen-year-old brother-in-law James Gifford died in Bertha's arms with similar symptoms.

Tragically, one man took to the stand to tell the grand jury how Bertha had nursed three of his children for small ailments that promptly turned into acute gastritis and ended in all of their deaths. In fact, horrifyingly, it seemed Bertha preferred children as patients whenever possible, perhaps because they were more easily talked into taking whatever substance she gave them.

According to further witness testimony, one man who had worked for the Giffords had complained that Bertha owed him wage . . . She paid the money back in time for it to be spent on his funeral.

The grand jury indicted Bertha for murder, but she still insisted that she had done nothing wrong. Her priority during the trial was to avoid getting photographed, and she was said to sit in her cell with a blanket that she threw over her head whenever she heard someone walking down the hallway. She refused to eat anything but ice cream.

The whole blanket + ice cream scenario honestly just sounds like a sleepover with Em.

Despite the fact that two of Bertha's victims were exhumed and found to have traces of arsenic in their system, Bertha was "found not guilty by reason of insanity" and was committed to the Missouri State Hospital #4, where she remained until her death in 1951. While there, she worked at the hospital's beauty shop before being transferred to the kitchen as a cook.

Bertha Gifford is buried in Church of God Faith of Abraham Cemetery in Morse Mill. Her grave is unmarked, and the undertaker's records list the balance of her burial as "unpaid."

TEAM WINE HAUNTS

JOHN D. MCGURK'S IRISH PUB & GARDEN
Haunted

BISSELL MANSION RESTAURANT & MURDER MYSTERY DINNER THEATRE
Haunted

THAXTON SPEAKEASY

BROADWAY OYSTER BAR

TEAM MILKSHAKE HAUNTS

CLEMENTINE'S NAUGHTY AND NICE CREAMERY
Woman-owned

TED DREWES FROZEN CUSTARD

BOARDWALK WAFFLES AND ICE CREAM

HAUNTED HOTELS AND BARS

MOONRISE HOTEL

CHASE PARK PLAZA

MORSE MILL HOTEL

LEMP MANSION

SPOOKY TOURS

TRUE CRIME STORIES TOUR

ST. LOUIS MOB HISTORY TOUR

HAUNTED STL TOURS

LEMP MANSION HAUNTED TOUR

ST. LOUIS HAUNTED HISTORY WALKING TOUR

MISSOURI STATE PENITENTIARY TOUR

FANTASTIC CAVERNS
Ride-through cave tour

OTHER WEIRD (WTF) PLACES TO CHECK OUT

WORLD'S LARGEST TOY MUSEUM

LYLE VAN HOUTEN'S AUTOMOTIVE MUSEUM
Abandoned gas station with mannequins

GLORE PSYCHIATRIC MUSEUM

HANNIBAL HAUNTED HOUSE WAX MUSEUM

BONNIE AND CLYDE SHOOTOUT CABIN

RIDGE PARK CEMETERY: GRAVE OF JIM THE WONDER DOG

CAVE VINEYARD AND WINE TASTING

HEATON-BOWMAN-SMITH AND SIDENFADE CHAPEL FUNERAL MUSEUM—JESSE JAMES'S CASKET

THE EXORCIST HOUSE

ZOMBIE ROAD

FUN FACTS

St. Louis is known for its butter cake, which was created by accident when the baker added too much sugar.

Home of peanut butter and the first ever kindergarten class.

SOUTHWEST

PHOENIX, AZ

Phoenix was the first place we came to for the start of our 2020 tour! I remember being so nervous that our audience might not like the new format of our show, and we were stumbling all over ourselves since we hadn't fully mastered what to say or our timing. But what I loved the most about this show was the overwhelmingly positive response we got from the crowd. It made everything we had been working on that much more worth it. The first time we came to Phoenix, though, was in 2019, when I went to an oddity shop called Curious Nature and found some great gifts for my equally creepy-leaning friends. I also tried out MacAlpine's Soda Fountain, which has been open since the 1930s. I only had a really delicious milkshake, but for anyone looking for something new to try at the local diner, MacAlpine's has nearly 100 different flavored sodas. The firefighting museum called the Hall of Flame is also worth your time!

Oh, Phoenix . . . you always make us feel so welcome! As Em said, we kicked off our 2020 tour (RIP) in Phoenix, and the crowd was, for lack of a better word, kick-ass. The venue even came up with a custom menu for the night featuring drink specials like the "True Crime," the "Paranormal," and the "Podcast Bucket"! If I ever doubt our new tour format in the future, I'll just have to imagine myself in Phoenix, grabbing a local beer out of the Podcast Bucket and cheers-ing the beautiful Arizonan crowd.

PARANORMAL

JEROME GRAND HOTEL

200 HILL ST · JEROME, AZ

The next time you find yourself in central Arizona and in desperate need of a nearly guaranteed paranormal experience, might we suggest the Jerome Grand Hotel? This national landmark started its story back in 1917 as a hospital for miners and later became the United Verde Hospital. United Verde was not only considered one of the most modern hospitals in the West, but it was by definition an aboveground bomb shelter, able to withstand 130-ton blasts of dynamite from its friendly neighborhood land mines.

The hospital saw over 9,000 deaths during its time and has been famously haunted since the 1920s, when many of the patients died during the flu epidemic. The most famous death on site was the unsolved case of maintenance man Claude Harvey, who was found with his head crushed under the elevator in 1935. By 1950 the hospital shut down, and in 1996 it was turned into the terribly haunted hotel you see today. After its renovations, the building kept 95 percent of its original structure, which leaves us with two fun facts: this hotel has been deemed the best-preserved building in Arizona, and many parts of the hospital property have been eerily repurposed as hotel utilities (i.e., current trash chutes were once used to dispose of "surgical waste").

Today the hotel embraces its spirits and at different times has kept records of spooky activity, invited paranormal teams to investigate, and offered ghost tour packages for visitors. This place runs the gamut of paranormal activity. There are alleged apparitions of medical staff, miners, maintenance workers, and children all over the hotel, and disembodied sounds range from footsteps to laughter to heavy breathing to screams. People have also heard sounds of cocktail parties in empty rooms, their name being called, and—a personal favorite—someone whispering at 3 a.m., "Be careful; I am in here." How could it get creepier? If you guessed, "The ghost of a little boy stares at you and hides at the foot of your bed," you're right! People also report their blankets getting yanked off of them, feeling someone sitting on them while they sleep, and banging on their closet doors by an unknown force. (It's without a doubt that creepy-as-shit kid but yeah, okay, "unknown force.") Water faucets, fans, televisions, and lights will all turn on and off by themselves, furniture will rearrange itself, and doors will lock and unlock as well as open and close on their own. People have smelled flowers, whiskey, tobacco, and baby powder for no reason at all, and there are reports of gurneys squeaking down the hall even though the hotel is now carpeted. Shadow figures are said to shamelessly move around you and vanish before your eyes, and the spirits like to mess with employees until they get yelled at to stop. A plaque has been seen lifting itself off of its nail, items in the gift shop fly off the shelves, and the front desk gets phone calls from empty rooms—sometimes hearing people on the other end!

During one investigation, over forty hours of paranormal evidence were collected, and of course, Mr. Bagans himself has been here for an episode of *Ghost Adventures*. The only spiritual redemption I can find here is the hotel's ghost cat. Many guests have said they hear meowing and purring in their room and will feel the cat brush up against them. They will even invite the kitty to sleep in their bed, and the next day find paw-shaped imprints on the linens! It's also rumored that this phantom feline can be seen in pictures after your visit. So if you're looking for a run-in with one of the 9,000 potential spirits at the Jerome Grand Hotel, hopefully yours is just a selfie with the cutest, furriest one.

FUN FACTS

Jerome Grand Hotel has Arizona's oldest self-servicing elevator, which was installed in 1926. (Yes, the same elevator that killed Claude Harvey.)

Most of Jerome is at a 30-degree incline, making it the "World's Most Vertical City." Due to its steepness, Jerome Grand Hotel is only structurally possible because its concrete was poured on a 50-degree slope.

TRUE CRIME

WENDI ANDRIANO

In the early morning hours of October 8, 2000, 30-year-old Wendi Andriano asked a neighbor to watch her kids while she took her husband, Joe, to the hospital. Joe had been diagnosed with cancer back in 1998, and it had since spread throughout his body. When the neighbor arrived, she noticed Joe lying on the floor in the fetal position, barely breathing. Wendi told her friend she hadn't yet called 911, so her neighbor made the call before waiting outside for paramedics.

When EMTs arrived only minutes later, Wendi had locked the doors, refusing to let paramedics enter and treat her husband. Eventually, she came out of the back door and around the building, seemingly freshly showered. She told paramedics that she had things under control and that no medical care was needed. With no other recourse, emergency services left.

It was only an hour later, at 3:30 a.m., that Phoenix police received another 911 call from Wendi. This time, though, she told a different story. Wendi told police Joe had flown into a rage when he noticed she wasn't wearing a wedding ring. Joe grabbed a belt, and Wendi grabbed a barstool. Wendi claimed this had all happened before the aforementioned neighbor had even arrived. She explained that as soon as the neighbor and paramedics had left, Joe became physical again and attempted to strangle her with a telephone cord, so she grabbed a knife and stabbed him in the neck. The neighbor, however, later swore that upon her arrival she had seen neither blood nor a barstool anywhere near Joe.

Upon closer inspection, police noticed barely any of the alleged "defensive wounds" on Wendi's body. When Joe's friends and family insisted he was far too terminally ill to have taken part in a physical altercation, police knew something was up. While Wendi waited in the interrogation room, she stupidly called a coworker and asked her to hide some paperwork for her—all while police watched from the other room. They decided to conduct a search of her office.

During the search, police discovered Wendi had been leading a secret life. She was having multiple affairs and oftentimes told her family she was working when really she was partying at nightclubs. Wendi's coworkers told police she had been disciplined for "looking up inappropriate things" at work. I know what you're thinking—it must have been porn, right? WRONG! Believe it or not, her searches were even more outrageous, including keywords like "poison" and "how to kill people."

Quick piece of advice from yours truly: If you spot a coworker googling murder instructions, please alert the appropriate authorities.

The case really broke when police took a look at the mysterious paperwork Wendi had asked her coworker to hide on her behalf. The documents were shipping invoices for sodium azide, an extremely deadly poison. In order to access it, Wendi had created a fictitious business license, using the tax ID form from her workplace, a Xerox copier, and an X-Acto knife. But now they needed their smoking gun: where was the poison?

Police searched the Andriano apartment, sampling every food item in their home, including Joe's last meal: a pot of beef stew. Meanwhile, investigators uncovered a storage unit containing a box, within a box, within a box, within a box ... You get the picture. At the center of this charming set of nesting boxes was an aluminum foil–wrapped bottle of sodium azide, complete with a kitchen measuring spoon. (Did she think the searchers would just get tired of opening boxes and give up halfway through?!) The poison was also found in the beef stew and Joe's stomach contents.

Police theorized that Wendi had grown embittered as her husband battled his cancer and had plotted to poison him in an attempt to end his life. He did indeed have a heart attack after consuming the poison, so she called the neighbor and claimed she was taking him to the hospital. Hence her not calling 911.

But when the neighbor went out to wait for paramedics, Wendi realized the poison hadn't taken its toll the way she thought it would. Instead of waiting any longer, she sent the paramedics away and proceeded to hit Joe with a barstool repeatedly before stabbing him with a knife, ending his life.

Wendi's trial took place on November 18, 2004, four years after Joe's death. She was sentenced to death by lethal injection, becoming only the second woman on Arizona's death row, where she remains to this day.

Learn more about both Wendi Andriano and the Jerome Grand Hotel in Episode 107: "Ghostly Cat Toes and a Box-in-a-Box-in-a-Box."

TEAM WINE HAUNTS

UNDERTOW

STARDUST PINBAR
Stardust Pinbar offers over a dozen themed pinball machines (including my favorite, the Addams Family)!

CASEY MOORE'S OYSTER HOUSE
Haunted

THE KETTLE BLACK KITCHEN + PUB
Black-owned

THE MIX UP BAR
Black-owned

TEAM MILKSHAKE HAUNTS

NOVEL ICE CREAM

ROLL IT UP ICE CREAM
Black-owned

SUGAR BOWL

HAUNTED HOTELS

HOTEL SAN CARLOS

JEROME GRAND HOTEL

HOTEL MONTE VISTA

WEATHERFORD HOTEL

SPOOKY TOURS

SPIRIT OF ARIZONA TOURS

PHX TOURS

HAUNTED DOWNTOWN FLAGSTAFF TOUR

JEROME GHOST TOWN

GOLD KING MINE & GHOST TOWN

YUMA TERRITORIAL PRISON TOUR

OTHER WEIRD (WTF) PLACES TO CHECK OUT

FIREFLY INFINITY MIRROR ROOM

THE MYSTERY CASTLE

CURIOUS NATURE—CURIOSITY SHOP

BICENTENNIAL MOON TREE IN FLAGSTAFF

THE 1898 COURT HOUSE

IGNITE SIGN ART MUSEUM

TUCSON'S VALLEY OF THE MOON WHIMSY PARK

MINI TIME MACHINE MUSEUM OF MINIATURES

CASTLE DOME GHOST TOWN AND MINING MUSEUM

YUMA'S LITTLE CHAPEL

FUN FACTS

L. Ron Hubbard lived in Phoenix when he started writing about Scientology.

There is NO daylight saving time in Phoenix.

LAS VEGAS, NV

We may not have gone to Vegas on tour yet, but Christine and I still made memories here during her bachelorette party! Together we did the High Roller Ferris wheel (it comes with drinks!), which is the tallest observation deck wheel in the world and shows you all of the Las Vegas Strip. We also had drinks at the Golden Tiki and braved the many creepy rooms, dolls, and curses of Zak Bagans's Haunted Museum. The only things we didn't get to check out that I'd been hoping to do were some of the roller coasters on top of the city high-rises and the Pioneer Saloon, which is said to be haunted by multiple spirits still watching over the bar. While there, Allison and I tried the SlotZilla Zipline, which was a blast, and the Marvel Museum called Avengers S.T.A.T.I.O.N., which just rocked my world. Check out any of these things next time you're in town and you'll leave with happy memories!

I will never be the same after the bachelorette party Em planned for me in 2018. Not only did my own mother witness me getting a sensual lap dance by some Chippendales, but also we narrowly avoided being cursed by a certain doll who shall not be named . . . I know most people want what happens there to stay there, but I don't think I'll ever stop telling stories from that trip! Can't wait for my grandkids to see my Chippendales pics someday.

PARANORMAL

ZAK BAGANS'S
THE HAUNTED MUSEUM

600 E CHARLESTON BLVD · LAS VEGAS, NV

I couldn't write a book about haunted locations and neglect the one, the only, Zak Bagans's the Haunted Museum (aka what I consider the only appropriate destination for a bachelorette party). This 11,000-square-foot mansion has more haunted items in one location than anywhere else in the world, and with that comes an endless supply of spirits.

The original structure was owned by Cyril Wengert and built in 1938. Locals have reported that dark magic was practiced down in the basement during the 1970s—an area that allegedly has such intense paranormal activity that it is still off limits to general admission. Zak bought the building back in 2015 and has since filled its over thirty rooms with his personal collection of all things macabre. Here you can find several of Zak's haunted pieces on display, including the founder of the Church of Satan's chalice, Bela Lugosi's mirror, the "Crying Boy" paintings, and the actual staircase from the "Demon House," which during the museum's rebuild left construction workers running out of the house and never coming back.

Another item is the dybbuk box, said to be the most haunted item to exist and the inspiration for the movie *The Possession*. Some employees won't even go into this item's exhibit and ask tour guests for additional verbal assent before letting them in the room alone. (Only AFTER I agreed to go in this room did the guide say, "Oh, and a solid black mass is seen floating in that corner!") The Devil's Rocking Chair is also here, which was used in the exorcism of David Glatzel. The chair has such powerful energy connected to it that the exhibit was temporarily shut down after enough guests had something evil attach to them. People, including Zak, have had frightening experiences with it, including some who dared to sit in the chair and then developed back issues requiring corrective surgery.

One last item worth noting is the doll whose name I won't even write, in fear that she'll curse our book sales. (Although we're smart enough to not mention her name, we were stupid enough to go to the museum, stand alone in a closed room with her, look her in the eyes, and speak to her.) The Haunted Museum also has an extensive collection of "murderabilia," including original art by John Wayne Gacy and Richard Ramirez, Charles Manson's dentures, Ed Gein's cauldron, Ted Bundy's glasses, Michael Jackson's "propofol chair," and Dr. Kevorkian's van.

However, there are some less terrifying items on display, such as Zak's non-haunted (but equally creepy) collection of clowns and original props from the *Ghostbusters* movie franchise. I would love to list all of the paranormal experiences that have happened here, but that list would probably be longer than this book. Let's just say staff and guests regularly hear, see, and feel things, from the mild cases to the extreme. Just a handful of these moments have been documented on Zak's creepiest series to date: *Ghost Adventures: Quarantine*.

PSA (because I wish someone would have told me): be prepared for some very dark rooms with items used during gruesome murders. These rooms will 100 percent make your stomach churn (and bum you the fuck out). You may not run into these rooms, as exhibits are constantly being changed out, but please come to the museum prepared for it. Zak has called his museum "a sick, twisted, 'It's a Small World' at Disneyland" and "a hostel for the afterlife."

That being said, the Haunted Museum does not guarantee you will experience anything paranormal. The goal of the museum is to respectfully learn about these items' histories, and if something wants to present itself to you along the way, it will. When we went on the tour, we didn't witness anything, but I promise that didn't make our time there any less spooky. If you happen to be a more serious thrill-seeker, the museum also offers a Flashlight Night Tour where you are given free rein of the museum for ninety minutes. (*"There are things in this that we will never fully understand"* . . . like who would choose to do this.)

Whichever tour you select, you will have to sign a waiver releasing the museum from your usual, everyday risks such as "spiritual detection" and "actions by unseen forces."

To learn more, listen to: Episode 85 (Bela Lugosi's Mirror), Episode 58 (the Demon House), Episode 11 (Dybbuk Box), Episode 213 (David Glatzel), Episode 5 (John Wayne Gacy), Episode 217 and 218 (Richard Ramirez), Episode 42 and 85 (Ed Gein), and Episode 51 (Ted Bundy).

TRUE CRIME

BROOKEY LEE WEST

In a town where most major crime stories revolve around casino heists and mob violence, the story of serial killer Brookey Lee West stands out.

In 1998, 65-year-old Christine Smith, who had long struggled with alcohol abuse, seemingly vanished. When questioned, Christine's daughter, Brookey Lee Smith, informed police that her mother had simply moved to California to live with her son. Police initially accepted this story, until Christine's body was found in a trash can at a Las Vegas storage unit owned by none other than Brookey herself. In an effort to explain herself, Brookey backtracked and claimed she'd panicked after her mother had died of natural causes, stuffing her body in a garbage can. *Sure, sure, sure, sure, sure...*

For obvious reasons, Brookey was arrested, and a forensic entomologist was tasked with analyzing the body. He noticed a lack of blow flies on the corpse, meaning the body was either put into the garbage can immediately after death or, more horrifyingly, perhaps while the person was still alive.

While Brookey's defense continued to claim Christine had died of natural causes, the prosecution asserted that Brookey had killed her mother in order to benefit from Christine's monthly $1,000 Social Security checks.

Brookey's difficult childhood and her toxic relationship with her mother only served to further this argument. Brookey had always been close to her father, who taught her witchcraft, Satanism, and violence at a young age. Meanwhile, her mother was said to have had repeated affairs, often neglecting Brookey and her brother.

With this information, the jury found Brookey guilty of murder, and she was sentenced to life in prison.

But wait, there's more!

Since Brookey's conviction in 2003, she has been linked to the deaths of two additional people, which, if accurate, would make her a serial killer. In 1993, Brookey's brother, Travis, disappeared. Although his body was never found, the crime was linked to Brookey when it was discovered that Travis's Social Security number was being used in association with Brookey's home address.

A year after her brother's disappearance, Brookey married a man named Howard Simon St. John. Only months into that marriage, Howard claimed Brookey had assaulted him with a .32-caliber handgun, but the charges were ultimately dropped. Only two weeks later, Simon's body was found in the Sequoia National Forest, the cause of death being gunshot wounds.

Although Brookey was never convicted of the other two crimes, the murder of her mother was enough to put her away for life. Brookey made headlines once again in 2012 when she attempted to escape from prison by donning a disguise and attempting to walk out of the front entrance of the jail while the other inmates were on their way to breakfast. She was apprehended and remains in prison to this day.

TEAM WINE HAUNTS

PIONEER SALOON
Haunted

INDIGO LOUNGE
Haunted

WEST SIDE OASIS
Black-owned

THE GOLDEN TIKI
Haunted. Featured in Season 2, episode 7 of *Ghost Adventures*!

TEAM MILKSHAKE HAUNTS

SLOAN'S ICE CREAM

HANDEL'S HOMEMADE ICE CREAM & YOGURT

LAPPERT'S ICE CREAM

HAUNTED HOTELS

MIZPAH HOTEL

GOLDFIELD HOTEL

FLAMINGO HOTEL AND CASINO

SPOOKY TOURS

HAUNTED VEGAS TOUR AND GHOST HUNT

SHADOWS OF SIN CITY GHOST TOUR

LAS VEGAS STRIP: HAUNTED GHOST EXPERIENCE

GHOST AND VAMPIRE TOURS IN VEGAS

VEGAS GHOST TOUR

THE MOB MUSEUM

VEGAS MOB TOUR

ZAK BAGANS'S THE HAUNTED MUSEUM

OTHER WEIRD (WTF) PLACES TO CHECK OUT

AREA 51

OMEGA MART BY MEOW WOLF

THE SIMPSONS' HOUSE (REPLICA)

THE GAMBLER'S GENERAL STORE

THE CAR BONNIE AND CLYDE DIED IN

BONANZA, THE WORLD'S LARGEST GIFT SHOP

DRIVE-THROUGH WEDDING SERVICE

LAS VEGAS ODDITIES AND ANTIQUITIES

AL CAPONE'S CAR

SIGN ON ROAD WARNING OF EXTRATERRESTRIALS

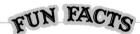

FUN FACTS

With its city so lit up, Las Vegas is the brightest spot on Earth.

On average, 300 weddings happen here every day.

SAN DIEGO, CA

San Diego is always fun to travel to on tour because it's relatively close to home, and my girlfriend and I always turn it into an excuse to have a long weekend away from LA. It's easy to get around, there's great tours, the Gaslamp District, Old Town, Coronado—all sorts of fun. There's even the Whaley House, where Christine saw her first (and last) ghost! But one of the main reasons I come to San Diego: it has my favorite dessert place, Extraordinary Desserts. I tell everyone visiting San Diego they absolutely must go there. They have tons of fancy-looking and fancy-tasting desserts without the fancy prices. They also have a massive selection of tea and really great sandwiches. Next time we're lucky enough to perform in San Diego, you know where to find me after the show.

I love touring in San Diego! While Em seeks out dessert, Eva and I usually find somewhere to grab seafood and margaritas. San Diego is also where Allison and I traveled before I introduced her to Em for the first time. It was a momentous trip: not only did I see my first ever ghost, but Allison proposed to me outside a Mexican restaurant in an attempt to convince the Whaley House owners to let us on the tour! (It didn't work, but we iced our wounds with some great margaritas afterward.)

PARANORMAL

HOTEL DEL CORONADO

1500 ORANGE AVE • CORONADO, CA

Are you looking for a place "free from malaria, hay fever, mad dogs, cold snaps, or cyclones"? Then come to the Hotel Del, where that's (for some reason) their slogan! A national landmark, one of the country's largest wooden buildings, and nicknamed both the "Talk of the Western World" and the "Lady by the Sea," this regal hotel has a lot to be known for, especially its many hauntings!

Opening in 1888 as the world's largest resort at the time, Hotel Del boasted 11,000 square feet of ballroom, 750 rooms, enough dining space for 1,000 people, a yacht club, and additional special features such as an Olympic-sized saltwater pool and an ostrich farm. ("Ostrich farm" was all I needed to hear.) In 1904, the Hotel Del also showcased the world's very first electrical Christmas tree.

Many notable people have stayed here, including Orville Redenbacher, who lived here for twenty years until his death (TBD if his ghost has *popped* by). Other notable guests have been presidents, actors, athletes, and at least two kings: King Edward VIII, who met his wife here, and Stephen King, who was inspired to write "1408" during his stay.

The store on the lower level, Kate's, is named after one famous guest of Hotel Del, Kate Morgan. She came to the hotel in 1892 and checked in under the name "Mrs. Lottie A. Bernard, Detroit." During her time here, people became suspicious of her identity. She told some people that she was there to meet her brother, she told others she was waiting for her boyfriend (I pray she was lying to at least one party so her brother and boyfriend might not be the same person), but nobody ever came to meet her. A few days later, Kate/Lottie died by suicide in her room, but the police could never find her family. Someone came forward and said her name was Kate Morgan, but there is no way to know whether that's true. The press ended up writing about her as the "Beautiful Stranger" and she was buried as "Lottie Anderson Bernard, aka Kate Morgan."

Some believe whomever she was waiting for actually did meet her at the hotel just to kill her and make it look like it was her doing. Kate is still said to haunt the Hotel Del to this day. Other regular activity comes from two rooms where, interestingly, pregnant women died by suicide in each room. There is also a little girl who died at the hotel and now haunts the building.

The most haunted rooms are booked over a year in advance, but luckily there are plenty of spirits to go around. Guests hear crying, whispers, laughter, footsteps by their bed, their name being called, and someone talking in their bathroom in the middle of the night. People get grabbed, their throats close up, their beds shake, they feel overwhelming sadness, and sometimes they experience vertigo or tinnitus. Dark shadows have pulled sheets off of guests, and a little girl is seen playing in some rooms.

Guests also report seeing objects move on their own and apparitions in Victorian clothing at the foot of their bed, gliding down halls, in the gift shop, staring out the windows, trying to unlock doors, or following them to their room. People wake up to floral scents next to their bed, flickering lights, drapes blowing without a draft, electronics turning on, shower curtains moving, or the pillows being stacked on top of each other across the room. One woman's necklace that was kept in the room's safe was later found with knots tied through it. Spirits of children will run into you; indentations of someone sitting on the bed won't smooth out, as if someone is still there; and one maid got a note under the door from a vacant room. Finally, some have also claimed to hear a low growl, but I'd bet it was just their stomachs manifesting Orville Redenbacher's paranormal debut.

FUN FACT

While filming here for *Some Like It Hot,* "Marilyn Monroe ate a chilled vanilla soufflé with merengue on top every day."

TRUE CRIME

"ANGRY BETTY" BRODERICK

Recently featured in season two of *Dirty John* on the USA Network, the story of Betty Broderick continues to find an audience, seemingly as compelling today as it was back in the '80s.

Betty and Daniel Broderick were a prominent San Diego couple in the '70s and '80s, living in the upscale coastal neighborhood of La Jolla. Betty had financially supported the family while simultaneously raising their four children as Dan got his medical and law degrees. To the outside world, the family appeared picture-perfect, when in reality the marriage was rocky and, according to some, abusive on both sides.

As early as 1983, Betty began suspecting Dan of having an affair with his legal assistant, 21-year-old Linda Kolkena. Two years later, Dan admitted to the affair and moved out. A bitter, drawn-out divorce ensued, which captured the fascination of women across the US, many of whom empathized with Betty's struggle to support her husband financially without appreciation or recognition.

By now, Dan had become a prominent lawyer, giving himself the world's douchiest nickname, the "Count du Money." Vomitous. Betty claimed Dan blocked her from finding good legal representation, using his power to take everything from her, including the kids, the house, and a large portion of her finances.

Four years into the divorce proceedings, Betty had become increasingly volatile. Despite numerous restraining orders, she spray-painted the inside of the home they once shared, rammed her car into Dan's front door, and left hundreds of obscene voicemail messages on Dan's answering machine.

When Dan and Linda married in April of 1989, Linda was understandably uneasy about Betty's increasing hostility, even urging Dan to wear a bulletproof vest to the wedding. Betty didn't crash the ceremony (neither figuratively nor literally with her car), but she did claim that Linda spent the coming months taunting her by mailing her facial cream and slimming treatment ads. These accusations haven't been confirmed.

At 5 a.m. on November 5, 1989, seven months after Dan and Linda's wedding, Betty drove to their home with a newly purchased revolver. She snuck into the couple's bedroom, stood beside their bed, and fired. Two bullets hit Linda, 28, in the head and chest, killing her instantly. Dan, 44, was hit in the chest by one bullet as he reached for the bedside phone.

Betty turned herself in to police and never denied having fired the gun five times. She did, however, claim the murder was not premeditated, despite evidence indicating that Betty had unplugged the couple's phone to prevent them from calling for help.

During the trial, Betty's defense team argued her actions were the result of years of psychological, physical, and mental abuse at the hands of her ex-husband. As expected, the prosecution argued the opposite, claiming that Betty had not been abused, but rather suffered from histrionic and narcissistic personality disorders, which led her to kill.

We may never know to what extent Betty's version of events hold true, but as of now she continues to serve her thirty-two-year-sentence at the California Institution for Women. She was most recently denied parole in January 2017 and will not be eligible again until January 2032.

TEAM WINE HAUNTS

FALSE IDOL

TRUST
Black-owned

LOUISIANA PURCHASE
Black-owned

CASA DE BANDINI
Haunted

TEAM MILKSHAKE HAUNTS

EXTRAORDINARY DESSERTS
"Hands down my favorite dessert place anywhere." —Em

MR. TRUSTEE CREAMERY

HAMMOND'S GOURMET ICE CREAM
Black-owned

HAUNTED HOTELS

HORTON GRAND HOTEL

GRANDE COLONIAL

COSMOPOLITAN HOTEL AND RESTAURANT

SPOOKY TOURS

GHOSTS AND GRAVESTONES FRIGHT-SEEING TOUR OF SAN DIEGO

WHALEY HOUSE TOUR

HAUNTED SAN DIEGO TOURS

MURDER N' MAYHEM TOURS

SPOOKS AND SPIRITS HAUNTED PUB CRAWL

RIDE THE HELLEVATOR

OTHER WEIRD (WTF) PLACES TO CHECK OUT

REPLICA OF HEAVEN'S GATE SCENE

HEAVEN'S GATE SUICIDE HOUSE

FORMER CEMETERY GRAVES STILL UNDER THE SIDEWALK

LEMON GROVE'S GIANT LEMON

1883 SCHOOLHOUSE

1895 LOOFF CAROUSEL

FLOWER FIELDS

MINI TACO BELL (ACROSS FROM A REAL TACO BELL)

FUN FACTS

The *Star of India*, which resides in San Diego, is the world's oldest active sailing ship.

The founder of Jack in the Box also opened the first drive-in restaurant here.

SAN FRANCISCO, CA

San Francisco always holds a special place in my heart. It has the best weather, some of the best tourist attractions, and I'm a sucker for Haight and Ashbury. Unfortunately, I have to say San Francisco now has a flaw, because there was a terrible audience member on the night of our live show: Lemon. That's right, the night before our first San Francisco show was the night Christine found Lemon under a bed in San Jose. Which means this show was the first one Lemon ever attended—on stage by the way—from Christine's pocket. Who knew he would become the monster—I mean, icon—he is today. During our second time coming to perform, chaos also ensued when . . . let's just say red wine spilled all over the white carpet backstage. Also, this venue had bread in the shape of life-sized baby alligators, and we still talk about it to this day.

I'd like to take this opportunity to say I plan on pursuing legal action against the other author of this book for libel. There is documented proof (in the form of the San Francisco live show recording) that Lemon is widely loved and adored and is in fact the perfect audience member, especially when propped up in his glass case. Between finding Lemon and eating animal-shaped bread, San Francisco is one of my favorite cities in the world.

PARANORMAL

CLAREMONT HOTEL

41 TUNNEL RD · BERKELEY, CA

In the 1800s, Bill Thornburg moved to California during the gold rush and built his wife her dream castle. (Note to self: if your partner won't build you your dream castle, it's a red flag and leave immediately.) Eventually, the Ballard family bought the property from the Thornburgs, and in 1901 a fire destroyed the castle.

After this, the property was handed over to Frank Havens, who is said to have won it in a poker game. Havens built the Claremont Hotel, which opened in 1915 with 276 rooms, spas, and fitness facilities, and it looked over the bay. Frank Lloyd Wright called the property "one of the few hotels in the world with warmth, character, and charm." However, there was one major problem: the hotel was too close to UC Berkeley to get an alcohol license. Havens had to go to court, and one UC Berkeley student actually came to defend Claremont Hotel—and thus earned free drinks for life once the hotel had its license.

And that's why they drink . . . for free!

In the Claremont's history, there are only a handful of documented deaths. Some guests died in fires in the hotel, and a woman in Room 417 died during her stay. There are several spirits here, though. The fourth floor is said to be the most haunted, especially Room 422, where a little girl was staying with her family. It isn't understood what happened, but she went missing for a few days and was found in the basement's laundry chute. To this day, people say they feel her sitting on their beds, and they can hear her running up and down the halls at night. A few people say they woke up to a girl giggling in their room while feeling like someone was tickling their face.

People also say they hear all sorts of noises from Room 422, including screaming, crashing, and loud parties going on, even when the room is vacant. Guests hear construction in empty rooms of the hotel and see shadow figures near their windows. A lot of people also swear they hear a disembodied baby crying. This includes San Antonio Spurs player Jeff Ayers, who stayed at the Claremont and says his room key wasn't working and he could hear a baby crying in his room even though nobody was in there. In Room 409, a woman in a wedding dress (there's always one!) throws items at staff, slams doors, and walks through the room's walls.

Visitors will complain about noises coming from the room upstairs, only to find out their room was on the top floor and nobody is above them. Others see lights flicker on their own, objects move on their own, and dresser drawers open and close. People also smell smoke and feel like their room is really hot at 3 a.m., as if a phantom fire was burning. Guests also report getting dizzy in the elevators and feeling something evil in the lobby bathrooms. People will experience their electronics not working until it is a very inconvenient moment. One guest said the TV would only turn on (and at full volume) once they had sat down on the toilet or got in the shower. (Funny, but mean.) Others have smelled and heard food cooking when food was no longer being served. (Just mean.)

Some guests say they have heard phantom "fighting" between people through the walls. One guy says his clothes were being yanked so hard that his pants fell to the ground. (PSA: wear belts at haunted hotels.) Some of the spirits, though, seem much creepier. People claim to roll over at night and think their hand has swung into the wall—but the wall isn't near their bed, so their hand just hit something standing next to their bed while they slept. Other spirts seem to try to suffocate you. One guest felt herself held down by her neck, and another saw and felt "something" climb into his bed then jump on him. The most unsettling story I've found about a haunted hotel so far is one couple who claims they heard knocks on their door and then watched their deadbolt unlock itself. If this sounds like your idea of fun, come on down to the Claremont in San Francisco, and also please don't invite me!

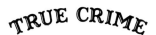

TRUE CRIME

ED KEMPER— THE CO-ED KILLER

Portrayed by Cameron Britton in the first season of the popular *Mindhunter* series, Ed Kemper reentered the zeitgeist in 2017, sparking a renewed interest in the twisted backstory of this notorious clinical psychopath.

Sometimes referred to as the Co-Ed Killer, Kemper began a life of crime at a young age. While other kids were jumping rope and playing hopscotch, Kemper cut the heads off his sisters' dolls and coerced his sisters to play a fun game he invented called "gas chamber," in which he pretended to writhe in pain until he "died." In the ultimate "that escalated quickly," at age fifteen Kemper killed both his grandparents simply to "see what it felt like."

After his release at age twenty-one, Kemper began targeting strangers in the Santa Cruz area. At first, he picked up female hitchhikers and let them go. But his restraint didn't last long. In May of 1972, Kemper picked up 18-year-olds Mary Ann Pesce and Anita Mary Luchessa in Berkeley. Their families would later report them missing when they never arrived at their intended destinations. Instead, Kemper subtly changed direction, driving the young women an hour into the woods before stabbing and strangling them both. He later confessed that during the struggle he had accidentally grazed one of Pesce's breasts and, embarrassed, apologized. An officer pulled Kemper over for a broken taillight on his way home, completely unaware there were two bodies in the trunk. Kemper evaded detection and brought the bodies home, where he engaged in necrophilia before dismembering and disposing of the bodies.

That September, Kemper picked up 15-year-old Aiko Koo, who had missed the bus to her dance class. He drove her to a remote area, where he choked her unconscious, raped her, and killed her. On his way home he stopped for a drink, the body still in his trunk. Like with Mary Ann and Anita, Kemper engaged in necrophilia before dismembering and disposing of the body.

Three months later, Kemper picked up 18-year-old Cindy Schall, before driving her to a wooded area and shooting her. He kept her body hidden in his mother's house overnight and dismembered her in his mother's bathtub the following morning. He later buried Cindy's severed head in his mother's garden facing up toward her bedroom, later explaining that his mother "always wanted people to look up to her."

If you haven't noticed it by now, Kemper's got mommy issues.

On February 5, 1973, Kemper picked up 23-year-old Rosalind Thorpe and 20-year-old Allison Liu, fatally shooting both before bringing their bodies home to his mother's house. He beheaded them in his car before taking the bodies inside and engaging in necrophilia with them.

On April 20, 1973, Kemper's mommy issues came to a head when he entered her room while she slept, bludgeoning her with a claw hammer and slitting her throat with a pen knife. He decapitated her and later explained that he "put her head on a shelf and screamed at it for an hour . . . threw darts at it," ultimately smashing her face in. In the ultimate act of symbolic defiance, he put her tongue and larynx down the garbage disposal.

After hiding his mother's body, Kemper called his mother's friend Sally Hallett and invited her over for a movie night. Kemper strangled her shortly after she arrived and hid her body in a closet.

Kemper fled town the following morning, three guns and hundreds of rounds of ammunition in tow. On his way to Colorado, he found a phone booth and called Santa Cruz police to confess his crimes. When asked why he gave himself up, Kemper would explain, "The original purpose was gone. . . . It wasn't serving any physical or real or emotional purpose. It was just a pure waste of time. . . . Emotionally, I couldn't handle it much longer. Toward the end there, I started feeling the folly of the whole damn thing, and at the point of near exhaustion, near collapse, I just said to hell with it and called it all off."

Kemper was indicted on eight counts of first-degree murder, ultimately being sentenced to eight concurrent life sentences, despite his request that he be "tortured to death."

Kemper is currently seventy-two, serving his sentence at the California Medical Facility in Vacaville. He has been referenced in numerous works of film and literature, including *The Silence of the Lambs*, in which he served as inspiration for the character of Buffalo Bill.

For a deep dive into Edmund Kemper, listen to Episode 40: "A Fashion-Forward Victorian Ghost and Workplace Triangulation."

TEAM WINE HAUNTS

TEAM MILKSHAKE HAUNTS

CAFE DU NORD
Haunted

MISSION BOWLING CLUB
Black-owned. Retro bowling alley
with six lanes, a full bar, and attached
restaurant

MOSS BEACH DISTILLERY
Haunted

UNGRAFTED WINE BAR
Black-owned

GAY NINETIES PIZZA CO.

FENTON'S ICE CREAM
Black-owned

MITCHELL'S ICE CREAM

BI-RITE ICE CREAM

HAUNTED HOTELS

CLAREMONT HOTEL

HOTEL EMBLEM

PALACE HOTEL

ST. FRANCIS HOTEL

SPOOKY TOURS

SF GHOST HUNT WALKING TOUR

HAUNTED HAIGHT WALKING TOUR

SF GHOSTS/GHOST HUNT

VAMPIRE TOUR OF SF

OTHER WEIRD (WTF) PLACES TO CHECK OUT

WINCHESTER MYSTERY HOUSE

GOOD VIBRATIONS VIBRATOR MUSEUM

INSTITUTE OF ILLEGAL IMAGES

ANDY GOLSWORTHY'S SCENIC WOOD LINE

MAGOWAN'S INFINITE MIRROR MAZE

SEWARD STREET SLIDES

GRAVE OF THE BLACK DAHLIA

DOROTHEA PUENTE'S HOUSE

FAIRYTALE TOWN

MASS GRAVE OF JONESTOWN MEMBERS

LOVED TO DEATH TAXIDERMY

SAN FRANCISCO DUNGEON ADVENTURE

PRESIDIO PET CEMETERY

FUN FACTS

The California bear's name is Monarch.

In 1867, San Francisco made an "ugly law," keeping people with "ugly" faces from walking around in public.

Oh no, Em, you better cover your face!

LOS ANGELES, CA

LA was the very first show we played, and it was one of the most nerve-wracking but most rewarding nights I'll probably ever have. Before getting on stage, I tried to tell myself to not be nervous and that this wasn't "that" big of a deal. Seconds later the staff told us that legendary Zach Galifianakis had just gone on before us, and my anxiety went from zero to sixty. Thank god we have such supportive listeners because they couldn't have been sweeter throughout and after the show. Since then, we've performed in LA again and in other cities nearby, and every time our listeners who come to see us are just as lovely. That being said, my favorite part of LA shows is that instead of ending the night in a hotel in a town I don't know, I get to eat at my local late-night spots (shoutout to Daniel's Tacos and Wokcano) and go home! (Although it is always a weird feeling to come home after a show: people were just watching me on stage an hour ago, and now I'm in my pajamas yelling at a rerun of *Cake Boss*.)

Em is right. LA shows are the best! Our local listeners always embrace us with open arms. It might be the only town where Blaise, Allison, and Xandy get more pics with their fans than we do! Plus, it was always great to come home to Gio and June after a long night.

PARANORMAL

THE CECIL HOTEL/STAY ON MAIN

640 S MAIN ST · LOS ANGELES, CA

Welcome to LA's most notorious hot spot for all things scary as hell. Described as "total, unmitigated chaos," the Cecil Hotel's history is overflowing with serial killers, suicides, homicides, dark magic, and unsolved mysteries. It's rumored to be either cursed or infested with demonic energy (or both!) and is so creepy that it inspired season five of *American Horror Story*.

Built in 1924, the luxury hotel was intended for wealthy businessmen, but not long after its opening came the Great Depression, and the hotel tragically suffered. The Cecil became low-budget housing and lodging and gained a reputation for having runaways and criminals as its clientele. Some of the more heinous criminals that stayed here were Richard Ramirez, aka the "Night Stalker," and Jack Unterweger.

Richard Ramirez murdered at least thirteen people and stayed at the Cecil in Room 1419 during some of his killing spree. He would take off his bloody clothes out back and walk to his room naked, never looking out of place given the behaviors of Cecil's other guests. Jack Unterweger murdered several sex workers while working as an investigative journalist and reporting on his own crimes. He murdered at least three women while he was staying in Room 712.

Other noteworthy guests have been the Black Dahlia and Elisa Lam. Elizabeth Short, aka the "Black Dahlia," was seen here three days before being murdered, and Elisa Lam was staying in Room 412 and was found dead in one of the rooftop water tanks after behaving erratically in the elevator. She was only found when people started complaining about the poor water pressure and that the water "tasted off."

The Cecil Hotel has also seen other tragic deaths, many of which were people jumping from the top floors, one even landing on a pedestrian on the sidewalk and killing him on impact. Former hotel manager Amy Price alleges to have dealt with thousands of 911 calls and about eighty deaths while in

charge, saying people sometimes call this place "Hotel Death." Some former guests even reported they would never stay on the upper floors because that was where people started dying.

In recent years, the Cecil Hotel has since changed its name to the "Stay on Main" (but literally nobody calls it that) in an effort to rebrand from its dark history. Obviously with such a checkered past, the Stay on Main (ugh, I can't do it—the Cecil . . .) has countless spirits and is considered one of the most haunted places in Los Angeles. People claim to see the Black Dahlia herself in the bar right before items move on their own. People get grabbed, scratched and shoved and hear all sorts of sounds, from footsteps to knocking to scream- ing. People feel their bedsheets being tugged, their items go missing, they see shadow figures everywhere, and they feel phantom hands wrap around their neck. Their hair and clothes get pulled, faucets turn on by themselves, lights turn on and off, doors slam, and closed windows that people have jumped from are found open.

Many people claim the elevators, where Elisa Lam was last seen alive, have a dark energy. The doors will open by themselves, and the elevator will travel to random floors you did not select. People also get very panicky and irrita- ble and have seemed to be dazed and not themselves according to peers. It's suggested a dark entity does this to people (including Elisa Lam) and lures them into harm's way. This was further corroborated by evidence that *Ghost Adventures* got during their investigation. Some of the spirits that made con- tact said they were pushed out of fire escapes and that a "being" did this to them.

Also during this episode, the spirit of Jack Unterweger cracks a "your mom" joke to Zak. (How does this show not have an Emmy yet?) Although the Cecil Hotel's background seems completely grim, there is one happy point in its history worth mentioning. On October 30, 2017, one ethereal soul had his very first Puppachino while parked out front of the hotel. While his owner wanted to get to the bottom of this building's mysteries, Gio was getting to the bottom of his Pup Cup.

To learn more, listen to: Episode 217 and 218 (Richard Ramirez), Episode 34 (Jack Unterweger), Episode 3 (Black Dahlia), and Episode 11 (Elisa Lam).

Learn more about the Cecil Hotel in Episode 89: "Violent Tickling and a Hollywood Bonfire."

TRUE CRIME

THE BLACK DAHLIA

Listen, I love LA, but I gotta admit that it was nearly impossible to pick a story for this chapter. Between the Night Stalker, Charles Manson, and countless other high-profile stories, the options seemed endless. In the end, I decided on a classic, unsolved case that never fails to give me the creeps: the Black Dahlia.

Many of us know the basics of this one already, but if you're unfamiliar, consider this your warning: this one's gory.

On January 15, 1947, a woman out walking with her daughter stumbled upon what looked like pieces of a mannequin. She would soon discover that she had actually found the body of 22-year-old Elizabeth Short. When police arrived, they discovered the body had been severed at the waist and completely drained of blood. Her face had been slashed from the corners of her mouth to her ears, a form of mutilation sometimes called a "Glasgow smile."

Police also noted several cuts on Elizabeth's thighs and breasts. Entire portions of her flesh had been cut off. What's more, the lower half of her body had been positioned a foot away from the upper, and her intestines had been "tucked neatly beneath her buttocks." The body was posed with her hands over her head, her elbows bent at right angles, and her legs spread apart. Nearby, police discovered a cement sack filled with watery blood.

I told you it was gory.

Once word got out, reporters from the *Los Angeles Examiner* contacted Elizabeth's mother in an effort to get the scoop on Elizabeth's backstory. But rather than approach the situation with tact, they instead lied to Elizabeth's mother, telling her Elizabeth had won a beauty contest and they needed more information about her backstory for the feature. It wasn't until the end of the conversation that the reporters admitted to Mrs. Short that her daughter had actually been brutally murdered.

The media took the story and ran with it, nicknaming Elizabeth Short the Black Dahlia. Some believe the name came from a film noir murder mystery called *The Blue Dahlia*, which had been released the year before.

Over the years, hundreds of people confessed to the murder, though most of them were almost immediately ruled out. When discussing this phenomenon in Episode 3, Em referred to this scenario "a psychologist's wet dream."

Listen to Episode 3: "Paranormal Bitchslaps and the Body Examiners."

The most promising lead at the time was a US Army corporal who had been out drinking with Elizabeth a few days before her body was discovered. He admitted to police that he'd blacked out with no idea what he'd done until he came to in a cab outside Penn Station. Elizabeth was known to have an affinity for servicemen, so at the time this seemed like a promising lead. When asked whether he thought he had committed the murder, the corporal said yes. Fortunately for him, investigators were able to confirm the man was actually on the military base with multiple witnesses on the night of the murder.

Suspect number two surfaced a few years later, when a woman doing hypnotherapy to retrieve repressed memories became convinced that her father had been the murderer of Elizabeth Short. Police dug up the man's house and backyard, yet nothing connected him to the murders. Although, fun fact: they did find a collection of costume jewelry and farm tools buried in the backyard … perhaps that'll be a story for another chapter.

Suspect number three is the most recent and, in my opinion, the most promising lead. A detective named Steve Hodel is convinced he knows who murdered Elizabeth Short: his own father. Hodel became convinced his father, the late Dr. George Hodel, had killed the Black Dahlia after finding photos of her in his father's belongings after he passed away. It's worth noting that the Black Dahlia was said to have been dismembered by someone with a medical background and surgical precision. Dr. Hodel was indeed a surgeon.

According to *Time*, soil samples taken from Dr. Hodel's Hollywood estate in 2012 tested positive for chemical markers for human decomposition, and to this day the LAPD considers Dr. Hodel the most likely suspect of the crimes, though the case remains unsolved. Today, there are twenty-two viable suspects, seven of whom are doctors.

You can see Dr. Hodel's former mansion, sometimes known as the Black Dahlia House, at 5121 Franklin Avenue in Los Feliz. Designed by Frank Lloyd Wright, the building is a marvel in and of itself. (Bonus: House of Pies is just down the street if you need a pick-me-up after immersing yourself in this tragedy.)

TEAM WINE HAUNTS

MUSSO AND FRANK GRILL
Haunted

HOLLYWOOD'S OLDEST RESTAURANT

THE DRESDEN
Haunted. Have a martini and watch iconic jazz couple Mary and Elayne perform nightly. Then stop at House of Pies down the street for a shake!

HMS BOUNTY
Haunted

FORMOSA CAFÉ
Haunted

THE PARLOR
Black-owned

EASTSIDE LUV WINE BAR
Latinx-owned

TEAM MILKSHAKE HAUNTS

MCCONNELL'S FINE ICE CREAM
One of Em's favorites! Get the chocolate-covered strawberry!

AFTER'S ICE CREAM
Another one of Em's favorites! Get the frozen hot cocoa flavor!

LITTLE DAMAGE

HOUSE OF PIES

HAUNTED HOTELS

HOLLYWOOD ROOSEVELT

QUEEN MARY

GEORGIAN HOTEL

HOTEL NORMANDIE

SPOOKY TOURS

HAUNTED TALES OF DTLA

HOLLYWOOD HAUNTED TOURS

LA GHOST TOURS

HAUNTED PASADENA WALKING
TOUR

OTHER WEIRD (WTF) PLACES TO CHECK OUT

ECHO PARK TIME TRAVEL MART

HOUSE THAT INSPIRED *AMERICAN HORROR STORY*

HOLLYWOOD FOREVER CEMETERY

MUSEUM OF DEATH

MANSON MURDER HOUSE

ROOM JANIS JOPLIN DIED IN

MUSEUM OF JURASSIC TECHNOLOGY

HOUSE FROM *A NIGHTMARE ON ELM STREET*

MEMENTO MORI CURIOSITY SHOP

BEARDED LADY VINTAGE & ODDITIES

FUN FACTS

Hollywood was originally named Hollywoodland.

The Hollywood Walk of Fame has over 2,500 stars.

Home of *And That's Why We Drink!*

SALT LAKE CITY, UT

Salt Lake City was our last show of the 2019 tour! It was supposed to have happened a few months earlier but was pushed back due to a "bomb cyclone" in Colorado, which is as dramatic as it sounds. I remember Christine and I accidentally matched for the show, both of us wearing black tops, black bottoms, and white shoes, which I still think was just a precious nod to how much time we had spent together (so much so that it was beginning to affect our fashion choices). We had a blast celebrating our finale show and stayed up all night hanging out together in the hotel. We ended up ordering pizza from a place called Big Daddy's (because, obviously) and watched *Ghost Adventures* (because, obviously) for our final night on the road together before starting to prep for our 2020 tour (that a pandemic ruined)!

Not me over here getting teary-eyed at Em's description of our time in Salt Lake. We did indeed match for the show, and we took a picture in front of a Lisa Lampanelli poster we found in the lobby. (Hi, Aunt Lisa!) We were sad to see our 2019 tour come to a close but starry-eyed and hopeful for our next tour in 2020 . . . If only we knew.

PARANORMAL

OLD TOOELE HOSPITAL, AKA ASYLUM 49

140 E 200 S · TOOELE, UT

About thirty minutes out of Salt Lake City, this structure was built in 1873, and over the years it's been turned into different facilities to help the community. By 1953 the building was the Tooele Valley Hospital, but it held the unfortunate nickname the "Hospital of Death." Despite its state-of-the-art technology, it had too few facilities, minimal restrooms, and no morgue. This means that when people died, their bodies were stacked in an unventilated storage space until they could get signed off by a coroner.

At the turn of the century, Old Tooele was closed when another hospital opened nearby, sat abandoned, and was later converted into a nursing home. ("Here, Mom, I'm sending you to live at the former Hospital of Death! I said *former!*") Soon after Side A of the hospital became a nursing home, Side B became a full-contact jump-scare attraction called Asylum 49, meaning the whole building has an increased likelihood of heart attacks, no matter the demographic. And did I mention the ambient sounds of mahjong tiles clinking paired with teenagers screaming on the other side of the wall?

Somebody make that a track for my "Study Music" playlist!

Since owners Kimm and Cami Andersen bought the space and created Asylum 49, there has been a lot of paranormal activity throughout the building. On their first day, Kimm felt and watched his pants moving by an unknown force. Multiple spirits are said to reside here. One is Robert, who spends his days watching over the child spirits, balling up bedsheets, jumping out from around corners, and cracking jokes through paranormal equipment. There is also Tabitha, who likes when people bring her toys and enjoys when the haunted house attraction is open for the season. People also see the spirit of a patient pulling her IV drip around and the spirit of a doctor standing behind actors who were dressed as doctors (I assume critiquing their performance). There is also a spirit named Wes who will pin people (including Zak) against the wall if you go in his room, and an exorcism allegedly took place here during which people were attacked by dark energies.

During paranormal investigations, some of the EVPs that have been caught are: "We died here," "Caught a bullet," "I'm going with you," and "You'll be mine." Allegedly, some of the spirits enjoy confusing visitors in the attraction and luring them to dead ends to get them lost.

Pro tip: turn on Find My Friends before entering.

There is also a little girl who likes to follow you in the attraction with the literal goal of scaring the guests—à la my worst nightmare. One time Kimm even saw the spirit of the little girl crying because, as she said, "I want to scare people too." Kimm told her she could scare the visitors but not the employees and to hide under the set's hospital bed until the next group came in. That night multiple people witnessed a black mist floating under the bed in wait. To me that means this spirit is actually much more sinister than we know, or she just has a theatrical streak and too much time on her hands. Either way, get her on the payroll! As for the nursing home half of this building, many believe that the child spirits are actually escorts to the other side and have become an omen that someone is about to pass.

Interestingly, deaths in the nursing home almost always seem to happen in threes. And if the children don't scare you in the nursing home, the "Man in Black" sure will. Often manifesting around 3 a.m., this figure has been seen walking into a patient's room and locking the door behind him. Once the staff were able to get back into the room, the patient had passed. All of this to say, you will never find me in Tooele.

TRUE CRIME

KIDNAPPING OF ELIZABETH SMART

Christine, I've never actually had a problem with any of the stories we've told yet . . . Can I spend the night?

On June 5, 2002, fourteen-year-old Elizabeth Smart was abducted from her bedroom in the wealthy Federal Heights neighborhood of Salt Lake City. Her nine-year-old sister, Mary Katherine, witnessed the abduction from her bed across the room. She pretended to be asleep as she watched a man force her sister out of bed at knifepoint. She thought she recognized his voice but couldn't quite place it.

Once Mary Katherine felt the intruders were gone, she woke her parents to tell them what had happened. Her father insisted it was all a bad dream . . . until he noticed a window screen that had been cut open with a knife.

After police were called, a massive search for Elizabeth began, but any early leads quickly dried up. It wasn't until October of that year that Mary Katherine had a sudden realization. She knew where she'd heard the intruder's voice before. She insisted it was a man named "Emmanuel," who had worked at their house for one day the previous November. The Smart family was known to hire people who were down on their luck, so a lot of people went in and out of the home doing odd jobs. One of these men, Brian David Mitchell, who called himself "Emmanuel," had helped out on the roof raking leaves for about five hours back in November.

Police were skeptical of Mary Katherine's revelation, so initially they didn't follow through. The Smart family believed their daughter, though, and promptly hired a sketch artist to re-create Emmanuel's face. They released the images to the media, leading John Walsh to reveal it on *America's Most Wanted*.

This girl deserves a trophy for (a) remembering such a minute detail almost a year later and (b) going through all this trauma to begin with.

The day after the episode aired, a man bicycling in Sandy, Utah, noticed a man walking with two women wearing veils that covered every part of their body except their eyes. The man alerted the police, who picked up the young woman wearing a gray wig, sunglasses, and veil. When Elizabeth was approached by police, she said, "Oh, I know who you think I am. You think I'm that Elizabeth Smart girl." And indeed she was.

It wasn't until police took Elizabeth in for questioning that they learned the true horrors of her experience. After he kidnapped Elizabeth from her bedroom, Emmanuel and his wife, Wanda, made Elizabeth hike up the mountains behind her family's house, keeping her chained to a tree in the hills behind her own home for several months. On the first night of her captivity, Emmanuel held a "wedding ceremony," proclaiming Elizabeth his bride. He raped her daily for her entire nine-month captivity.

Perhaps the most chilling revelation after Elizabeth's rescue was that she had actually been among the community, undetected for several months. A few months into Elizabeth's captivity, Emmanuel regularly began taking her with him into town. During these outings, Elizabeth never spoke up in public, perhaps out of fear or perhaps due to the effects of Stockholm syndrome.

On one occasion, Emmanuel, Wanda, and Elizabeth attended a party in town, where Elizabeth recognized a number of people. Elizabeth wore her veil and remained undetected. The host of the party remembers being slightly taken aback when he saw Emmanuel trying to force the young woman to drink absinthe despite her refusals. She was fourteen.

On another occasion, the trio went to the library and were confronted by a homicide detective suspicious of the young women's outfits. He asked Elisabeth to take off her veil, but Emmanuel intervened, claiming their religion was being threatened. The officer questioned him for fifteen minutes but ultimately let him go.

Although I don't feel Emmanuel/Mitchell is worth the paper this is printed on, a brief sojourn into his past might be useful to the story. According to his son, Mitchell had taken a large amount of LSD in the desert one afternoon and realized that he was the messiah. He proceeded to write his own set of scriptures, ultimately leading to his excommunication from the LDS Church. The week of his excommunication was the week he kidnapped Elizabeth, leading some to believe the event was a trigger.

Elizabeth, whose married name is Elizabeth Gilmour, is a kick-ass woman, turning her trauma into life-saving work for others. She is an advocate for missing persons, an American child safety activist, and a commentator for *ABC News*. Meanwhile, Mitchell continues to serve a life sentence in federal prison, where he belongs.

To hear even more details of the case, listen to Episode 6: "The Human Hair Version and the Worst Social Studies Class."

TEAM WINE HAUNTS

CLAIM JUMPER STEAKHOUSE
Haunted

GRAY CLIFF LODGE RESTAURANT
Haunted

DIVERSION SOCIAL EATERY
Black-owned

SHOOTING STAR SALOON
Haunted. Oldest saloon in Utah

TEAM MILKSHAKE HAUNTS

DOLCETTI GELATO
Oldest gelato shop in Utah

KOI D BAR AND BOBA TEA

MONKEYWRENCH
Vegan

HAUNTED HOTELS

KIRK HOTEL

HOLIDAY INN EXPRESS

SILVER FORK LODGE

BIGELOW HOTEL

BEN LOMOND HOTEL

SHILO INN

SNOWED INN

SPOOKY TOURS

GRIMM GHOST TOURS

OGDEN AND SLC GHOST TOURS
(MULTIPLE)

PARK CITY GHOST TOURS

OTHER WEIRD (WTF) PLACES TO CHECK OUT

ROAD SIGN ART INSTALLATION

PYRAMID OF MODERN
MUMMIFICATION

MORMON HISTORY MUSEUM

VIRGIN MARY IN A STUMP

GILGAL GARDEN

COLONEL SANDERS STATUE

FUN FACT

Home to Kentucky Fried Chicken.

As a Kentuckian now, I feel it's my duty to point out that
Colonel Sanders first sold his chicken here in Kentucky, but yes,
Salt Lake is home to the first KFC franchise.

DENVER, CO

Ah, Denver, I remember it well, because who could forget the experience of intense altitude sickness. The second we landed, Christine and I both started feeling really sick, and I inexplicably couldn't breathe well all day. I shrugged it off as a panic attack and went on my merry way. When we got to the venue, though, one of the employees said, "How are you handling the altitude?" and once I realized there was a reason for why I felt this way, I officially acknowledged it, and thus, my symptoms became tenfold. We were backstage chugging coconut water and putting our heads between our knees up until our intro music came on. I remember being on stage, looking out into a sea of smiling faces, and thinking "I'm going to pass out, and they're going to watch me do it." Lucky for me, my stage fright beat out my body's demand for oxygen, and I was able to power through, for both nights!

If there's one piece of advice you take from this book, let it be this—altitude sickness and wine don't mix. That said, I'm not usually known for taking my own advice, so I threw caution to the wind and had a great time drinking-and-almost-fainting alongside Em in Denver. Eva and I were so loopy we entertained ourselves with Silly Putty backstage.

PARANORMAL

MOLLY BROWN HOUSE

1340 PENNSYLVANIA ST • DENVER, CO

In 1893, J.J. Brown struck gold, literally. J.J. quickly became very rich, and when he got his first big paycheck, rumor has it he hid the money in the oven to surprise his wife, Margaret, when she got home. Well, quelle surprise, Margaret came home and immediately started preparing dinner, lit the oven, and burned it all away.

What was J.J.'s endgame here? Even if she found a check that big in the oven, her husband still put a check in the oven. Was she supposed to brag to her friends about that? Best-case scenario, the *surprise* would be her realizing she married someone with such terrible judgment.

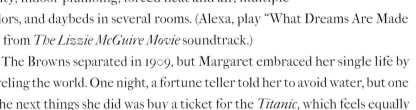

Lucky for him this was only his first payment. With money still coming in, the socialites moved to Denver. They moved into a 7,000-square-foot Victorian home for $30,000, nearly $900,000 today. The house had electricity, indoor plumbing, forced heat and air, multiple parlors, and daybeds in several rooms. (Alexa, play "What Dreams Are Made Of" from *The Lizzie McGuire Movie* soundtrack.)

The Browns separated in 1909, but Margaret embraced her single life by traveling the world. One night, a fortune teller told her to avoid water, but one of the next things she did was buy a ticket for the *Titanic*, which feels equally as reckless as her husband's decision-making (re: putting your money in the fucking oven).

The night the *Titanic* went down, Margaret: (1) realized her fortune teller was not a fraud and (2) did the exact opposite as Billy Zane, for she stayed onboard as long as she could to help others onto lifeboats. She also pulled people from the water and took charge in helping women row to safety. She was later the head of the Survivors Committee, and when asked why she did not sink with the *Titanic*, her reply was, "Hell, I'm unsinkable." This elevated her celebrity status even further, and with said fame, the "Unsinkable Molly Brown" inserted herself wherever she could to work toward social reform.

Margaret founded organizations, helped preserve historic buildings, earned a French Legion of Honor medal, participated in several relief efforts, fought for women and children's rights, and ran for senate multiple times. (Girl Boss Energy!!!) When Margaret died in 1932, her house was sold and later became a gentlemen's-only boarding house, then a girls' home, and then was restored to its original 1910 appearance. The Molly Brown House, also known as the House of Lions, is on the National Register of Historic Places and is one of the most haunted places in Denver. People have seen a rocking chair move on its own and apparitions of Margaret, J.J. smoking, and a maid dusting in the library.

People also smell cigars where J.J. has been seen and rose perfume, which Margaret was known to wear. Spirits are seen in many forms pacing the halls. People have heard humming, knocking, whistling, footsteps, talking, and throat clearing when alone in the house. People also hear the sounds of a party in empty rooms. There have also been reports of people feeling like they're being stared at, cold spots, and the sensation of someone grabbing them. Windows, doors, and curtains have all been said to open and close on their own, sometimes in front of people, and apparitions will appear in the reflections of the windows too.

People most often claim to see a man around the stairs on the first floor, as well as a woman in a Victorian dress sitting at the dining table, standing in a corner, or looking out the window toward the yard. Sometimes these spirits will be seen walking down halls and turning the corner into dead ends where they vanish. Other spirits have been known to move furniture around and mess with electronics. Sometimes light bulbs have also unscrewed themselves and lights will turn themselves off. One of the more common reports all around the house is seeing a woman sitting in a chair. Maybe she just loves relaxing? I'll tell you what, bring back one of those nap-only daybeds and in the future people will report seeing my ghost in the Molly Brown House too.

FUN FACT

Margaret Brown went by "Margaret" or "Maggie," never "Molly"— it was the press who dubbed her this. The nickname was then perpetuated by the 1960 musical, *Unsinkable Molly Brown*.

TRUE CRIME

JILL COIT, COLORADO'S BLACK WIDOW

Jill's story begins innocently enough with a high school crush. In fact, there's no evidence to suggest Jill's childhood in Louisiana was anything but carefree and uneventful. Unfortunately, Jill didn't need a head injury or a fire obsession to inspire her life of crime.

In 1961, Jill dropped out of high school to marry her crush, 18-year-old Larry Ihnen, before promptly filing for divorce and liquidating their shared bank accounts. The following year, Jill married again, this time to a man named Steven Moore. Shortly after the birth of their son, Jill filed for divorce. One evening while out on the town, Jill fell in love with a wealthy engineer named William Clark Coit Jr.

Now twenty-three years old, Jill married William, but not before her divorce with Stephen had been finalized. Small details, right? Jill and William had two more sons. On the surface everything seemed fine, but while William traveled for work, Jill engaged in a number of extramarital affairs. After

William discovered her escapades and accused her of marrying him for his money, Jill filed for divorce.

Eleven days later, on March 29, 1972, William Clark Coit Jr. was found dead in his home, having been shot twice in the back. Jill was suspected of the murder, but police couldn't find enough evidence to charge her. When told there would be further questioning, she checked herself into a psychiatric hospital and was able to avoid it. Sneaky, sneaky.

Shortly after William's death, Jill skipped town and moved to California, where she persuaded a wealthy 90-year-old man to adopt her.

Did I miss something? Is this an option in life?

When the man passed only a year later, Jill inherited a large portion of his estate.

Jill's fourth husband was a US Marine Corps major named Donald Brodie. This two-year marriage was pretty uneventful and was followed by a marriage to Jill's fifth husband, Louis D. DiRosa. Wanna guess how they met? Get this— Louis was her attorney when she was suspected of murdering her third husband, William Coit! She must have been one helluva charmer.

Jill and Louis got married in 1976. Throughout Jill's and Louis's marriage, they separated several times, even getting divorced and remarried. During one of their separations in 1978, Jill married a new man, a guy from Ohio named Eldon Duane Metzger, who became Husband #6. Jill wanted to divorce her attorney, Louis, for real this time. But for whatever reason, she decided to travel to Haiti to file for divorce . . . meaning the divorce was not legally recognized in the US.

Now, I know I probably lost you as early as paragraph one, but stick with me: Jill decided to divorce Eldon Metzger shortly into their marriage, but she was technically still married to Louis because of the whole Haiti thing. During this kerfuffle, Jill married ANOTHER man, a schoolteacher from Indiana named Carl V. Steely, who became Lucky Husband #7. (This lady puts Em's and my parental divorce stories to shame.)

Jill and Carl separated after less than a year of marriage, and guess where Jill went to divorce him? Haiti. (Again, am I missing something here?) By 1991, when she was forty-seven, Jill had moved on to her eighth husband, Gerry Boggs, one of the wealthiest men in Colorado.

Jill and her sons began renovating a bed and breakfast, but she would often visit Gerry at his hardware store in Steamboat Springs. Unfortunately for Jill, Gerry's brother grew suspicious of Jill's "excessive" interest in her husband's finances, so he hired a private investigator to check her out. The PI discovered that Jill was a fraud: she had been married nine times, had several aliases, and had perpetrated a number of insurance scams. She was also still married to her seventh husband and had even invented a pregnancy, despite having had a hysterectomy.

Gerry understandably annulled his marriage to Jill after only seven months, after which they became entrenched in a hostile lawsuit over the bed and breakfast. During this time Jill FINALLY divorced Carl Steely, but instead of trying to make it up to Gerry, she began dating a new man named Michael Backus.

In 1992, while dating her new boyfriend Michael, Jill moved to Las Vegas, where she married Husband #9: a man named Roy Carroll. Jill moved with Roy to his hometown in Texas, but by the end of the year they were divorced, and she and Michael Backus had not only gotten back together but also gotten married. And thus, Michael became Husband #10.

I know we all have a headache at this point, but I promise it's worth sticking through to the end.

Jill was still entrenched in her lawsuit with Gerry, and there was a hearing coming up regarding the case. One week before the hearing, on October 22, 1993, Gerry Boggs was found shot and beaten to death in his Colorado home. Police would soon find out that Jill and her new husband, Michael Backus, had put on disguises (including fake mustaches), had broken into Gerry Boggs's home, and had beaten him, shocked him with a stun gun, and finally shot and killed him.

Jill confided in her son about the murder and asked for his help in covering it up. Her son was like *"sure-sure-sure-sure-sure"* . . . and went straight to the police. He said his mother had told him in advance that she had plans to kill Gerry, then called him on the night of the murder to say, "Hey, baby. It's over, and it's messy."

On December 23, 1993, Jill and Michael were arrested for the murder of Gerald Boggs. During the trial, the prosecution brought forward witnesses who testified that both Jill and Michael had tried to talk them into killing Gerry Boggs before deciding to do it themselves. One of Michael Backus's coworkers, Troy Giffon, said Michael had offered him $7,500 to kill Gerry. Troy said once he saw the news that Gerry had been murdered, he went to Michael and was like, "Dude—I know you had something to do with this because you offered me money to kill this guy and now he's dead," and Michael said, verbatim, "I was hoping you would forget that."

Several other witnesses testified that they saw Jill and Michael wearing disguises near Gerry's home the day he was killed and that they saw them "passing by" his funeral. When spotted at the funeral, Jill was described as wearing a fake black mustache and driving a red sports car. (Girl. Get it together.)

In March of 1995, Jill Coit and Michael Backus were convicted of first-degree murder and conspiracy to commit murder and were both sentenced to life in prison.

But of course, Jill couldn't stop there. In May of 1998 she created a super cool website called "Cyberspace-Inmates.com" and posted an online personal ad reading, "Want U.S. citizenship? Marry an inmate." The United States Department of Immigration shut the site down before she could find any takers.

As of today, all of Jill's appeals have been denied. She's now seventy-six years old and is still serving her life sentence at the Denver Women's Correctional Facility.

TEAM WINE HAUNTS

TEAM MILKSHAKE HAUNTS

BRASS TACKS
Haunted

NEON BABY DANCE CLUB
Haunted

RAICES BREWERY
Latinx-owned

THE L

BONNIE BRAE

LITTLE MAN ICE CREAM

SWEET ACTION

HAUNTED HOTELS

HAND HOTEL B&B

BROWN PALACE HOTEL & SPA

BROWN PALACE HOTEL

IMPERIAL HOTEL

OXFORD HOTEL

SPOOKY TOURS

DENVER BREWS CRUISE

DENVER TERROR TOURS

NIGHTLY SPIRITS

DARK SIDE OF DENVER GHOST TOURS

DENVER GHOST WALKING TOUR

OTHER WEIRD (WTF) PLACES TO CHECK OUT

THE SOUNDWALK
Public audio park

DENVER FLEA MARKET

THE LEARNED LEMUR ODDITIES

THE TERRORIUM SHOP

THE ROOM OF LOST THINGS SHOP

MILE HIGH COMIC MEGASTORE

FIFTY-TWO 80S SHOP

CHURCH OF CANNABIS

ABANDONED TV WALK OF FAME

ALFRED PACKER RESTAURANT AND GRILL
Named after Colorado's most famous cannibal

FUN FACTS

The Denver Mint has $100 billion worth of solid gold bars.

The first permanent structure here was a saloon.

Some believe Denver International Airport was built by a secret society and contains underground tunnels leading to secret meeting facilities for the world's elite.

HOUSTON, TX

Our first time playing Houston was one of our one and only double-show nights, where we did two shows in one day. During our first tour, we would cover different local stories each show, which meant we did two different sets of material that day. I still remember being humiliated when I accidentally researched a topic that was nowhere near Houston and found out only an hour before going on, and I just had to run with it. That didn't seem to bother anyone, though, because Houston was and still is one of our loudest audiences whenever we go there. The last time we went to Houston, I tried out Katz's Deli after a show, where I had their "Chicken in the Pot" and their "Cheesecake Sandwich" for dessert, which was just *chef's kiss.*

Like Em said, we were overwhelmed by our task of performing two different sets in one evening, but if we had to do it anywhere, I'm glad it was Houston. Damn, were y'all loud!!! It felt like I was drinking with the audience rather than in front of them, and I can't wait to go back.

PARANORMAL

HOTEL GALVEZ

2024 SEAWALL BLVD · GALVESTON, TX

An hour drive from Houston there is a massive hotel right on the beach that happens to be not only the oldest hotel in Galveston but also the most haunted. During the hurricane of 1900, Galveston Island was destroyed, including the St. Mary's Orphan Asylum. A nun attempted to save all of the children; however, only three survived. The storm killed upward of 8,000 people on the island.

After the storm passed, the townspeople began rebuilding their home, and in 1911, they also built Hotel Galvez for future guests to the island. It was nicknamed the "Queen of the Gulf" since it overlooked the Gulf of Mexico, and also the "Playground of the Southwest" since it was a "playground" for the wealthy upper class. Some of these elite guests include several presidents, Frank Sinatra, and General MacArthur. This hotel was known for hosting some very important people, but as mentioned earlier, it still hosts many spirits.

Hotel Galvez's most popular hauntings include the spirit of a heartbroken bride-to-be (there's always one in every hotel, I swear). In the 1950s, a woman named Audra stayed here while waiting for her fiancé to come home from war. One day, Audra heard that he died during a shipwreck, and out of grief she hung herself in the bathroom of her room, number 501. To this day Audra, or the "Lovelorn Lady," is well known for haunting the fifth floor. Guests have seen her roaming the halls and sitting on their bed and have heard electronics turning themselves on and off, doors slamming, and a woman crying. Staff have also reported seeing a light from under the door and heard humming in the room when nobody is staying there.

A lot of the times the key cards to Room 501 will malfunction, and all phones have difficulty working in there, including your own. (But how am I supposed to livestream the experience?!) When asked by visitors, "What happened to you?" Audra has given us EVPs of the words "bathroom" and "rope." She has also said "drawer," which is super creepy because in Room 501's dresser there are books about her. Some have claimed that when they flip through the books, Audra will give another EVP of the word "rescued" when they turn to the pages that mention her fiancé. Some unlucky guests on the fifth floor have also claimed to see the spirit of a woman levitating by their bed as if being hanged, which could be the residual haunting of Audra's final moments.

There's also the spirit of a little girl in early-1900s garb, who can be seen running through the halls, on the staircase, and in the gift shop, often bouncing a ball. She has also been seen by construction workers during renovations, and they are known to ask the front desk to tell the guests' children to not run through their work spaces. This little girl has also been heard giggling, singing, and talking to other child spirits. (Great, so there's more of them.)

Many guests have complained to staff the next day that kids were running up and down the halls all night when nobody was up there. The child spirits are sometimes seen in the lobby, sometimes playing on the piano. Some say that all of these child spirits could be the orphans who passed in the storm over 100 years ago. The bathrooms of Hotel Galvez seem to be a hot spot for ghosts, where there can be children laughing, knocks and shaking on the stall doors, toilets flushing by themselves, lights turning off, and toilet paper in your stall disappearing (oh my god). Some apparitions have been seen walking through rooms and vanishing, new machines break down for no reason, and dishes and glassware will shatter on their own. Many also claim to see a nun by the water's edge during storms, possibly the same nun who died saving the orphanage's children in 1900. If you read all of this and still want to go, rest assured, Hotel Galvez also offers a beachfront spa. Might I suggest using these services to relieve any tension, both before and after your spooky stay (and on the way out, steal some of their toilet paper in case that bathroom ghost tries to prank you later).

TRUE CRIME

THE ICEBOX MURDERS

One of Houston's most infamous unsolved crimes, the Icebox Murders, takes "chilling" to a new level (sorry). Let's head back to June of 1965, a month I'm assuming was hot and humid AF. Elderly couple Fred and Edwina Rogers, 81 and 72, respectively, had seemingly dropped off the face of the earth. They hadn't answered their phone in days, and knocks from concerned relatives elicited no answer. Nephew Marvin Marlin (no, that's not a typo) grew increasingly concerned and requested police do a welfare check.

Two Houston officers arrived at the apartment and promptly kicked the door in. I'm not sure what they expected to find, but what they found, well . . . it took everyone by surprise. One of the officers opened the fridge, moved aside the boxed Franzia,* and discovered what he initially thought were stacks of "hog meat." Think again, buddy. Turns out, as the *Amarillo Globe-Times* reported the next day, "On all the shelves and in the freezer compartment were the dismembered bodies, cut in unwrapped, washed off pieces smaller than individual joints." (Vomitous.) It was once they found two heads in the vegetable crisper that officers knew they had found the bodies of Fred and Edwina. Their organs were nowhere to be found.

Edwina had been shot in the head, while Fred had been bludgeoned to death with a hammer. The killer had then dragged their bodies to the bathroom, where they were drained of blood, chopped into pieces, and stacked neatly in the fridge. In other words, this was a meticulous and organized murder by someone who knew what they were doing, according to the medical examiner.

* I may or may not have taken some artistic liberty here.

Several days later, the missing organs turned up in a nearby sewer. They'd been ... get this ... flushed down the toilet. As for the crime scene itself, it was nearly immaculate. The home had been cleaned after the murders, and there was barely any blood to be found. (Where's that good old *Forensic Files* luminol when you need it?!) What little blood was discovered, however, led to the bedroom of none other than Fred and Edwina's 43-year-old son, Charles Rogers.

Charles was a smart cookie. He spoke seven languages, had a degree in nuclear physics, and worked for a time as a pilot in the navy before serving in the Office of Naval Intelligence. Despite his career success, he had abruptly quit his job without explanation in 1957 and become what *Houstonia Magazine* called "a recluse." He had moved in with his parents, with whom he communicated solely via notes slipped under the bedroom door, and was rarely seen by neighbors. In Charles's attic bedroom, police found clothing, a hot plate, and a collection of ham radios. They also found a bloody keyhole saw, assumed to be the tool used in the dismemberment.

Once police had zeroed in on their suspect, an international manhunt commenced. You see, Charles had left behind all his all his priceless hot plates and radios and fled. Spoiler alert: he was never seen again. And I know this sounds like the end of the story, but wait—there's more!

A lot more. In fact, things are about to get real noodles up in here. Turns out, at some point during his post-naval career as a seismologist for Shell Oil Company, Fred had met a man named Fred Ferrie, who would later be suspected of involvement in the plot to assassinate President John F. Kennedy. Remember when I told you Charles had quit his job abruptly and become a recluse? Well, some believe Charles himself was one of the men who assassinated JFK. (I told you it got noodles!)

In their book *The Man on the Grassy Knoll*, authors John R. Craig and Phillip A. Rogers argue that Charles was a CIA agent until the mid-1980s, having helped murder John F. Kennedy before hiding out in his parents' home. Craig and Rogers argue that Fred and Edwina had been listening in on his CIA phone calls, and, as in every cliché spy novel ... *they knew too much*. So they had to be killed. And chopped up into pieces in the fridge . . . ? In my opinion, this theory falls apart a bit at the seams, but what do I know.

Another (perhaps more plausible) theory was put forth in 1997 by forensic accountant Hugh Gardenier and his wife, Martha. While their book, *The Ice Box Murders*, did acknowledge Charles's dealings with the CIA, they argue that he didn't kill his parents for secret-spy reasons but instead as a result of the abuse he suffered as a child. The Gardeniers argue Charles was emotionally and physically abused by his father throughout childhood and once again when he moved into the attic. In my opinion, their theory holds some water. Consider this—investigators determined Charles's parents had been killed *on Father's Day* of all days. Plus, turns out his dad's privates had been . . . ahem . . . removed. One could argue (and the Gardeniers do) that the Rogers' murders and mutilation were a result of years of abuse.

But their theory doesn't end there. The Gardeniers believe Fred and Edwina had been defrauding their son, forging his signature to take out loans in his name before pocketing the money. In their version of events, the Gardeniers argue that Charles fled to Mexico after the murders, eventually ending up in Honduras, where he was killed over a wage dispute with miners. It's important to note, however, that both the *Houston Press* and *Publishers Weekly* considered *The Ice Box Murders* "fact-based fiction and supposition."

Regardless, the truth of the matter is that we may never know what really happened to the Rogers or where Charles ended up. Despite the international manhunt, Charles was never found, and he was declared legally dead in July of 1975. The murders of Fred and Edwina Rogers remain unsolved to this day, with their son, Charles, as the only suspect.

TEAM WINE HAUNTS

 **LA CARAFE**
Haunted

TREZ WINE BAR
Black-owned

 **MOLLY'S PUB (DOWNTOWN)**
Haunted

MONKEY'S TAIL
Latinx-owned

TEAM MILKSHAKE HAUNTS

FAT CAT CREAMERY
Woman-owned

AMY'S ICE CREAM
Woman-owned

HANK'S ICE CREAM PARLOR
Black-owned

HAUNTED HOTELS

HOTEL GALVEZ

HOTEL ICON

SPOOKY TOURS

HOUSTON GHOST TOUR

NIGHTLY SPIRITS

HOUSTON HISTORICAL HAUNTED TOURS

HOUSTON HAUNTED PUB TOUR

OTHER WEIRD (WTF) PLACES TO CHECK OUT

WILDE COLLECTION CURIOSITY SHOP

NATIONAL MUSEUM OF FUNERAL HISTORY

ART CAR MUSEUM

HILLENDAHL PARKING LOT CEMETERY

HUMAN BODY PARTS MUSEUM

THE ORANGE SHOW FOLK ART

DISCOVERY GREEN PARK'S LISTENING VESSEL SCULPTURES

THE BEER CAN HOUSE

WORLD'S LONGEST CAR WASH

BETHEL CHURCH PARK
Park inside church ruins

SPACE CENTER HOUSTON

HOBBIT CAFE

FUN FACTS

Houston has over 150 museums.

The Houston Livestock Show and Rodeo is one of the most popular
and biggest rodeos in existence.

SAN ANTONIO, TX

I have to be honest here: my first time in San Antonio was brutal, and anyone who was there knows why. The night of our San Antonio show was also opening night for *Avengers: Endgame*, aka the movie I had waited on for years of my life, and I've never been more conflicted about doing a show. Everyone kept coming up to me afterward saying they were about to go see it and have the "opening night audience reaction" experience I would be missing. The Marvel nerd in me was struggling, but luckily I took solace in the retail therapy I got during our pit stop at Buc-ee's, and it really got me through. I'm pretty sure I would've bought out the store if I could, but I settled for one of each shirt and ten of each snack available. The second time we came to San Antonio I had a much better time considering no bucket list items were also occurring that day! We also went back to Buc-ee's for some more retail therapy regardless!

We stayed on the Riverwalk, and it was every bit as cool as everyone told me it would be! Unlike Em, I was fortunate enough not to be missing any major pop cultural milestones and enjoyed San Antonio's many tacos and margaritas without a care in the world. Just like Em, I purchased an entire new wardrobe at Buc-ee's and spent the evening in the hotel sharing Beaver Nuggets with Eva. What a time to be alive!

PARANORMAL

THE ALAMO

300 ALAMO PLAZA • SAN ANTONIO, TX

The Alamo. One of the most famous sites in San Antonio, where tourists flock and local children are dragged to for every field trip. For those of you who don't fall into either category, here is a crash course on its history. Belonging to the Payaya people, this land became a Franciscan mission called San Antonio de Valero in 1724. In 1803 it became a military post nicknamed the Alamo, and in 1806 Texas's first hospital was built on the second floor. In 1835, Texas gained control of San Antonio, and the Battle of the Alamo started soon after. General Santa Anna and the Mexican army came in to take control of the Alamo and fought the Texans.

They won, killing nearly every Texan defender and refusing to give them proper burials. Santa Anna instead ordered his men to stack the Texans' bodies into piles and burn them. Three weeks later, Sam Houston defeated Santa Anna in the Battle of San Jacinto and Texas gained its independence. After his loss, Santa Anna was worried that people would see the Alamo as a shrine to Sam Houston and those who rebelled. He had his men attempt to burn down the Alamo but they couldn't do it, because they claim when they got to the Alamo, "six diablos" with flaming swords came out of the front doors, shouting, "Do not touch the Alamo; do not touch these walls!"

Usually a location will gradually become super haunted, but this place said, "Fuck it, start strong with aggressive, patriotic demons."

In a second attempt, more of Santa Anna's men tried to burn it down but ran off after seeing a spirit on the roof holding two balls of fire. After that, neither General Santa Anna nor his men came back to the Alamo. By the late 1800s, most of the building was torn down, and it became a general store, police headquarters, and jail. It is now a museum and gift shop for all of your Alamo souvenir needs.

Including Indigenous people, Mexican soldiers, Texas defenders, and others, the property is said to have had over 1,000 deaths and burials on the land. So not shocking then that this place is one of the most haunted places in Texas. (I mean, it literally started its paranormal career with demons on day 1.) In fact, I like to call this place "the melting pot of ghosts," because the range of spirits here is unmatched. In the 1890s, the *San Antonio Express News* even wrote about activity at the Alamo, that manifestations could be heard until five o'clock in the morning.

When it was a jail, both officers and prisoners complained about the sounds at night, and shadow figures are still seen pacing the grounds and on the roof. People also see spirits in 1830s clothing walking around, the spirit of a boy in windows of closed-off rooms, the spirit of Davy Crockett in the chapel, and apparitions walking out of the Alamo's walls. Visitors have also seen a cowboy, a general, soldiers, Franciscan monks in the courtyard, Presidents Lincoln and Grant, and John Wayne, who was an Alamo history buff (and starred in *The Alamo*). There are spirits of Indigenous people on the grounds, two little boys who follow you on tours, and a young soldier named Jamie who tells children about his time at battle. There is also the spirit of a man on the highway walking toward the property with his rifle in hand. When asked where he's going, he's told drivers, "To the Alamo, where I belong."

People hear screams, explosions, trumpets playing, horses galloping, banging on doors, and heavy footsteps. There is also a residual haunting that people have witnessed of a man covered in bullet holes being stabbed by soldiers with bayonets and an apparition that looks like a real person but is soaking wet and "melts into the air." If you're thinking, "With that many ghosts, you couldn't pay me to go there," what if I told you that going might mean stumbling across $13 million? That's right, the Alamo is rumored to have $540,000 worth of treasure buried somewhere on the property, which is about $13 million today. It's also rumored that some of the spirits know where the treasure is, so if they like you, they just might nudge you in the right direction. That's why if I ever go to the Alamo, you'll find me with a box of conversation starters, vintage candy, a Ouija board, and a metal detector.*

Learn more about the Alamo in Episode 143: "Portal Ripping Muscles and Vampire Rumors."

TRUE CRIME

OTTO KOEHLER AND THE THREE EMMAS

Ever heard of the Pearl Brewing Company? A few days in San Antonio and you probably will. But did you know its original founder was part of a murderous love triangle?! Buckle up, pals!

In 1883, the San Antonio Brewing Association was founded by German-born Otto Koehler, who quickly becoming a leading citizen of San Antonio and one of the wealthier men in the nation. He built a mansion near the brewery (now called the Koehler House) and married a lovely lady from St. Louis named

---

* I am 100 percent kidding: do not bring a Ouija board or metal detetector anywhere near this place. Or conversation starters, unless you want to be that "weird" guest. Do bring the candy.

Emma Benson. She stood by Otto's side through his successes, even helping him run the brewery, which at the time was virtually unheard of.

Unfortunately, a major car accident in 1910 left Emma with severe injuries. Otto hired a live-in nurse from Germany named Emma Dumpke to care for his wife. Fortunately, she was nicknamed "Emmi" so we can tell them apart. *Un*fortunately, however, Emmi was young, lively, and, well . . . a looker. I wish I could say Otto kept his hands to himself and stayed true to his lovely wife, but alas, this is a murder story, and what would a murder story be without its fair share of alcohol and infidelity?

Otto and Emmi began an affair, prompting Emma to kick Emmi out of their home. But don't go feeling sorry for her, folks, because she moved out of Otto and Emma's home and straight into the cottage that Otto had just purchased for her. Once Emmi settled into her new home, she invited her best friend to move in. This friend had also emigrated from Germany, and her name was . . . you guessed it . . . Janet. Just kidding, it was Emma.

Otto would visit the Emmas' cottage about once a week or so, usually at night, for two to three hours at a time. He paid all the expenses and gave Emmi a stipend of $125 a month in spending money, which equates to about $40,000 *a year* in today's currency.

Finally, Emmi confessed to Emma 3 that she and Otto were having an affair, to which Emma 3 responded, "Um. This is awkward. I'm kinda-sorta sleeping with him too."*

Otto was seemingly smitten with both of them and had somehow created the most epic love rhombus ever. And before you go correcting my English,** there are four people involved, so the classic triangle has evolved!

After several years of this romantic chaos, Otto's worst fear came true when Emmi fell in love with and married another man.

---

* This is not a direct quote.
** It's not my first language.

Emma 3 was her maid of honor.

With Emmi out of the picture, the love trapezoid was demoted to a lowly love triangle, and Otto's interest in Emma 3 developed into an obsession. He gave her the equivalent of almost half a million dollars in today's money and flaunted her everywhere he went while his wife lay at home, still bedridden after all these years.

In November 1914, Otto asked Emma 3 to elope with him, but her guilt got the better of her. She couldn't bear for Otto to abandon Mrs. Koehler. Oddly, when Emma 3 broke the news, Otto suddenly became very amicable, fully agreeing to the breakup and offering her the cottage, but *only* if she'd meet him at a rooming house above a saloon the following evening. Suspicious that Otto was up to no good, Emma 3 insisted they meet at the cottage instead.

On November 13, 1914, Otto drove his horse and buggy to the cottage and entered to find Emma 3 holding a gun. She shot him in the neck, face, and heart, killing him almost instantly. A neighbor called the police and Emma 3 was arrested on murder charges, though she claimed self-defense.

The trial lasted one week, and the jury found Emma 3 not guilty. She must have had one hell of a charming persona, because one of the jurors, a man named J.W. Turley, fell in love with her. The two eloped in New Orleans before moving back to San Antonio and settling into the home Otto had once purchased for Emmi.

Once the dust settled, the OG Emma once again took center stage, miraculously healing from her injuries and taking over her late husband's business. Keep in mind women didn't even have the right to vote at this point, so running a business, let alone a brewery, was unheard of. But she kicked ass, and pretty soon Pearl became the largest brewery in Texas. Even during the prohibition years, which threatened to shut down the company, Emma managed to keep doors open by ingeniously switching to soft drinks and food production.

Rumor has it the company used the old brewery equipment for more than just soda, secretly making beer to sell on the black market. While it's unclear whether or not the rumors are true, what we do know is that within minutes of Prohibition's repeal in 1933, hundreds of beer-filled boxcars rolled out of the brewery grounds, distributing beer to the people of Texas. *Hooray!*

Emma became a social icon and philanthropist, hosting big parties in her mansion and donating eleven acres of land to build "Koehler Pavilion" in honor of Otto, with the stipulation that alcohol consumption be permitted in the park. I'm not sure if that's still the case, so report back to me.

In 1952 the San Antonio Brewing Association officially changed its name to Pearl Brewing Company, and in 2001 Pearl sold its product to Pabst Brewing Company, continuing the brand but closing the brewery.

Today the old Pearl Brewery is a posh hotel in San Antonio called the Emma Hotel. They serve an infamous cocktail called the Three Emmas in honor of all three women. The drink's base is grapefruit to represent Texas, gin to represent Emma 3, sherry to represent Emma 2, and finally rose syrup and Pearl beer itself to represent Emma 1.

Hotel staff has famously warned, "One Emma is great, but three will kill you."

TEAM WINE HAUNTS

REBELLE BAR, ST ANTHONY HOTEL

BAR 414 AT THE GUNTER HOTEL
Haunted

COLONIAL ROOM AT THE MENGER HOTEL
Haunted

LUNA
Latinx-owned. Regular live music and cocktails

TEAM MILKSHAKE HAUNTS

LICK HONEST ICE CREAMS

BOOZY'S CREAMERY & CRAFT

PACIUGO GELATO

HAUNTED HOTELS

MENGER HOTEL

EMILY MORGAN HOTEL

HOTEL INDIGO AT THE ALAMO

SPOOKY TOURS

SISTERS GRIMM GHOST TOURS

NIGHTLY SPIRITS TOURS
Includes a haunted pub crawl

ALAMO CITY GHOST TOURS

RJA GHOST TOURS

BAD WOLF GHOST TOURS

CURIOUS TWINS PARANORMAL AND
GHOST TOURS

GHOST CITY TOURS

SAN ANTONIO SEGWAY GHOST
TOUR

OTHER WEIRD (WTF) PLACES TO CHECK OUT

"JOHNNY LOVES VIVIAN" BENCH

CASTROVILLE HEARSE

1920S MINI GOLF

MANSPLAINING STATUE

GRAVES OF THE CATS OF
THE ALAMO

ASHES OF THOSE FROM THE ALAMO

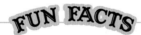

FUN FACTS

San Antonio holds the Guinness World Record for "Most Tamales Made in a
12-Hour Period," at over 17,000 tamales in 10 hours.

It also holds a second Guinness World Record for the tallest cowboy boots,
at thirty-five feet.

DALLAS, TX

Back in 2019, Dallas was our first stop on our full-fledged nationwide tour! We stayed for two nights, and since it was our first time all together out on the road, we spent the nights hanging out together in the hotel. While in town, I tried Houndstooth Coffee (which was amazing) and finally had my first Whataburger (which was AMAZING). This was also the first time I ever went to a Buc-ee's, the first time I tried Cauldron Ice Cream (purely for the name alone), and the trip when Christine ended up in Delta's Group 8 instead of Comfort Class. The next time we came here in 2020 was when I really explored the area. I especially enjoyed checking out the gravesites of Bonnie and Clyde, the Toilet Seat Art Museum, and a bar called Public School 972, which has some of the coolest decor I've seen in a restaurant. It also had a great sandwich called the Hot Mess and a cast-iron brownie.

Dallas was one of the few places we got to visit in 2020 before everything went to shit. We had an awesome time showing off our new tour format and restocking on Buc-ee's merchandise. If I had known it'd be one of our last stops before the pandemic brought everything to a screeching halt, I probably would have followed Em's lead and done more than just eat tacos the whole time! On second thought, that's probably what I would have done regardless.

PARANORMAL

MISS MOLLY'S HOTEL

109 W EXCHANGE AVE · FORT WORTH, TX

Next time you're in Forth Worth, check out the oldest bed and breakfast in Fort Worth: Miss Molly's Hotel! Although by "bed and breakfast," I mean just "bed" since it is technically only a hotel now (or what I call a bed and breakfast without the best part).

But don't panic, because the hotel makes up for it by having themed rooms!!! The seven themes are: Cowboys, Miss Josie's, Miss Amelia's, Cattlemen's, Rodeo, Gunslinger, and Railroader. Although my first instinct is to pay whatever I have to for a chance at the "Rodeo Room," I learned that for the spookiest experience, the best rooms are the ones with the "Cowboy" and "Cattlemen" themes.

Also, I'm sorry, but are cowboys and cattlemen not the exact same thing except one sounds like they got promoted? I digress.

In 1910, Fort Worth was getting so big that they needed to offer lodging to visitors, so a hotel called the Palace Rooms was built. During Prohibition it became a speakeasy and boarding house, and it later turned into a brothel until Texas made sex work illegal and the building was sold. In 1989, the property's ground floor became the Star Café and above it was Miss Molly's Hotel. During this history, cowboys, sex workers, and allegedly even some children died in the building, most of those deaths being from illnesses. As for the spirits, Miss Molly's is chock full of them.

The hotel even has a deal with Texas Christian University's "Paranormal Activity" class (WHAT?!) and offers regular visits for its students to investigate.

People see apparitions of a cowboy named Jake, kids in their room, a woman sitting on their bed, lamps turning on and off, doors opening and closing, covers getting yanked off, sinks filling themselves, and toilets flushing themselves. Staff will also report finding coins left all over rooms they just cleaned. (Hey, if being haunted means getting tipped for my services, I'm cool with it.)

As a former bordello, men often report being petted and held by someone, feeling someone kiss their cheek, and hearing a woman giggling. One investigative team called TEXPART asked the spirits who the president was and got an EVP saying "Grant." They also communicated with some spirits who knew the actual year, but some still thought it was the 1940s. Some of the spirits knew they were dead; others thought they were alive.

The general manager and former innkeeper, Paula Gowins, has had a lot of experiences with the spirits here. She has seen Cowboy Jake, seen boxes fly off shelves, and even heard a disembodied child's voice laugh at her when she looked in the mirror and said, "Whoo, I'm getting old." She also says she has had to yell at the ghosts when they mess with her stuff or go into her room. She'll shout, "You know the rules—get yourself out of here; you've got eight rooms out there to play in, and this ain't one of them." (Yesss, Paula, setting healthy boundaries!) Paula has said they love to bother her, especially in messing up places she has just tidied and locking her in rooms. The spirits are also the reason many employees leave the job, because "they can't handle the ghosts."

But Paula does state that the spirits here are mainly just annoying pranksters, but not harmful. This was further confirmed by one TCU student who brought a spirit box with her during her stay. While reading, the spirit box said the word "sentence," and the next sentence in her book read, "I hope that my presence does not frighten you." If Miss Molly's is too scary (or just fully booked), you can still have a chance at running into a ghost! According to Paula, the apparition of Cowboy Jake is also seen outside of the hotel, wandering the street and drinking at local bars.

TRUE CRIME

JOHN WESLEY HARDIN— THE MAN SO MEAN HE SHOT A MAN FOR SNORING

I think old-timey stories sometimes get a reputation for being less horrific than more recent ones, but I assure you that is not the case here, friends. Grab your box of wine and find somewhere comfortable to sit as I tell you the tale of John Wesley Hardin, one of the most notorious outlaws in Texas history.

Born outside of Dallas in 1853, John Wesley Hardin's life of crime began at a young age. At age fourteen, a classmate accused John of graffiti on the schoolhouse wall that insulted the "purity" of a girl in their class. John stabbed his accuser, nearly killing him.

The following year, John challenged a former enslaved person named Major "Maje" Holshousen to a wrestling match, which John won. When Maje approached him the following day for a rematch, John shot him five times. His father worried they wouldn't get a "fair trial" because they were in a Union-occupied state (big yikes), so he ordered John into hiding. When Union soldiers uncovered his location, John shot all three of them.

Quick recap: John is fifteen years old and had by then killed four men. This was when his time as a fugitive began. While on the lam, John taught school for a brief time, during which he shot a man's eye out to win a bottle of whiskey in a bet. That same year, John was playing cards with a man named Benjamin Bradley and was winning almost every hand. Bradley was angry and threatened to "cut out his liver" if he won again, then drew a knife. Hardin said he was unarmed and excused himself but claimed that later that night, Bradley came looking for him. Bradley fired a shot at John and missed, so John drew both his pistols and returned fire, killing him.

Witnesses later described John's unique setup: his holsters were sewn into his vest so that the butts of his pistols pointed inward across his chest. He crossed his arms to draw, claiming that this was the fastest way, and one he practiced daily.

Later that year, John shot a circus performer and, in the same month, killed a man trying to rob him. In 1871, he shot two more men in a card game as well as an Indigenous man "just for practice." In the summer of 1871, John began work as a cattle driver, heading toward Abilene. On the road, he killed a few cattle drivers because they cut him off.

Oh, and side note? John was only nineteen years old.

In August of 1871, John spent the night at the American House Hotel after an evening of gambling. Sometime that night, John was awakened by loud snoring coming from a neighboring hotel room. He shouted several times for the man to "roll over" and then, irritated by the lack of response, drunkenly fired several bullets through the shared wall in an effort to wake him. The man was hit in the head by the second bullet as he lay in bed and was killed instantly.

Half-dressed and still drunk, John exited through a second-story window onto the roof of the hotel, leapt into the street, and hid in a haystack for the rest of the night before stealing a horse and riding to the cow camp thirty-five miles outside of town. It's no wonder John earned the reputation as a man "so mean he once shot a man for snoring."

In early 1872, John met his future wife, a woman named Jane. Unfortunately, soon after their nuptials John was shot in the kidney during a gambling dispute. While recuperating from his wounds, he decided it was finally time to settle down. He surrendered to authorities, handed over his guns, and asked to be tried for his past crimes in order to clear the slate. . . . However, when he heard how many murders he would be charged with, he changed his mind and had his cousin smuggle in a hacksaw, which he used to cut through the bars of a prison window before climbing out and escaping.

John met back up with Jane and their young daughter, and they went (where else?) to Florida, adopting the fake last name "Swain."

On May 26, 1874, John met up with his friends to celebrate his twenty-first birthday. Yeah, you read that right. He was still only twenty-one years old. That day, John saw the local deputy sheriff arrive and invited him inside for a drink. As the sheriff followed him inside, John turned around and shot him for seemingly no reason whatsoever.

This act pissed off the town and prompted John and his family to go into protective custody. A $5,000 reward was announced for the capture of John Hardin. According to my trusty inflation calculator, that is $120,000 in today's currency!

Once again, Johnny Boy went on the lam. In August of 1877, local authorities found him on a train in Pensacola, Florida. In a very sitcom-esque moment, when John attempted to draw his cool double-crossed pistols, they got caught in his suspenders. (*insert laugh track*)

John was tried for murder and was promptly sentenced to twenty-five years in Huntsville Prison. He made several attempts to escape but ultimately adapted to prison life, where he studied theology and became the superintendent of the prison's Sunday school.

John was released from prison at the age of forty, after serving seventeen of his twenty-five-year sentence. He was pardoned by the state later that year (what?) and passed the Texas State Bar, officially becoming a licensed lawyer in the state of Texas (*what?!*).

I know this might come as a shock, but it turns out John hadn't fully changed his ways. According to a newspaper article from 1900, John made a $5 bet that he could knock a man off the soap box he was sitting on in one shot. I don't know what jackass agreed to this bet, but either way John "won," killing the man in the process.

In 1895, John headed to El Paso, where he exchanged heated words with local constable John Selman. That night, while John played dice at the very-cliché-sounding Acme Saloon, Selman walked up behind him and shot him in the head, killing him instantly. John had finally met his match, and he was buried the following day.

Because of his life events, some real and some exaggerated, John Hardin has become a legend of the Old West and an icon in American folklore. It is believed he killed anywhere from twenty-seven to forty-two people and is known as Texas's mostly deadly gunman.

You can visit John's grave in El Paso's Concordia Cemetery, but don't even *think* about trying to steal the body; his grave is surrounded by a cage to prevent people from digging up his corpse.

TEAM WINE HAUNTS

SNUFFERS
Haunted

HAPPIEST HOUR

SHOALS
Black-owned

SONS OF HERMANN HALL
Haunted

CATFISH PLANTATION
Haunted. This eatery is outside of
Dallas, but it's worth the drive to eat
at what many call the most haunted
restaurant in Texas!

TEAM MILKSHAKE HAUNTS

MILK CREAM
Asian-owned

**HYPNOTIC EMPORIUM ICE
CREAM & CANDY SHOP**

CAULDRON ICE CREAM
Asian-owned

HAUNTED HOTELS

STOCKYARDS HOTEL

LE MÉRIDIEN DALLAS, THE
STONELEIGH

RENAISSANCE DALLAS HOTEL

THE ADOLPHUS

SPOOKY TOURS

FORT WORTH GHOST BUS TOUR

NIGHTLY SPIRITS, DALLAS

STOCKYARDS GHOST TOURS

TRUE CRIME TOUR, DALLAS

OTHER WEIRD (WTF) PLACES TO CHECK OUT

OUTLAWS STATUE PHOTO OP
GRAVES OF BONNIE AND CLYDE

TATTOO RANCH
Home of the chainsaw from the original
Texas Chainsaw Massacre

LEE HARVEY OSWALD'S GRAVE

ADRIAN E. FLATT, M.D., HAND
COLLECTION

ALIEN GRAVE
"A spaceship crashed nearby in 1897 and the
pilot, killed in the crash, was buried here."

WHERE LEE HARVEY OSWALD
SHOT JFK

FUN FACTS

Laser tag was created in Dallas.

The Dallas Fort Worth International Airport is bigger than Manhattan.

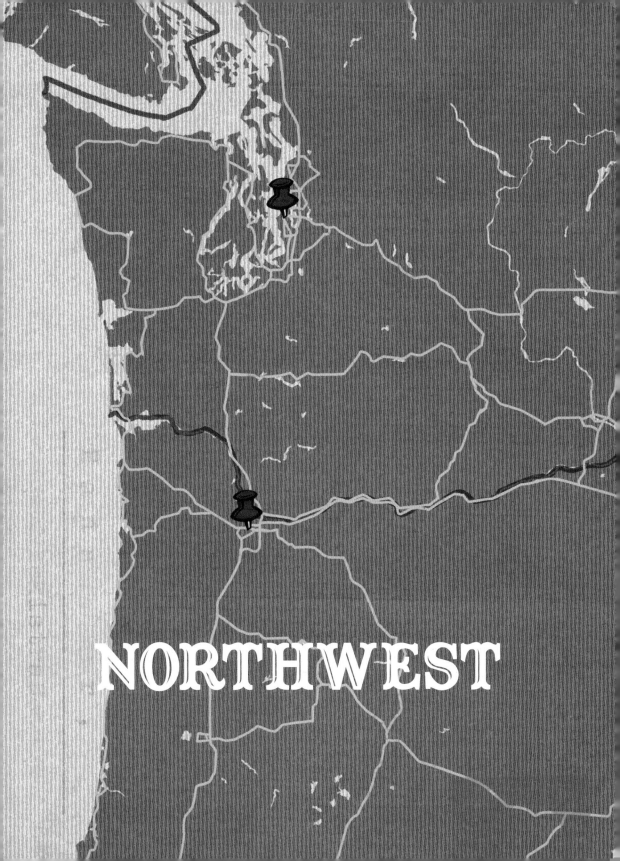

NORTHWEST

SEATTLE, WA

Seattle is always one of my favorite cities. We were lucky enough to do two shows there in 2019, but our third show was supposed to be on March 13, 2020, aka the official beginning of the pandemic shutdowns and the official ending to our 2020 tour. When we did get to perform there, we stayed at the Palladian Hotel. It not only looks like a library-speakeasy combo deal, but it offers you the chance to "sleep with a celebrity" by furnishing each room with a pillow designed to look like an oil painting of a celebrity. I'm happy to announce that I've slept with Will Smith and it was a pretty average experience. The hotel also had a dog running around in the lobby that we got to play with named Molly, and she was a dream hostess. My aunt and uncle were able to come see me and treated me to Dick's Drive-In after one of our shows, and it was the perfect midnight meal. Any place with multiple milkshake options until 2 a.m. is all right in my book.

Seattle was the first time I got to experience being both Em and Eva at the same time, and by that I mean Delta lost my luggage and I got to raid Em's and Eva's suitcases for a whole new wardrobe. I'm pretty sure I wore Eva's cat hat and Em's boxers on stage at the Neptune. I regret nothing.

PARANORMAL

MANRESA CASTLE

651 CLEVELAND ST · PORT TOWNSEND, WA

In the 1850s, Charles Eisenbeis immigrated to New York from Prussia, moved west, and settled in Port Townsend. He and his brother opened Pioneer Bakery and made a fortune baking for sailors (now that's Hoboken style, baby). He used his fortune to move into real estate, and he began building up businesses. He was one of the most successful men in town, later became Port Townsend's first mayor, and was one of the five men in Port Townsend who controlled the town's entire economy.

In 1892, a railroad was set to be constructed in town, so Charles built a hotel for future visitors. However, the plans for the train fell through, and Charles had a 120-room hotel with no use. He decided, "I always wanted my own castle," so he renovated it into his dream home and called it the Eisenbeis Castle. Not even twenty years later, Charles passed away. Later, his casket was damaged and had to be opened to be repaired. How does one find out a casket is broken when it's buried underground? I digress. When his casket was dug out, a child-sized Victorian coffin was found sitting on top of his. There was no record of a coffin being there, and to this day, nobody knows the child's relation to Charles. Charles's wife had remarried and left the home to a caretaker.

The castle was quickly sold off and became a home for nuns and then a monastery for ministry students. While it was a monastery, the building was renamed Manresa Castle in honor of the birthplace of St. Ignatius Loyola. In 1968 the castle was renovated back into a hotel with an attached restaurant.

During its time, the castle has seen many deaths. The first was one of Charles's sons, who died from a gunshot wound. Charles's granddaughter also died here after battling a heart infection. One of the priests who lived here drowned, and a woman jumped from Room 306's window. There is a rumored story that a priest in training hanged himself in the attic above Room 302. There is no record of this, but lore suggests it could have been covered up since it was a cardinal sin in a monastery.

As for spirits, Manresa Castle is riddled with them. People report all kinds of sounds, including voices and footsteps in empty rooms, chanting where the chapel was originally located, someone whispering your name, clocks chiming and phones ringing for no reason, and a woman singing in your bathroom in the middle of the night. One boy even heard crying in a neighboring room, and when employees went in, the room was empty but tissues were all over the floor. People have also smelled decomposition, or sometimes something pleasant if the spirit seems to like you. (*BRB, manifesting that I smell chocolate chip cookies if I ever visit.*)

Many visitors and staff also report feeling touched or grabbed, the sensation of someone sitting on your bed while you sleep, and their covers being pulled off while they're trying to sleep. One housekeeper even asked aloud for the spirits to leave her alone, and an unknown force punched her right in the face, apparently so hard that she claims she can't even punch that hard. Does it get worse? Yes! Electronics turn themselves on and off, doors open and close, pictures get thrown off walls, objects move on their own, and furniture rearranges itself. Not only that but your personal belongings get rearranged in the dresser drawers, people see hooded figures and translucent apparitions in Victorian garb, and people's shoes get taken. (Souls stealing soles? I'll see myself out.) Visitors also say they sometimes feel a phantom cat come up to them, and honestly, I've never hoped a cat was declawed until this moment. Arguably the worst paranormal activity is in the bar, where glasses will mysteriously be found stacked upside down, or will fly out of your hand, or just plain old explode when not being touched. The staff also say a pitcher of juice has slammed itself down on the counter, and dishwashers have felt someone holding their hand under the water. I'll end this with my favorite part of the *Ghost Adventures* episode of Manresa Castle: Zak intentionally taunts the spirits and then tells them to punch Aaron in the face—because of course he does.

TRUE CRIME

THE JAKE BIRD HEX

Okay, okay, yes . . . This story takes place in nearby Tacoma, not Seattle. That being said, I hope you'll forgive me on this technicality once you hear how majorly Goose Cam™–inducing it is. Let's meander back to the fall of 1947 in Tacoma, Washington.

On the evening of October 30, police were called to the home of 52-year-old Bertha Kludt and her daughter, 17-year-old Beverly, after neighbors had noted screaming coming from inside the residence. Police arrived on scene to find the bodies of both Bertha and Beverly, seemingly bludgeoned to death.

Fortunately, authorities arrived on time to spot a man fleeing from the scene of the crime. After a long chase, they ultimately captured the man, who was covered in blood and holding an axe. The man they'd captured was taken to the Tacoma City Jail and identified as 45-year-old Jake Bird, who had a lengthy criminal record including burglaries, assaults, and murder.

When asked for his background, Bird explained he had been born in a small town in Louisiana but didn't remember where. He left town when he was nineteen years old and never stayed in one place for long, often finding work with the railroad, which conveniently helped him move from town to town. He had also served a total of thirty-one years in various prisons over his lifetime, mainly in Michigan, Iowa, and Utah.

Bird quickly confessed to the murders of Bertha and Beverly, signing a confession in the presence of four police officers. By the time his trial rolled around, however, he had changed his tune, claiming the murders weren't intentional; in fact, the whole ordeal had simply been a burglary-gone-wrong.

Bird pleaded not guilty, but because his clothes were covered in Bertha's and Beverly's blood, his fingerprints were found in the house and on the axe, and his shoes had been left at the murder scene, Bird's fate was pretty much sealed. The jury deliberated only thirty-five minutes before finding Bird guilty of first-degree murder. He was sentenced to hang at the gallows of Washington State Penitentiary on Saturday, December 6, 1947.

After the verdict, Bird's attorney, a man named J.W. Selden, said he had done everything in his power to defend Bird and that no further appeals would be made. Selden further declared, "My heart does not beat in sympathy for this man, who fixes his life as more important than that of others. I feel whenever any man forty-five years old gets an idea that no lives are safe to anyone, except his own, that man is a detriment to society and should be obliterated."

Let's just say Bird didn't take that very well.

When the judge asked him if he'd like to give a final statement, Bird took that opportunity and ran with it. He addressed the court for twenty minutes, noting that his own lawyers were against him. "I was given no chance to defend myself," he declared. "My own lawyers just asked you to hang me. They apologized for defending me."

As he reached the end of his twenty-minute speech, Bird told the crowd,

"I'm putting the hex of Jake Bird on all of you who had anything to do with my being punished. Mark my words. You will die before I do."

Understandably, this threat was dismissed as mere dramatics. That is, until people started dying . . .

Within a month of sentencing Bird to death, the judge died suddenly from a heart attack. Soon after, the police officer who had interrogated Bird and the officer who wrote the official report had both died suddenly as well, followed by one of Bird's prison guards. Finally, the court's clerk, who had never missed a day of work in his life, quickly contracted pneumonia and died. If you've lost count, that's five deaths in a row.

When Bird was finally brought to Walla Walla to await his execution, he dropped a bombshell on police. He explained that over the past twenty years, he had been involved in forty-four other murders across the country. If they gave him a reprieve on his sentence, he said, he'd be willing to elaborate on these crimes, to "clear his conscience." Although everyone knew this was just a ploy to delay his execution, the state spent the next several days taking notes on Bird's many confessions, which they then compiled into a 174-page report for the governor's office.

Of the forty-four confessed murders, only eleven (I use the term "only" relatively here) were substantiated. That being said, Bird had more than enough knowledge about the others, so much so that he became the prime suspect in the remaining thirty-three murders throughout the US. In fact, Bird's confessions gave police from several states the opportunity to close the books on many of their unsolved cases. It turns out Bird had murdered people, mostly women, in Illinois, Kentucky, Nebraska, Oklahoma, Kansas, South Dakota, Ohio, Florida, Wisconsin, Michigan, Iowa, and Washington. His weapon of choice was an axe or a hatchet.

After his attempt to appeal his conviction failed, Bird was once again sentenced to hang. He was executed in front of a crowd of 125 witnesses on July 15, 1949, and was buried in an unmarked grave in the prison cemetery, identified only as convict no. 21520.

By this point, most people had forgotten about Jake Bird's hex. But on the one-year anniversary of Bird's hanging—to the day—his former attorney, J.W. Selden, the man who had openly regretted defending him, died suddenly of a heart attack.

As it stands today, the "Bird Hex" is still a mystery. As for Bird himself, if his victim count is accurate, that would make him not only one of the most prolific serial killers of the time but also the first recorded Black serial killer in America.

And while it can be argued that Jake Bird's hex was the real deal, it's interesting to note that the prosecutor who had Bird convicted, Pierce County attorney Patrick Steel, seemingly lived out the rest of his life with no concern. According to an interview in the *Modesto Bee* on November 27, 1948, Steel laughed when asked about the curse, responding, "Nothing to it. Never felt better in my life."

For more on Jake Bird, listen to Episode 121, *our crossover episode with* Wine & Crime: "The Plumbing Dutchman and a Murderous Glowup."

TEAM WINE HAUNTS

CANTERBURY ALE HOUSE
Haunted

MERCHANT'S CAFÉ AND SALOON
Haunted. Seattle's oldest bar and restaurant

KELL'S IRISH RESTAURANT AND PUB
Haunted

FOOTPRINT WINE TAP
Black-owned. Serves sustainable wine ...ON TAP!

COMMUNION RESTAURANT AND BAR
Black-owned

BATHTUB GIN & CO

TEAM MILKSHAKE HAUNTS

MOLLY MOON'S HOMEMADE ICE CREAM
Woman-owned

GELATIAMO
Woman-owned

FRANKIE AND JO'S
Woman-owned

HAUNTED HOTELS

HOTEL ANDRE

MAYFLOWER PARK HOTEL

THORNEWOOD CASTLE BED AND
BREAKFAST

SPOOKY TOURS

SPOOKED IN SEATTLE TOURS

NIGHTLY SPIRITS TOUR

UNDERGROUND PARANORMAL
TOUR

HAUNTED HISTORY GHOSTS OF
SEATTLE

SEATTLE TERRORS TOUR

OTHER WEIRD (WTF) PLACES TO CHECK OUT

MYSTERY SODA MACHINE

GREENWOOD SPACE TRAVEL
SUPPLY CO

TRAILER PARK MALL

YE OLDE CURIOSITY SHOP

MUSEUM OF BAD ART

METAPSHYICAL LIBRARY

STEVE'S WEIRD HOUSE

ARCHIE MCPHEE CATALOG STORE

MEOWTROPOLITCAN CAT CAFE

CENTER OF THE UNIVERSE SIGN

BALLYHOO CURIOSITY SHOP

RUBBER CHICKEN MUSEUM

BIG TOP CURIOSITY SHOP

NEVERTOLD CASKET COMPANY

FUN FACTS

This was the first major city to have a female mayor.

Seattle has more dogs than children.

PORTLAND, OR

Portland was a goddamn rollercoaster. The show itself was amazing—one of the loudest audiences I think we've ever had. After the show, my friends who live there said there was a great steakhouse I should try out with them. I thought, "This place must be amazing: a bunch of people at our meet and greet recommended the same place!" Well, my two friends and ALL OF YOU who suggested this place are, as Raven Baxter would say, "Ya nasties." I should have known when I was walking in and everybody was literally topless that this was not just your local Sizzler. It was called Acropolis, a strip club with some . . . experimental spaces. I'm all for sex positivity, but as a very nonadventurous person, all I wanted was steak, and I simply had no preparation for the things I saw (also, hi, Mom). Fun fact: One woman came up to us, lifted up her naked butt cheek, and let it slap down onto our table, and all I could think to say was, "Hey, watch it, you almost knocked over my Shirley Temple." I'm keeping it as PG as I can here, but let's just say Acropolis was not at all what I expected but also so much more. If this is your kind of scene, though, please go tip Musk, who absolutely deserves it (and order the Shirley Temple—it was fabulous). Long story short, the kitchen was closed and I never got my steak.

How the hell am I supposed to top that story? While I wish I could have seen Em's face in the Acropolis, I daresay it was almost *more* fun to hear Em regale me with tales of Musk that evening. To this day, it's my favorite bedtime story. While Em's fundamental worldview was being challenged somewhere in Portland, Eva, Blaise, and I had a perfectly family-friendly evening playing pinball at the Ground Kontrol barcade. Em and I just presented possibly the widest spectrum of activities, so now it's up to you how you enjoy your time in the City of Roses!

PARANORMAL

SHANGHAI TUNNELS

120 NW 3RD AVE · PORTLAND, OR

Come one, come all to the most popular and haunted attraction in all of Portland! Under these city streets are the Shanghai Tunnels, running from north to south and ending at the riverfront—these tunnels have been around ever since the nineteenth century. It all started when the businesses in town were fed up with bringing goods into the city through the constantly muddy streets. To avoid these paths, Portland decided it would be more efficient to dig tunnels under the city and begin bringing in imports this way.

The tunnels soon became part of darker activities, when more people, including gangs, started moving in. One of the main gangs was the Crimps. The tunnels soon became gang territory, and they were used as opium dens as well as gambling halls. The Crimps also made deals with sea captains and started using these tunnels to traffic people out to sea for labor on ships. This trafficking was called "Shanghai-ing." The captain would come into one of the gang-owned bars and signal to the Crimps by pointing out a bar patron that he wanted on his ship. The Crimps would drug the guy's meal, throw him down a trapdoor into the tunnels, starve him for days, and then feed him a huge (drugged) meal to make it easier to move him to the waterfront and sell him to the captain. By the time the victim would wake up, he was usually on a ship heading toward China.

Soon, Portland became the Shanghai capital of the world, with up to 3,000 people being trafficked each year. It only got easier to Shanghai people when Prohibition began and speakeasies started opening inside the tunnels. Around this time, sex work also became a high demand, and so sex trafficking also became common in the tunnels. Many captives died in the holding cells from drug overdoses or starvation. One of the more famous deaths here was a victim of sex trafficking named Nyna, who after trying to escape was found dead at the Merchant Hotel.

More deaths came from rival gangs getting in fights, including one where speakeasy patrons tried to run, got lost in the tunnels, and were murdered at a dead end. After World War II, the tunnels were officially closed to the public, but they have since been restored for tours. The tunnels to this day are still connected through the basements of storefronts on the main level, and the paranormal activity is intense. Just for starters, people have felt cold, wet hands grab them in the dark.

In the words of Randy Jackson, "It's a no from me, dog."

People have also seen dark shadow figures, felt something choking them or tripping them, and had bricks thrown at them. Visitors and staff have heard footsteps, screaming, crying, talking in the walls, and groans that get louder over time. When Zak Bagans and his team came to the Shanghai Tunnels, they got several intelligent responses during their spirit box session, including a male voice explaining, "I was wasted; I was beaten," and a female voice . . . propositioning Mr. Bagans. There are also several sets of chimes that hang in the tunnels that have swung as if smacked by someone. In the businesses attached to the tunnels, people have witnessed furniture and other items move on their own and seen spirits walking around. People in the bars have also felt as if people rushed past them and knocked over their drinks and chairs, even though nobody was there. In the hotels attached to the tunnels, people claim that the bed moves by itself at night while they're in it and they hear knocking from underneath the bed. In the words of Simon Cowell, "Absolutely not."

Learn more about the Shanghai Tunnels in Episode III: "A Ghost Tour by Em and a Mother of Pearl Pie Tin."

TRUE CRIME

RICHARD LAURENCE MARQUETTE

Yes, Portland is known for its hipster culture and craft beer, but what you might not know is that the beautiful town is also home to the first person ever to be added as an eleventh name on the FBI's Ten Most Wanted List. Back in 1961, Richard Marquette, sometimes fittingly nicknamed "Dick," perpetrated what Oregon Governor Mark Hatfield called "the most heinous [crime] in Oregon history." Let's crack into it!

It was June 8, 1961, when Portland police received a phone call from a frantic woman whose dog had brought home a dismembered foot in a paper bag. While detectives were at the house investigating, the dog returned *again*, this time with a severed hand. (Someone get this dog on payroll!)

A search of the area revealed several more body parts, none of which had been buried. Even more ominous, the parts were fresh and had all been bled dry, the veins and arteries having been completely drained of blood. (Vomitous.) The foot was determined to have belonged to a woman, and its slightly webbed toes had been painted bright red.

Police scanned missing persons reports and found one that seemingly fit the bill: Joan Caudle, a 23-year-old Portland housewife who'd recently been reported missing by her husband. At first, Joan's husband was questioned carefully. He told police his wife had been out shopping for Father's Day gifts when she vanished but that she may have stopped by a bar due to a recent bout of depression. When asked if his wife could be having an affair, Mr. Caudle vehemently denied the possibility, explaining that there was no way Joan could have found the time. Finally, when asked if she had webbed toes, he had absolutely no idea. Apparently, this was something that had never come up between the two of them . . .

With Mr. Caudle's answers not getting them very far, police turned to the public. They found a local woman who claimed to have seen Joan in a bar on June 7. At the time the witness had been talking to a charming man who'd introduced himself as "Marquette." Though they were seemingly hitting it off, Joan had arrived and (luckily for the witness) stolen Marquette's attention.

When police arrived at the home of this mysterious man, whose full name was Richard Laurence Marquette, they didn't find him. They did, however, find body parts. A lot of them. That's right, Mr. Marquette was storing tidy stacks of newspaper-wrapped body parts in his fridge.

A manhunt began, and an appeal to the FBI prompted them to add an eleventh name to their infamous Ten Most Wanted list. It worked. Marquette was arrested the following day in California, with arresting officers noting that he seemed almost relieved at his arrest.

Marquette claimed that he was in a bar when he spotted Joan Caudle, who recognized him from elementary school and approached him. (*BRB, adding another reason to avoid socializing with past acquaintances to my list.*) Marquette took Joan to a few more bars before they headed back to his place, where she allegedly agreed to have sex with him. Afterward, he claimed, they'd gotten into an argument and Marquette choked Joan to death. In a "panic," he dismembered her body in the shower before storing it in the fridge.

For obvious reasons, officials were dubious about Marquette's version of events, especially the claim that the sex was consensual. That being said, he was the only witness to the crime, so there wasn't much they could do. While

Marquette was found guilty of first-degree murder, the jury recommended leniency (really, guys?) and he received parole in 1973 after only eleven years as a "model prisoner." Yuck.

I'm not sure what anyone expected, but two years later another body was discovered floating in a shallow slough in Marion County, Oregon. The body had once again been bled dry, mutilated, and dismembered before being dumped. Police determined the remains were those of 37-year-old Betty Wilson, a North Carolina native who'd recently left home to escape a life of poverty and abuse. Betty was last seen alive in a crowded nightclub in Salem.

With her husband's rock-solid alibi of being literally across the country at the time of the murder, suspicion immediately fell on our good pal Marquette. A search warrant helped police to uncover several pieces of evidence that tied him to the crime, and only fifty-five hours after the remains had been found, he was arrested and brought in for questioning.

Marquette's story was familiar—he claimed he'd brought Betty back to his house, where she first agreed to sex before changing her mind. Marquette strangled and dismembered her with surgical precision, which was clearly not a result of "panic" but rather as part of his sick MO.

Marquette surprised authorities when he confessed to yet another murder from 1974. He claimed the woman agreed to come back to his place, where he choked her to death and dismembered her body. Marquette led detectives to her grave, but sadly her remains were mostly skeletal so an ID couldn't be made. Marquette claimed he never got her name, and the woman is known simply as "Jane Doe" to this day.

Marquette was sentenced to life imprisonment with no possibility of parole. Interestingly, a review by criminal psychiatrists concluded that Marquette was a seemingly "normal," well-adjusted individual until a woman turned him down, after which he would fly into a murderous rage. (Doesn't sound exactly well adjusted to me, but what do I know.)

Marquette has been incarcerated at the Oregon State Penitentiary in Salem since June 1975. He is eighty-six years old.

TEAM WINE HAUNTS

OLD TOWN PIZZA AND BREWING
Haunted

ABBEY CREEK WINERY: THE CRICK
Black-owned

KELLS IRISH PUB
Haunted

RAVEN'S MANOR
A haunted mansion-themed cocktail bar in Old Town

PALOMAR

TEAM MILKSHAKE HAUNTS

WIZ BANG BAR

HEARTBREAKER NEIGHBORHOOD KITCHEN

WHAT'S THE SCOOP?
Woman-owned

HAUNTED HOTELS AND BARS

HEATHMAN HOTEL

WHITE EAGLE SALOON AND HOTEL

THE BENSON

MCMENAMIN'S EDGEFIELD

HOOD RIVER HOTEL

MCMENAMIN'S GRAND LODGE

OLD TOWN PIZZA AND BREWERY

SPOOKY TOURS

BEERQUEST WALKING TOURS

HAUNTED PUB TOUR

PORTLAND OLD TOWN GHOST TOUR

PORTLAND GHOSTS TOUR

BEYOND BIZARRE GHOST TOUR

PORTLAND HAUNTED BREWERY CRAWL

OTHER WEIRD (WTF) PLACES TO CHECK OUT

HAT MUSEUM

VACUUM MUSEUM

MUSEUM OF ODD HISTORY

ZYMOGLYPHIC MUSEUM

KIDD'S TOY MUSEUM

FREAKYBUTTRUE PECULIARIUM AND MUSEUM

END MILLS PARK
The world's smallest park

PAXTON GATE ODDITY SHOP

RIMSKY-KORSACOFFEE HOUSE

ONE OF A KIND WEATHER MACHINE IN DOWNTOWN PORTLAND

FUN FACT

Portland was going to be named either Portland or Boston;
it was decided by a coin toss.

PACIFIC STATES

HONOLULU, HI

I would love to visit Hawai'i one day, take in the sights, and do *some* touristy activities like the hedge maze, La Mariana, and this scenic urinal I keep seeing on the internet. However, visitors of Hawai'i (myself included) need to be aware of how we fit on the islands as tourists and learn all we can before traveling there. Please take time to become a more conscious visitor before heading here: educate yourself on their history with the US, respect the locals' culture, beliefs, and spirits, and shop at local businesses. It will make you a better traveler and give you a better appreciation for the visit!

What Em said! With the rise in travel post-Covid, tourists are putting a real strain on the state of Hawai'i. While this book is technically a road atlas, and we're pretty sure you didn't drive here, if you do make the trip to beautiful Honolulu, please be respectful of the local people, culture, and economy. I went to Honolulu as a kid, and my favorite memories included visiting local bakeries before spending every day at the beach.

So whether you're headed to Hawai'i for a family vacation, for your honeymoon, or to join in the hunt for the still-at-large Honolulu Strangler, we think you'll love your time in the Aloha State. Now if only we could convince our tour manager to book a live show here . . .

PARANORMAL

HUAKA'I PO,
AKA THE NIGHT MARCHERS

Hawai'i is known for some of the best history, the best food, and the best sights. But it's also known for having some very powerful spirits, arguably the most popular of which are the infamous Night Marchers!

For some background, Hawai'i was once a caste system, with multiple chiefs called "ali'i" and the higher-ranking chief called the "ali'i nui." Ali'i nui and ali'i were said to hold incredible spiritual power called "mana," and they were thought to be physical representations of the gods. Each island had its own ali'i with their own set of "kānāwai," or strict rules and laws that dictated what was "kapu," or forbidden to citizens.

One of the most serious kapu you could commit was looking directly at or even being in the presence of the ali'i nui, because you could potentially steal some of their mana. Even if done by accident, interacting with the ali'i nui was punishable by death. So to prevent people from running into him and inadvertently committing kapu, the ali'i nui would often travel at night with a procession of guards who would blow a conch to alert others that they were nearby.

> **SIDE NOTE**
> When visiting Hawai'i, if you see "kapu" written anywhere, it can mean "forbidden" or "sacred." Either way, be respectful and stay out!

Okay, but that's the nicest practice I've heard a leader do for their people . . . ignoring the whole "we would have to kill you otherwise" aspect, of course.

The ali'i that marched with him would also carry torches and drums, and they would chant to warn others of their presence so that they had time to leave the area. It is said that the ali'i continue their high-ranking duties after death, and these are the "huaka'i po," also known as the Night Marchers. Night Marchers have been seen for centuries, but the first written evidence only dates back to the 1880s, when the spirit of King Kamehameha the Great was seen walking with several spirit soldiers behind him. People who have seen the Night Marchers from afar say that they have heard drumming and conch shells, smelled a "death-like" odor, and even spotted lit torches and groups of warrior spirits walking by. It's said if you were to come face to face with the Night Marchers, one deadly look could kill you for committing kapu.

The group of warriors are sometimes seen floating slightly off of the ground, but others say they leave giant footprints in the dirt. They are also said to be preceded by bad weather that comes out of nowhere, and they sometimes appear in pictures as shadow figures with torches or spears. The Night Marchers are most often seen on pō Kāne, which is the night at the end of the lunar cycle, and are most frequently seen traveling between sacred sites, important cultural spaces, and historic routes. They have also been known to escort the spirits of the recently deceased to a place where the spirit can properly cross over. (Again, I'm ignoring all of the terror and just focusing on how precious this is.)

It's not just Hawai'ian residents who need to be careful of running into the Night Marchers. Tourists are also at risk of spotting them and are warned to stay away from certain paths at night. Night Marchers will walk through the walls of buildings that are in their way, unless people have planted Ti leaves in their home, which are said to keep spirits away. (Note to self: Carry Ti leaves 24-7 whether or not I'm in Hawai'i.) The Night Marchers do show mercy for some people who run into them: their descendants. Those related to the warriors who have stumbled upon them have heard one of the spirits shout, "na'u," which means "mine," claiming them as someone to not harm. Some people have even reported seeing the Night Marchers and not knowing they were a descendant until they heard someone in the procession say so. It's been said to never whistle at night or else you risk summoning them, and if you do hear their drums, hide, cover your eyes, and play dead (or maybe just avoid all of this by checking the lunar calendar before you head out).

Learn more about the Night Marchers in Episode 193: "An Afterlife Guard and a Rosé Colored Flag."

TRUE CRIME

THE HONOLULU STRANGLER

If there's one thing I've learned from hosting *ATWWD*, it's that no place is immune to evil. It should come as no surprise, then, that even the gorgeous state of Hawai'i has a dark side.

In this case, the darkness came in the form of a series of murders that took place in Honolulu between May of 1985 and April of 1986. The Honolulu Strangler, as he would come to be known, took five lives that year. His first victim was 25-year-old Vicki Gail Purdy, who is most often described as a "military spouse" (*insert eyeroll here*). In an effort to give her a more well-rounded description, I did some digging* and found that Vicki worked at a local video rental store. Originally from North Carolina, Vicki was described by her husband, Gary, as tough, streetwise, and someone who packed a mean punch.

On May 29, 1985, Vicki left to go clubbing with her friends in Waikiki, but she never arrived. She was reportedly last seen alive by a taxi driver who had dropped her off at the Shorebird Hotel around midnight, apparently to pick up her car. When Vicki failed to come home that night, Gary grew worried, relentlessly paging her to no avail. It wasn't until the following day, May 30, 1985, that Vicki's body was found on an embankment near the Keehi Lagoon, a place with easy access to the Pacific Ocean and considered secluded in the 1980s. Her hands had been bound behind her back, and she had been sexually assaulted and strangled to death.

Police received their first lead from Gary, who told them of Vicki's job at the Wahiawa Video Rental Store. The shop was known to handle pornographic films, so detectives considered the possibility that an unhinged customer had stalked and killed her. This theory was bolstered by the fact that two women— an employee and the store's co-owner—had been stabbed to death at the store the previous year. Unfortunately, this lead turned out to be a red herring (albeit a pretty interesting one), as the two cases were never linked.

The Honolulu Strangler struck again on January 14, 1986. Leilehua High School student Regina Sakamoto, age 17, was last heard from at 7:15 a.m. when she called her boyfriend to let him know she had missed her usual bus and was running late for school. Her body was found the following day, once again at Keehi Lagoon. Like Vicki, Regina's hands were bound behind her back, and she had been raped and strangled. According to the *Honolulu Star-Bulletin*, Regina was known as shy but friendly and was very close with her mother. Originally from Kansas, she was planning on attending Hawai'i Pacific University in the fall.

The Strangler's third victim was 21-year-old Denise Hughes, who worked as a secretary for a local telephone company. Originally from Washington, Denise was known for her bright smile and had recently earned a raise at work

---

* Borrowed my brother's newspapers.com account.

for her stellar performance. Denise didn't arrive at work on January 30, 1986, and her body was discovered just two days later. Three fishermen stumbled upon the body in Moanalua Stream. Not only had the killer diverged from his usual dumping ground, but he had also added a new element to his MO: Denise's body had been wrapped in a blue tarp. That being said, the similarities to the previous crimes were too noteworthy to ignore: Denise's hands had been bound behind her back, and she had been sexually assaulted and strangled. Interestingly, she was also known to use Honolulu's bus system to get around.

Despite the slightly shifting MO, detectives knew they had a serial killer on their hands. On February 5, the Honolulu Police Department formed a serial killer task force. But pinpointing their suspect wouldn't be easy: not only was Hawai'i home to a large military population, but it was also home to thousands of migrant workers, drawn in by Oahu's recent telecommunications boom. What's more, 10.5 million tourists visited Hawai'i between 1985 and 1986. In other words, the killer could have come from any of these populations.

Unfortunately, the task force didn't manage to capture the Strangler before he attacked his next victim. On March 26, 1986, 25-year-old Louise Medeiros had just returned from a trip to Kauai, where she had met her family after the tragic death of her mother. After the get-together, she boarded a red-eye flight back home to Oahu, where she planned to take a bus home from the airport. After disembarking from the plane, Louise was never seen alive again. Her body was found on April 2 near Waikele Stream. Her body was found in a similar state to the previous victims. The Honolulu Strangler had struck again. Louise's family described her as finally being "centered and motivated" after several years of turbulence and financial instability. Louise was three months pregnant when she was killed.

The Honolulu Strangler's last-known victim was 36-year-old Linda Pesce. Linda's roommate reported her missing when she didn't arrive home after work. The case took an unexpected turn when a man named Howard Gay came forward and told police that a psychic had informed him of the location of Linda Pesce's body (WTF?!). Her body wasn't found in that location, but it would later be discovered nearby, also having been sexually assaulted with her hands behind her back.

Turns out, Howard Gay Dutcher was not so much a good Samaritan as he was a really, really suspicious dude. In fact, clues started to quickly add up when police took a closer look at his life. His girlfriend described him as a "smooth talker." She and his ex-wife also told police of his interest in bondage, more specifically tying their hands behind their backs. Furthermore, his ex-wife explained that on evenings they fought, he would leave the house and not return until morning. He also happened to work near the preferred dumping grounds of the Strangler. Unfortunately, police didn't have enough to arrest him—even after he failed a polygraph test.

Fortunately, a new witness came forward before the Strangler had a chance to strike again. She told police she had seen Linda with her killer the night of her murder. The witness was brought to a police lineup, where she immediately picked Howard out as the killer. Her cooperation stopped there, though, because she was certain Howard had seen her the night of the murder, and she was afraid for her safety.

This is the part where I tell you that things didn't end "happily ever after." In fact, despite a $25,000 reward, no other strong leads ever came up, and Howard Gay was never officially charged with the crimes. It's worth noting, though, that when Howard fled to the mainland, the crimes came to an abrupt halt. He died in 2003, and many believe that with his death, any chance of closing the case for good was also lost. That being said, the case is still considered open.

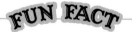

FUN FACT

The Honolulu Strangler is known as Hawai'i's first serial killer.

TEAM WINE HAUNTS

SKULL & CROWN TRADING CO.

HANA KOA BREWING

MOKU KITCHEN

OFF THE WALL CRAFT BEER & WINE

TEAM MILKSHAKE HAUNTS

MAGNOLIA ICE CREAM & TREATS

FROSTCITY

BANAN WAIKIKI BEACH SHACK

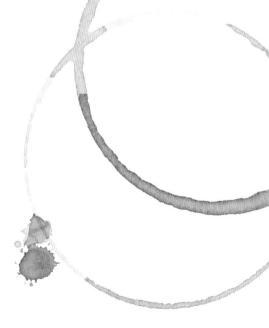

HAUNTED HOTELS

MOANA SURFRIDER

THE BLAISDELL HOTEL

HILTON HAWAI'IAN VILLAGE

SPOOKY TOURS

MYSTERIES OF HAWAI'I TOUR

HONOLULU HAUNTS

SPIRIT EXPEDITIONS

OTHER WEIRD (WTF) PLACES TO CHECK OUT

DOLE'S PINEAPPLE GARDEN MAZE

THE TOILET BOWL SWIMMING HOLE

ZOO'S BURIAL MOUND

HAWAI'I'S OLDEST TIKI BAR

HOTEL KONA'S SCENIC URINAL

MACADAMIA NUT VISITOR CENTER

UFO PEACE PARK

THE BASKIN ROBBINS WHERE OBAMA WORKED

POSTANUT
Mail a coconut

BEES MUSEUM AND TOUR

FUN FACTS

Honolulu does not have daylight saving time.

Honolulu is the creator of casual Fridays.

OUTRO

Oooooh, we're at the conclusion! Should we drive this book home with a sappy thank-you? Some sage advice? Or maybe a cheeky play on words?

Just like our podcast episodes, we have no idea how to end this. But hopefully, this smattering of creepy cities has inspired you to explore a nearby town or plan a spooky trip for yourself in the future. We have been lucky enough to visit so many of these areas, but after researching their local "haunts" while writing this book, we can't wait to go back and discover each town all over again!

Thank you so much to everyone who has read this book, come to our shows, or checked out our podcast. We are so grateful for all of you (nothing says "we appreciate you" more than Em agreeing to write a literal book), and we can't wait to visit, report on, and maybe even write extensively about more places and their sinister histories. (There's that sappy thank-you!)

In the meantime, continue listening wherever you get your podcasts and keep an eye out for any future projects (the sage advice).

As this guide has let on, the world's a scary place . . . *And That's Why We Drink* (the play on words . . . I swear we should have been writing books together years ago)!

—Em and Christine

ACKNOWLEDGEMENTS

To Leona, my brave little lion, who hung out in my womb throughout the entirety of the writing process. You are my whole heart. (But you're not allowed to read this book until you're 18.)

To Blaise, whose endless patience and nonstop snack deliveries made this book possible. Thanks for always making space for me to grow, learn, and thrive. I love you.

And finally, to our listeners, our inimitable Boozers & Shakers: Thank you from the bottom of our hearts for going on this wild, spooky journey with us. *"Love you, mean it!"*

—Christine

To my best friends in Fredericksburg, for spending every night of high school hanging out on some abandoned, haunted property with me.

Thank you for being there for my first ghostly encounters. Out of all of the spooky stories I've ever told, ours are my favorite.

Also to my mom, for not grounding me when she found out about it.

—Em

REFERENCES

BOSTON

"Boston Strangler Strikes Again." www.history.com

"Boston Strangler." www.britannica.com

"The Boston Strangler." www.crimemuseum.org

"Boston Strangler Case Solved 50 Years Later." www.abcnews.go.com

"Spiritualism." www.newworldencyclopedia.org

"When Houdini Came To Williamsport – To Expose Fake Mediums." www.wusquehannavalley.blogspot.com

"Harry Houdini and Arthur Conan Doyle: A Friendship Split by Spiritualism." www.thegaurdian.com

"Overlooked No More: Rose Mackenberg, Houdini's Secret 'Ghost-Buster.'" www.nytimes.com

"The Female Ghost Buster Who Rooted Out Spiritual Fraud for Houdini." www.atlasobscura.com

"Harry Houdini – The Occult and Spirit Mediums." www.thegreatharryhoudini.com

"In 1926, Houdini Spent 4 Days Shaming Congress for Being in Thrall to Fortune-Tellers." www.atlasobscura.com

"Spiritualist Practices Then and Now: The Lasting Legacy of Victorian Mediums." www.keen.com

"Sir Arthur Conan Doyle and Victorian Spiritualism." www.victorianweb.com

"Houdini's Greatest Trick: Debunking Medium Mina Crandon." www.mentalfloss.com

"Mina Crandon, Psychic Fraudster." www.headstuff.org

"Mina Crandon & Harry Houdini: The Medium and The Magician." www.historynet.com

"Margery (Mina) Crandon – Physical Medium." www.the-voicebox.com

"The Two Faces of Margery." www.michaelprescott.freeservers.com

"Mediums and Channelers – Mina 'Margery' Stinson Crandon (1888–1941)." www.unexplainedstuff.com

NEW YORK

"The Curious Case Of Michael Malloy – 'Rasputin Of The Bronx.'" www.allthatsinteresting.com

"Iron Mike Malloy: The Donegal Man They Tried Nine Times to Kill." www.thejournal.ie

"The Murder Trust of Mike Malloy: The Strange Tale of an Insurance Scam and a Man Who Refused to Die." www.prospectmagazine.co.uk/

"The Man Who Wouldn't Die." www.smithsonianmag.com

"15 Minutes with Olive Thomas, Former Follies Girl and Full-time Ghost" www.catapult.co

"The Ghosts of Broadway" www.playbill.com

"The Haunted History of Broadway's Palace Theatre." www.ny.curbed.com

"The Haunting of Broadway's Spirited Belasco Theatre." www.ny.curbed.com

"Belasco Theater." www.nyghosts.com

"Scandals and Secrets of the Supernatural: The Stories Behind Broadway's Haunted Theatres." www.playbill.com

"Broadway's Most Haunted Tale." www.medium.com

"The Real-Life Ghost Stories Behind Broadway's 9 Haunted Theatres." www.playbill.com

"The Creepiest Stories of Broadway Ghosts." www.grunge.com

"A Guide to Broadway's Theatre Ghosts." www.cityguideny.com

"Ghosts, Curses, & Charms: Theater Superstitions – Part 4." www.rickontheater.blogspot.com

"The Most Haunted Theater on Broadway: The Reprise of Mr. Belasco." www.jimharold.com

WASHINGTON, DC

"The Worst Marriage in Georgetown." www.nytimes.com

"Albrecht Muth Found Guilty of Murdering His Wife, Viola Drath Muth." www.washingtonian.com

"Viola Drath Murder: Husband Albrecht Muth, Fake Iraqi General, Found Guilty." www.theguardian.com

"Albrecht Muth Sentenced to 50 Years in 2011 Slaying of His Socialite Wife, Viola Drath." www.washingtonpost.com

"Is the White House Haunted? A History of Spooked
Presidents, Prime Ministers and Pets." www.
washingtonpost.com
"White House Ghost Stories." www.
whitehousehistory.org
"Knock, Knock! Whoooo's There? Spooky Stories
from Children of the White House." www.
ourwhitehouse.com
"Is Any DC Home More Haunted Than the White
House?" www.wtop.com
"Know About the 'Haunted' Places in and around the
White House." www.indiatvnews.com
"Ghostly Tales and Spirited Stories from the White
House." www.travelchannel.com
"The Attic Ghosts of the White House." www.
theresashauntedhistoryofthetri-state.blogspot.com
"The White House's Basement Demon Cat That
Foretells Disaster." www.hauntjaunts.net
"The White House's Best Ghost Stories." www.
constitutioncenter.org
"5 Famous Ghosts Haunting the White House." www.
stranglingbros.com
"The White House." www.dcghosts.com
"Over 200 Years, Only 10 People Have Ever Died
Inside the White House – Here's the Full List."
www.businessinsider.com
"The White House Building." www.whitehouse.gov
"'The Obstinate Mr. Burns' and the First White
House." www.boundarystones.weta.org
"Ghosts in the White House." www.history.com
"Does Abraham Lincoln's Ghost Haunt the White
House?" www.budgettravel.com
"Lincoln's Ghost." www.potus-geeks.livejournal.com
"Is the White House Haunted? These Presidents All
Think So." www.cheatsheet.com
"Ghosts of Presidents Past: Who's Haunting the
White House?" www.blogs.ancestry.com
"The Haunted White House." www.
americanhauntingsink.com
"White House Ghosts." www.haunted-places.com

PITTSBURGH, PA
"Pittsburgh's Greatest Scandal: Mrs. Soffel and the
Biddle Brothers." www.hauntedpittsburghtours.
com
"Jack and Ed Biddle." www.wikipedia.org

"Let's Learn from the Past: Biddle Brothers' Escape."
www.post-gazette.com
"Is Love a Crime? The Story of the Biddle Brothers'
Infamous Escape." www.wesa.fm
"Mrs. Soffel and the Biddle Boys." www.
heinzhistorycenter.org
"Warden's Lonely Wife Helped Two Notorious
Brothers in Daring Escape from Pittsburgh Prison
in 1902." www.nydailynews.com
"The Warden's Wife: Kate Soffel & the Biddle
Brothers, 1902." www.historicalcrimedetective.com
"Hill View Manor – New Castle, Pa." www.
pennsylvania-mountains-of-attractions.com
https://www.discoveryplus.com/video/ghost-
adventures/hill-view-manor
"History of Hill View Manor." www.
hauntedhillviewmanor.com
"The Ghosts of Newcastle's Hill View Manor." www.
hauntedrooms.com
"Haunted Histories Part 2: Hill View Manor." www.
ithappenedwhilewriting.wordpress.com
"Hill View Manor." www.hauntedjourneys.com
"The Most Haunted Places in All of Pennsylvania."
www.thrillist.com
"Hillview Manor – History." www.
ironcityparanormal.com
"The Parajournal: Hill View Manor." www.youtube.
com
"Our Hill View Manor Experience – EctoVision
Paranormal." www.youtube.com

PHILADELPHIA
"Witch's Brew: How the 'Philadelphia Poison Ring'
Exploited Unhappy Wives and Killed 100+ People."
www.thoughtcatalog.com
"Philadelphia Poison Ring." www.absolutecrime.com
"Arsenic and No Lace: The Bizarre Tale of a
Philadelphia Murder Ring." by Robert James
Young Jr. on www.jstor.org
"Philadelphia Poison Ring." www.en-academic.com
"My Neighbor's Chestnut Hill Mansion is (Probably)
Haunted." www.billypenn.com
"The 16 Most Haunted Locations in Philly." www.
philly.curbed.com
"Baleroy Mansion." www.wikipedia.com
"The Baleroy Mansion." www.deadblack.net

"The Haunting of Baleroy Mansion and the 'Death Chair.'" www.discover.hubpages.com

"Baleroy Mansion and the Blue Room." www.pennsylvaniaparanormal.tumblr.com

"Magickal Compendium – Hauntings – The Baleroy Mansion." www.lulusenchantedgems.com

"Baleroy Mansion." www.creativespirits.net

Ep. 24: "The Baleroy Mansion." *Realm of Unknown.* www.realmofunknown.com

"The Haunted Baleroy Mansion, Home to the Death Chair." www.linkedin.com

NEW ORLEANS

"The Axeman of New Orleans Preyed on Italian Immigrants." www.smithsonianmag.com

"The Axe Murderer Who Loved Jazz." www.wbur.org

"The Murder Mystery Behind the Crazed Axeman of New Orleans." www.filmdaily.co

"The Axeman of New Orleans." www.legendsofamerica.com

"The Year of the Axeman." www.nola.com

"Delphine LaLaurie." www.wikipedia.com

"Delphine Lalaurie." www.64parishes.org

"What Happens When a Haunted House is TOO Scary? Three Spooky Stories about Haunted Houses and the Plaintiffs That Sued Them." www.bethune-law.com

"How to Avoid the Ghosts of Murdered Slaves on Your Next Visit to New Orleans." www.funeralwise.com

"The LaLaurie Mansion 1832." www.blackpast.org

"Marie Delphine MaCarty LaLaurie." www.findagrave.com

"The Dark Side of the Quarter." www.frenchquarter.com

"Madame Lalaurie of New Orleans." by Fred R. Darkis, Jr. on www.jstor.org

"Delphine Lalaurie – The Stirring of Brains (Graphic)." *Unfortunate History.* www.unfortunatehistory.com

"Filming Locations for American Horror Story Coven." www.thegeographicalcure.com

"Slaveowner Madame LaLaurie Tortured and Killed Her Slaves for Fun." www.historyofyesterday.com

"Madame LaLaurie's House of Horrors." www.emmaraeshalloween.com

"This Woman Caught Pictures of Ghosts on Her Phone and I'm Done." www.totallythebomb.com

"Nicholas Cage Once Blew $150 Million on a Private Island and a Dinosaur Skull – Here's Everything He Bought." www.cnbc.com

"Can I Go Inside the LaLaurie Mansion?" www.ghostcitytours.com

"Womens History Month: Madame Delphine LaLaurie." www.neworleanslegendarywalkingtours.com

New Orleans Ghost and Vampire Tour, 2019

New Orleans French Quarter Phantoms, 2019

NASHVILLE

"Janet Gail Levine March." www.charlieproject.org

"A Good Thing Gone Bad." www.nashvillescene.com

"March Memories Linger in Mexico." www.mexconnect.com

"Notorious Nashvillian Perry March Sues over Prison Food." www.tennessean.com

"The Hermitage." www.hauntedhouses.com

"Greetings from Nashville, Tennessee." www.kathrynrjones.wordpress.com

"Rachel." www.thehermitage.com

"Do the Spirits of Andrew Jackson and His Wife Still Linger at the Hermitage?" www.wkrn.com

"The Hermitage." www.nashvilleghosts.com

"Nashville Haunted Hotels: These Lodgings Are to Die For!" www.nightlyspirits.com

"The History of the Hermitage Hotel." www.thehermitagehotel.com

"Hermitage Hotel Men's Bathroom." www.atlasobscura.com

"America's Best Bathroom Found in Tennessee." www.nbcnews.com

"Get Spooked by History and Haunts at the Hermitage." www.herlifeinruins.com

"The Hermitage Hotel." www.nashvillehaunts.com

"Fronted Haunted TN, Andrew Jackson's Hermitage Mansion." www.youtube.com

JACKSONVILLE

"'I Didn't Want To Kill Nobody,' Serial Killer Says After Murdering 6 Men and Shoving Items in Their Mouths." www.oxygen.com

"Serial Killer Who Preyed On Gay Men, Was Dubbed 'I-95 Killer' Is Executed in Florida." www.nbcnews.com

"Gary Ray Bowles." www.murderpedia.org

"Haunted Guide to the Old Jail." www.ghostsandgravestones.com

"Henry Flagler." www.wikipedia.org

"Saint Augustine Jail." www.panicd.com

"Old Jail." www.visitstaugustine.com

"Haunted Places in St. Augustine: The Old Jail." www.haunted-places-to-go.com

"Saint Augustine Jail." www.hauntedhouses.com

"The Devil's in St. Augustine's Old Jail Museum." www.oldcityghosts.com

"In St. Augustine Florida, It Looks Like the Prisoners Are Running the Old Jail." www.youtube.com

ORLANDO, FL

Murder in the Tropics by Stuart McIver

www.historicalcrimedetective.com

www.palmbeachpast.org

"The True Spirit of Cassadaga." www.medium.com

"Cassadaga, Florida." www.wikipedia.org

"A Thin Veil Among the Scrub: Spiritualism and Cassadaga." www.thehistorycenter.org

"Cassadaga: Florida's Most Spirited Town." www.weirdus.com

"Sarasota Vortex." www.vortexhunters.com

"Siesta Beach." www.wikipedia.org

"Cassadaga Encounter the Spirit Night Tour." www.visitwestvolusia.com

"Cassadaga, NY." www.ufo-hunters.com

"Cassadaga, Florida." www.florida-backroads-travel.com

"Communing with Spirits in Cassadaga, Florida." www.buckettripper.com

MIAMI, FL

"The Mysterious Clues of the 'Liquid Matthew' Case." www.horrorhistory.net

"Blotter Liquid Matthew." www.audienceseverywhere.net

"The Bizarre 'Liquid Matthew' Case of 1983." www.insidemystery.com

"The Biltmore Hotel." www.miamitiamo.com

"Tours Give Glimpse of History at the Biltmore Hotel, a Storied Name in Miami Luxury Hotels." www.hotel-online.com

"Biltmore Hotel and Golf Coral Gables 4 Star Resort." www.miamiairport411.com

"Miami Biltmore Hotel." www.wikipedia.org

"The Biltmore Hotel." www.hauntedhouses.com

"Biltmore Hotel Miami – Coral Gables." www.travellermade.com

"Biltmore Hotel." www.frightfind.com

"Biltmore History." www.biltmorehotel.com

"Spooky Miami: Biltmore Hotel Haunted by Gangsters and WWII Soldiers (PHOTO)." www.miaminewtimes.com

www.sun-sentinel.com

"The Biltmore's Strange Guest List (1988)." www.youtube.com

ATLANTA

"Who Was the Atlanta Ripper?" www.crimecapsule.com

"The Untold Truth of the Atlanta Ripper." www.grunge.com

"The Unsolved Atlanta Ripper Case." www.medium.com

"Marc Hoover: The Atlanta Ripper." www.clermontsun.com

"17 Gruesome Facts about The Atlanta Ripper, the American South's Own 'Jack'." www.ranker.com

"The Atlanta Ripper: Unsolved American Murders." www.troytaylorbooks.blogspot.com

"The Fox Story." www.foxtheatre.org

"The Atlanta Fox Theatre." www.dobywood.com

"Fox Theater Ghost Tours a Delightful Haunt." www.emorywheel.com

"A Haunted Night Inside the Fox Theater." www.sites.gsu.edu

"Fox Theatre." www.nps.gov

"Meet the Ghosts Who Live at the Fox this October." www.ajc.com

"Fox Theatre: A Haunted History." www.youtube.com

Inside the Ghost Tour at Fox Theatre (Atlanta)." www.youtube.com

"Backstage Spirits Take the Spotlight at Fox Theatre." www.youtube.com

CHARLOTTE

"The Taco Bell Strangler, Henry Louis Wallace: Does He Have More Victims?" www.themurdersquad.com

"Serial Killer Henry Louis Wallace." www.thoughtco.com

"Henry Louis Wallace." www.wikipedia.org

"10 Fast Facts About Biltmore." www.biltmore.com

"Biltmore Estate." www.wikipedia.org

"What is a Vortex?" www.ravenwolfvortexjourney.com

"How the Vanderbilts Went from the Richest Family in the World to Mostly Broke in Just a Few Generations." www.celebritynetworth.com

"Biltmore Estate." www.ashevilleterrors.com

"At the Biltmore Estate, Keeping Track of a Railroad Baron's 23,000 Books." www.archive.nytimes.com

"Richie Rich (Biltmore Estate)." www.vamonde.com

"A Behind-the-Scenes Visit to Biltmore." www.ourstate.com

"A Gem in George Vanderbilt's Library." www.biltmore.com

"Ghosts of the Biltmore House." www.northcarolinaghosts.com

"The Biltmore – North Carolina." www.everymilesamemory.smugmug.com

"Biltmore Estate and George Vanderbilt History." www.romanticasheville.com

"Biltmore Estate's Secret Passages." www.atlasobscura.com

"Discover George Vanderbilt's Railroad Ties." www.biltmore.com

"Behind the Biltmore Estate: 7 Things You Didn't Know About America's Largest Home." www.ncfieldfamily.com

"Touring Biltmore: America's Most Public Private Home." www.wsj.com

"Biltmore Mansion." www.hauntedjourneys.com

"The Vanderbilts Who Never Left Biltmore Estate." www.americashauntedroadtrip.com

"Biltmore Mansion: One of the Most Haunted Places in America! Why the Dead Family is Still There?" www.thesocians.com

"Haunted Biltmore." www.soulintentarts.com

CHARLESTON

"Lavinia Fisher." www.legendsofamerica.com

"Lavinia Fisher of Charleston: Nation's First Female Serial Killer or Wrongly Accused?" www.postandcourier.com

"Lavinia Fisher." www.murderpedia.org

"Lavinia Fisher the First Female US Serial Killer." www.charlestonterrors.com

"The Story of Lavinia Fisher." www.ghostcitytours.com

"How Being Hanged, Drawn, and Quartered Became the Most Brutal Punishment in History." www.allthatsinteresting.com

"Execution by Quartering." www.lordsandladies.org

"The Haunted Jail Tour." www.trustedtours.com

"Lavinia Fisher." www.wikipedia.org

"The Old Haunted Charleston Jail." www.nightlyspirits.com

Ep. 55: "The Old Charleston Jail." *History Goes Bump*

"The Haunted Old Charleston Jail." www.ghostcitytours.com

"Tour Charleston's Most Haunted Building: The Old City Jail." www.discoversouthcarolina.com

"The Haunted Wheel Chair at the Old City Jail." www.youtube.com

"The Unbelievable Horrors of the Old City Jail." www.youtube.com

"Bulldog Tours: Old City Jail." www.youtube.com

MINNEAPOLIS

"The December 3, 1894 Murder of Catherine "Kitty" Ging Near Lake Bde Maka Ska." www.original.newsbreak.com

"The Minneapolis Svengali." www.murderbygaslight.com

"Kitty Ging Murder." www.mplspolicemuseum.org

"Harry Hayward: A Murder that Shocked Minneapolis." www.hennepinhistory.org

"Gangster History at the Wabasha Street Caves." www.wanderthemap.com

"Video: We Visited the Haunted Wabasha Street Caves." www.bringmethenews.com

"Wabasha Street Caves Closing in November, Another Victim of the Coronavirus Pandemic." www.twincities.com

"Wandering the Wabasha Street Caves." www.olioiniowa.com

"Wabasha Street Caves." www.hauntedjourneys.com www.wabashastreetcaves.com

"Wabasha Street Caves – St. Paul, Minnesota." www.hauntedbarguide.com

"Happy Halloween!!!" www.gingerring.com

"St. Paul Gangsters Looking for a Good Time at the Wabasha Street Caves Tours." www.daytripper28.com

"Wabasha Street Caves Reopening in St. Paul." www.audacy.com

"MN's Most Haunted: Wabasha Street Caves." www.kare11.com

"Wabasha Street Caves." www.hauntedhouses.com

"MN's Most Haunted: Gangster Ghosts at the Wabasha Street Caves." www.youtube.com

MILWAUKEE

"Walter E. Ellis." www.murderpedia.org

"Milwaukee Strangler Dies Three Years into Life Sentence." www.nbcnews.com

"Six Serial Killers Who Left Deep Scars on Wisconsin." www.madison.com

"Historic Hotels of America." www.thepfisterhotel.com

"A Historic Milwaukee Hotel." www.thepfisterhotel.com

"Pfister Hotel." www.hauntedhouses.com

"Milwaukee Hotels that Famous People (Briefly) Called Home." www.onmilwaukee.com

"Ghost Story | Pfister Hotel in Milwaukee." www.ghostlyactivities.com

"Batter Up: The Strange Connection between MLB and the Pfister Ghost." www.onmilwaukee.com

"Pfister Hotel." www.hauntedjourneys.com

"Milwaukee Brewers Opponents Tell Crazy Stories of Staying in Haunted Hotel." www.sportscasting.com

"Joey Lawrence Reports Haunting Experiences at Pfister." www.mkeghosts.wordpress.com

"Scary Stories form Baseball's Haunted Hotel." www.mlb.com

"Travelocity Names Top 10 Haunted Hotels." www.businesswire.com

CHICAGO

"H.H. Holmes." www.britannica.com

"H.H. Holmes." www.crimemuseum.org

"H.H. Holmes." www.biography.com

"Did Serial Killer H.H. Holmes Really Build a 'Murder Castle'?" www.history.com

"Inside the Incredibly Twisted Murder Hotel of H.H. Holmes."

https://www.discoveryplus.com/video/ghost–adventures-serial-killer-spirits/john-gacy-prison

"Tours to Start at Old Joliet Prison, a Ruin of Busted Glass and the Stuff of Nightmares." www.chicagotribune.com

"'Dark and Damp': Touring the Rusty and Decaying Cells of Old Joliet Prison." www.roadtrippers.com

"The Old Joliet Prison Is Now a Haunted House." www.wgntv.com

"He Designed the Chicago Water Tower, Joliet's Prison, and This House." www.chicagobusiness.com www.jolietprison.org

"The Haunting of Joliet Prison: The Prison Cemeteries." www.chicagohauntings.com

"Where's Jake's Cell? At Old Joliet Prison, That's the Big Question." www.inquirer.com

"City's First Execution: Killer Hanged in 1866." www.will.illinoisgenweb.org

www.facebook.com/Theoldjoliethauntedprison/

"Adolph Luetgert, the Sausage King Killer of Chicago." www.crimecapsule.com

"Joliet Correctional Center." www.wikipedia.org

"Outside Chicago Historic Old Joliet Prison Is Open for Tours – At Least for Now." www.washingtonpost.com

"Warden's Wife Killed in 1915 Local Mystery." www.will.illinoisgenweb.org

"Ghost-Themed Tours Begin at Old Joliet Prison." www.chicagotribune.com

"Tormented Spirits Are Haunting Old Joliet Prison: Ferak Column." www.patch.com

CINCINNATI

"Donald Harvey Was Just an Unassuming Nurse's Aide When He Killed Dozens of Patients While on Duty." www.allthatsinteresting.com

"Donald Harvey." www.murderpedia.org

"'He Just Liked Killing': Donald Harvey Convicted of 37 Murders." www.fox19.com

My Ghost Story S4E10

"Sedamsville Rectory." www.paranormalmilwaukee.com

"The Ghosts of Sedamsville Rectory." www.
  ghostcitytours.com
Ghost Adventures S7E6
Ghost Adventures: Aftershocks S1E4
"Zak Bagans Investigates the Cincinnati Sedamsville
  Rectory on Ghost Adventures." www.heavy.com
"Paranormal Presence at Historic Sedamsville
  Rectory Is a Hoax or a Reality, Depending on Who
  You Ask." www.wcpo.com

DETROIT

"St. Aubin Street Massacre: 1929 Detroit Family
  Murders Still Unsolved." www.clickondetroit.com
"The Evangelista Occult Murders." www.
  americanhauntingsink.com
"St. Aubin Street In Detroit Has A Dark And Evil
  History That Will Never Be Forgotten." www.
  onlyinyourstate.com
"Inside Eloise Hospital: Metro Detroit's Most
  Haunted Asylum." www.aoibhneastravels.com
"Eloise." www.detroitparanormalexpeditions.com
"When We Called the Insane Asylum Eloise." www.
  fornology.blogspot.com
"Touring History: Inside Eloise Asylum." www.
  detroitnews.com
"Halloween Is Your Last Chance to Tour the Creepy
  Eloise Asylum before It Gets Redeveloped." www.
  metrotimes.com
"We Dared to Enter Michigan's Abandoned, Haunted
  Eloise Asylum, Turned Real-Life Halloween
  Attraction." www.mlive.com
"Eloise's Long-Hidden Basement: 'You Sense
  Someone Else Is Down There.'" www.freep.com
Destination Fear S1E5
"Asylum's Dark past Relived as Cycle Ends." www.ajc.
  com
"Through the Gates of Eloise (Eloise Hospital,
  Formerly Known as the Wayne County Poorhouse
  and Asylum)." www.kristinascarcell.com
"The Horror of Eloise Hospital: Haunted Michigan
  Mental Asylum Goes up for Sale." www.
  theguardian.com
"Scary Encounters Coming to Eloise Asylum." www.
  hometownlife.com

"Scary Encounter from Eloise Psychiatric Hospital."
  www.youtube.com
"Eloise Psychiatric Hospital, Door Slam with an EVP."
  www.youtube.com

ST. LOUIS

"A Darkness 'Round the Bend." www.berthagifford.
  com
"Bertha Alice Williams Gifford (1871-1951)." www.
  findagrave.com
"Bertha Gifford." www.murderpedia.org
"Night at the Mineral Springs Hotel." www.
  bumpinthenight.net
"Our Past: Mineral Springs Hotel Opened June 1914."
  www.thetelegraph.com
"On the Road with Great Rivers & Routes: Why
  Alton Is America's Most Haunted Small Town."
  www.fox2now.com
"Mineral Springs Hotel: The True Story of One
  of Alton's Most Haunted Location." www.
  hauntedillinois.com
"Mineral Springs Hotel." www.riseupparanormal.com
Ghost Adventures S17E12

PHOENIX

"Women on Death Row: Wendi Andriano." www.
  popculturecrime.medium.com
"Wendi Andriano." www.deadlywomen.fandom.com
"Wendi Andriano." www.murderpedia.org
"Wendi Andriano Women on Death Row." www.
  mycrimelibrary.com
"Hotel History – Jerome Grand Hotel 1994 – Present
  / United Verde Hospital 1926 – 1950." www.
  jeromegrandhotel.net
"Is Jerome Grand Hotel the Most Haunted Place in
  Arizona?" www.azcentral.com
"A Look Back at How Jerome, Verde Valley Dealt with
  1918 Pandemic." www.verdenews.com
"Jerome Grand Hotel." www.hauntedhouses.com
"Jerome Grand Hotel." www.wikipedia.com
"Jerome Grand Hotel." www.frightfind.com
"Did You Know: Jerome Grand Hotel Home to
  Arizona's First Self-Service Otis Elevator." www.
  fronterasdesk.org
"The Haunts of the Jerome Grand Hotel." www.
  prescottazhistory.blogspot.com

"Jerome Grand Hotel: One of the Most Haunted Buildings in Arizona." www.12news.com
"Jerome Grand Hotel – Real Haunted Place." www.azhauntedhouses.com

LAS VEGAS
"Convicted Killer May Get New Trial." www.lasvegassun.com
"Murderer Attempts Escape from Women's Prison in North Las Vegas." www.reviewjournal.com
The Truth, Revealed by Bugs: The Case of Brookey Lee West. www.nytimes.com
"Brookey Lee West, Serial Killer – Nevada, 1998." www.unknownmisandry.blogspot.com
"Late Night Flashlight Ghost Tour Experience." www.thehauntedmuseum.com
"The Not-So-Haunted Museum of Zak Bagans." www.skepticalinquirer.org
"The Trickery and Silly Kitsch of a Supposedly Haunted Museum in Las Vegas." www.hyperallergic.com
"About Zac Bagans' The Haunted Museum." www.thehauntedmuseum.com
Quarantine: Perimeter of Fear S1E1
"Zak Bagans' Haunted Museum Presents Creepy Collection in October." www.reviewjournal.com
"The Possession: The True Story Behind the Dybbuk Box." www.screenrant.com
"Zak Bagans Closes Devil's Rocking Chair Exhibit after Museum Haunts, Chilling Encounter in His Home." www.newsweek.com
Ghost-Hunting For Dummies by Zak Bagans

SAN DIEGO
"There Is No Villain in Dirty John: The Betty Broderick Story." www.vulture.com
"One Angry Better." www.lamag.com
"The Eye-Opening Case of Betty Broderick: Rage, Deception, Divorce and Double Murder." www.eonline.com
"Hotel del Coronado – Coronado, CA." www.waymarking.com
"The Haunted Hotel Del Coronado in California." www.haunted-places-to-go.com
"Revisiting the Del Coronado Hotel, Scene of a Classic Film – And My Best Childhood Holiday." www.thetelegraph.com

"A National Historic Landmark." www.hoteldel.com
"Throwback Thursday: Myths and Legends—The Ghost of Kate Morgan." www.mikesirota.com
"Haunted Hotel Del Coronado." www.stormynighttales.blogspot.com
"Hotel del Coronado." www.wikipedia.com
"The Duchess of Windsor and the Coronado Legend, Part I." www.sandiegohistory.org
"1408: The Creepy True Story That Inspired the Movie." www.screenrant.com
"Kate Morgan Mystery Begins." www.hoteldel.com
"The True Story of Kate Morgan, The Ghost of the Hotel Del Coronado." www.alltahtsinteresting.com
"Haunted Hotel Del Coronado" www.seeksghosts.blogspot.com
"Paranormal Activity at the Hotel del Coronado – Have You Seen Kate Morgan?" www.coronadotimes.com
"Spend the Night in Hotel del Coronado's Haunted Rooms." www.oklahoman.com
"Why the Ghost of Kate Morgan Still Haunts Hotel Del Coronado." www.anomalien.com
"Haunted Lodgings: Hotel del Coronado." www.4girlsandaghost.wordpress.com
"Hotel del Coronado." www.gothere.com
Haunted Happenings Tour

SAN FRANCISCO
"The Disturbing Crimes of Ed Kemper, the 6'9" Serial Killer Who Saved His Grisliest Murder for His Own Mom." www.allthatsinteresting.com
"Edmund Kemper." www.biography.com
"Edmund Kemper: The 'Co-Ed Butcher' of Hitchhiking Students." www.investigationdiscovery.com
"Edmund Emil Kemper III." www.murderpedia.org
"The Claremont Hotel Club and Spa, Ghosts and Hauntings." www.facebook.com
"Claremont Hotel." www.localwiki.org
"History of Claremont Hotel & Spa." www.hauntedrooms.com
"Creepy Stories and Legends about the Claremont Hotel." www.ranker.com
"Spurs' Jeff Ayers and Tim Duncan Share 'Creepy' Experience at Hotel." www.cbssports.com
"Ghosts at the Claremont Resort (My Own Experience)." www.kathleendavenport.blogspot.com

LOS ANGELES

"The Black Dahlia." www.fbi.gov

"Has the Black Dahlia Murder Finally Been Solved?" www.rollingstone.com

"10 Shocking Facts about the Black Dahlia, Hollywood's Most Famous Unsolved Murder." www.mentalfloss.com

"I Know Who Killed the Black Dahlia: My Own Father." www.theguardian.com

"The Chilling History Of Murder And Hauntings Inside Los Angeles' Cecil Hotel." www.allthatsinteresting.com

"Sick Crimes of Cecil Hotel Killer Jack Unterweger Who Strangled 12 Women with Their Own Bras & Raped Them with Branches." www.the-sun.com

"9 Chilling Facts about the Cecil Hotel, an Infamous Los Angeles Landmark That Inspired Netflix's Newest Show." www.insider.com

"Spending a Night at the Cecil Hotel, Where Serial Killers and Eerie Deaths Abound." www.lamag.com"

"*American Horror Story: Hotel.*" www.wikipedia.com

Ghost Adventures S21E5

"The Horrifying History of the Infamous Cecil Hotel." www.travelchannel.com

"Cecil Hotel (Los Angeles)." www.wikipedia.com

"What Did Netflix Crime Scene: The Vanishing at the Cecil Hotel Didn't Tell You about Elisa Lam and Cecil Hotel." www.showflik.com

"Cecil Hotel's Funny-Tasting Water Led to Horrific Discovery of Elisa Lam's Dead Body." www.mirror.co.uk

"Where Is Amy Price Now? The Cecil Hotel Manager from the Netflix Documentary." www.thetab.com

SALT LAKE CITY

"Elizabeth Smart: A Complete Timeline of Her Kidnapping, Rescue and Aftermath." www.biography.com

"Elizabeth Smart." www.biography.com

"Elizabeth Smart Says She's Sharing Her Abduction Story with Her Children: 'Never Want to Hide What Happened.'" www.people.com

Ep. 225: "Asylum 49." *History Goes Bump*

"The History behind the Haunting." www.smannionitsligo.wordpress.com

"True Terror Real Ghosts of the Asylum 49 Haunted House." www.backpackerverse.com

"A Haunting of the Living and the Dead: Asylum 49." www.slugmag.com

Ghost Adventures S4E25

DENVER

"Jill Coit." www.crimemuseum.org

"Jill Coit." www.murderpedia.org

"Jill Coit: Some Snow Job." www.forensicfilesnow.com

"The 'Unsinkable' Molly Brown House." www.waymarking.com

"Strangeography: The Molly Brown House – Ghosts and an Egyptian Curse?" www.myhauntedlibrary.com

"The Collection That Made Us: Historic Denver, INC. Restoration of the Molly Brown House Museum." www.mollybrown.org

"Margaret Brown." www.wikipedia.org

"The Story Behind Denver's Most Haunted House Will Give You Nightmares." www.onlyinyourstate.com

"Molly Brown House." www.hauntedhouses.com

"Molly Brown House Museum." www.americashauntedroadtrip.com

"Margaret Brown." www.encyclopedia-titanica.org

"Molly Brown House." www.wikipedia.org

"About 'the Ghosts of the Molly Brown House.'" www.hauntworld.com

"Molly Brown House Unveils Stunning Restoration after 3 Years of Work, $2 Million Campaign." www.theknow-old.denverpost.com

Denver Nightly Spirits Tour, 2021

Denver Terrors Tour, 2021

HOUSTON

"The Chilling Tale of the Icebox Murders" www.houstoniamag.com

"Cold Case: Revisiting Houston's Infamous Ice Box Murders." www.mentalfloss.com

"The Case of the Grisly Ice Box Murders That Horrified Houston in 1965." www.allthatsinteresting.com

"Everything We Know About the Icebox Murders." www.grunge.com

"True Crime Tuesday: The Ice Box Murders." www.heresthefuckingtwist.com

"Hotel Galvez and Spa Named Most Haunted Hotel in Texas. Here's Why It's a Great Place to Ghost Hunt." www.crhon.com

"The Spooky History of Hotel Galvez & Other Texas Haunts to Visit This Halloween." www.texalifestylemag.com

"The Ghosts of St. Mary's Orphanage." www.ghostcitytours.com

"Hotel History – Hotel Galvez Key Step in Galveston's Recovering Following 1900 Storm." www.pressroom.mitchellhistoricproperties.com

"Truly Terrifying in Texas: The Killing Fields, Hotel Hauntings and Ghostly Galveston." www.fox23.com

"Hotel Galvez." www.wikipedia.org

"The Haunted Hotel Galvez." www.ghostcitytours.com

"Haunted Galveston: The Reoccurring Hanging Ghost of Hotel Galvez." www.backpackerverse.com

"The Haunted Hotel Galvez in Galveston, Texas." www.hauntjaunts.net

"Hotel Galvez Story of Ghost Bride and Other Ghost Stories." www.pressroom.mitchellhistoricproperties.com

"Hotel Galvez, Galveston, TX." www.hauntedrooms.com

"My Stay in the Haunted Room 501 of the Hotel Galvez in Galveston." www.getoffthecouch.co

"Ghosts in Galveston? 'Oh Yes, Everywhere.'" www.freep.com

www.galvestonghost.com

"Hotel Galvvez." www.frightfind.com

"Galveston Ranks as One of Nations Most Haunted Places." www.houstonchronicle.com

"Courtesy Flush: The Haunting of the Hotel Galvez." www.jmplumbley.com

SAN ANTONIO

Wise About Texas Podcast

"The Tale of Pearl Brewery's Three Emmas." www.sanantoniomag.com

"The Dark Story behind the Hotel Emma That Is Keeping Guests up at Night." www.boredomthearpy.com

"Payaya People." www.wikipedia.org

"Alamo History Chronology." www.drtinfo.org

"San Antonio: The Alamo – Spanish Hospital." www.flickr.com

"Skeletons in Buckskin at the Alamo." www.historynet.com

"Ghosts of the Alamo." www.legendsofamerica.com

"Ghosts of the Alamo: History & Hauntings of One of America's Greatest Landmarks." www.militaryghosts.com

"A Tale of Competing Interests in the Alamo." www.thealamo.org

"Alamo's Buried Past." www.expressnews.com

"Americas Great Treasures Still Waiting to be Found." www.lovemoney.com

"Chilling Tales of Ghostly Experiences at the Alamo." www.texasescapes.com

"The Ghosts of San Antonio." www.nightlyspirits.com

"The Ghosts of the Alamo." www.ghostcitytours.com

"Remember the 'Haunted' Alamo?" www.warhistoryonline.com

"Spooky Stories of the Haunted Alamo." www.texashillcountry.com

DALLAS

"John Wesley Hardin." www.famoustexans.com

"John Wesley Hardin." www.britannica.com

"The Killing of John Wesley Hardin." www.texasescapes.com

"John Wesley Hardin." www.murderpedia.com

"More About Miss Molly's." www.missmollyshotel.com

"Miss Molly's B&B." www.hauntedhouses.com

"Haunted Miss Molly." www.holatexas.us

"Haltom City Investigation." www.texpartparanormal.com

"Is Miss Molly's Hotel in the Fort Worth Stockyards Haunted?" www.dallasobserver.com

"Miss Molly's Haunted????" www.stonehousebedandbreakfast.tripod.com

"Paranormal experiences at Miss Molly's Hotel in Fort Worth." www.youtube.com

"Justin & Jeremy in the morning Ghost Hunt at Miss Molly's Hotel." www.youtube.com

"Haunted Tales Of Miss Molly's Hotel In The Fort Worth Stockyards." www.youtube.com

PORTLAND

"154. Richard Laurence Marquette." www.fbi.gov

"Richard Lawrence Marquette." www.murderpedia.com

"Richard Marquette Case Shocked Oregonians after 'Butcher' Slayer Scored Parole, Killed Again." www.oregonlive.com

"The Shanghai Tunnels." www.portlandghosts.com

"A Brief History of Portland's Shanghai Tunnels." www.theculturetrip.com

"Portland's Shanghai Tunnels." www.hauntedhouses.com

"Portland's Shanghai Tunnels." www.atlasobscura.com

Ghost Adventures S6E1

"Why Is Portland So Haunted?" www.portlandghosts.com

"The Mysterious Shanghai Tunnels of Portland." www.mysteriousuniverse.org

"Portland, Oregon Underground – Shanghai Tunnels." www.legendsofamerica.com

"The Haunted Shanghai Tunnels in Portland, Oregon." www.haunted-places-to-go.com

"Shanghai Tunnels Case." www.parachills.com

Ep. 147: "Shanghai Tunnels." *History Goes Bump*

"The Truth about Portland's 'Shanghai Tunnels.'" www.oregonlive.com

Shanghai Tunnel/Portland Underground Tour, 2019

HONOLULU

"Hawaii: The Honolulu Strangler." www.sites.psu.edu

"This Was the First Victim of the Honolulu Strangler." www.grunge.com

"The Mystery of Hawaii's Honolulu Strangler Still Baffles People Today." www.onlyinyourstate.com

"The Honolulu Strangler (He Totally Did It)." *The Midnight Train Podcast*

"Honolulu Strangler." www.serialdispatches.com

"10 Terrifying Facts of the Honolulu Strangler." www.listverse.com

Ep. 189: "Hawaiian Night Marchers (with Kamuela Kaneshiro)." *Spirits* Podcast

Phantom Night Marches in the Hawaiian Islands by Katharine Luomala

"Pele, Goddess of Fire and Volcanoes." www.hawaii.com

"Hawaii – History and Heritage." www.smithsonianmag.com

"Legends of Hawaii's Night Marchers." www.olukai.com

"The Legend of the Mysterious Night Marchers of Hawaii." www.people.howstuffworks.com

"Friday Night Frights: The Legend of Hawai'i's Night Marchers." www.honolulumagazine.com

"The Legend of the Night Marchers." www.to-hawaii.com

"Huaka'I Pō: The Legend of the Hawaiian Night Marchers." www.theculturetrip.com

"Nightmarchers." www.wikipedia.org

"Night Marches of Oahu." www.youtube.com

INDEX